Fertility, Reproduction and Sexuality

GENERAL EDITORS:

David Parkin, *Director of the Institute of Social and Cultural Anthropology, University of Oxford*

Soraya Tremayne, *Co-ordinating Director of the Fertility and Reproduction Studies Group and a Research Associate at the Institute of Social and Cultural Anthropology, University of Oxford; and a Vice-President of the Royal Anthropological Institute.*

MODERN BABYLON?

Prostituting Children in Thailand

Heather Montgomery

Berghahn Books
New York • Oxford

First published in 2001 by
Berghahn Books
www.BerghahnBooks.com

Editorial offices:
604 West 115th Street, New York, NY 10025, USA
3 NewTec Place, Magdalen Road, Oxford OX4 1RE, UK

Library of Congress Cataloging-in-Publication Data
Montgomery, Heather.
 Modern Babylon? : prostituting children in Thailand / Heather
 Montgomery.
  p. cm. -- (Fertility, reproduction, and sexuality ; v. 2)
  Includes bibliographical references and index.
  ISBN 1-57181-318-7 (pb. : alk. paper) -- ISBN 1-57181-829-4
 (cl. : alk. paper)
  1. Child prostitution--Thailand. 2. Sex-oriented businesses--
 Thailand. 3 Child abuse--Thailand. 4. Child welfare--Thailand.
 5. Thailand--Social conditions. 6. Thailand--Economic conditions.
 I. Title. II. Series.

HQ242.55.A5 M66 2001
306.74'5'09593--dc21   2001049936

British Library Cataloguing in Publication Data
A catalogue record for this book is available
from the British Library.

Printed in the United States on acid-free paper.

ISBN 1-57181-829-4 (hardback)
    1-57181-318-7 (paperback)

To my mother and father

In ancient times, if we may believe the myths of Hellas, Athens, after a disastrous campaign, was compelled by her conqueror to send once every nine years a tribute to Crete of seven youths and seven maidens. The doomed fourteen, who were selected by lot amid the lamentations of the citizens, returned no more. The vessel that bore them to Crete unfurled black sails as the symbol of despair, and on arrival her passengers were flung into the famous labyrinth of Daedalus, there to wander about blindly until they were devoured by the Minotaur …

The fact that the Athenians should have taken so bitterly to heart the paltry maiden tribute that once in nine years they had to pay to the Minotaur seems incredible, almost inconceivable. This very night in London, and every night, year in and year out, not seven maidens only, but many times seven, selected almost as much by chance as those who the Athenian market place drew lots as to which should be flung into the Cretan labyrinth, will be offered up as the Maiden tribute of Modern Babylon. Maidens they were when this morning dawned but tonight their ruin will be accomplished, and tomorrow they will find themselves within the portals of the maze of London brotheldom … Multitudes are swept irresistibly on and on to be destroyed in due season, to give their place to others who will also share their doom.

William Stead, 'Maiden Tribute of Modern Babylon', Pall Mall Gazette, July 1885.

Contents

LIST OF TABLES

ACKNOWLEDGEMENTS

There are many people who helped me considerably when I was writing this book and whose help I gratefully acknowledge. Their support has been much appreciated.

It almost goes without saying that I owe a huge debt of gratitude to the people of Baan Nua for their patience and understanding. Others in the resort were equally kind. The people of the NGO where I was based welcomed me with open arms, looked after me and taught me so much. Michelle, Aileen, Lek, Lampa and Wanee were unfailing patient and generous with me and I should never have been able to complete fieldwork without them. In Bangkok, the staff at ECPAT, especially Kob, Sudarat and Nicola, looked after me when I first arrived in Thailand and helped me settle in. In Chiang Mai, Leif Jonsson and Graham Fordham coaxed me gently through fieldwork, contributing ideas and support. I am particularly grateful to Graham for his continuing support and comments on innumerable drafts of this book.

I studied for my PhD in Cambridge, where many people generously gave me the benefit of their considerable expertise. My supervisor, Helen Watson, and faculty advisor Francis Pine provided excellent advice and creativity which were very much appreciated. Alan Macfarlane, Virginia Morrow, Shigeharu Tanabe and Marilyn Strathern all commented on earlier drafts of the work and helped clarify my thinking. My fellow students and friends in Cambridge, Cathy Alexander, Tom and Sarah Hall, Terry Roopnaraine and Edmund Waite provided ideas, support and motivation. They made four years go very quickly. Jean La Fontaine, my external examiner, was a great help in suggesting improvements and ways of turning the thesis into a book. Judith Ennew has been an enormous influence on my ideas about children and childhood. I count myself lucky to have her as both a mentor and a friend.

I have been equally fortunate at Oxford. David Parkin and
Soraya Tremayne both read earlier versions of the book and have
been extremely encouraging and supportive in getting it published. Marina de Alarcon, Marcus Banks, Sandra Dudley, Maria
Fusaro, Clare Harris, Senia Paseta, Peter Rivière and Marie-Louise
Weighill have all provided much needed assistance and encouragement when, at times, it looked as if it would never be finished.

My mother, Tessa Montgomery has been an excellent proof
reader. She, along with my father, Ian, and my sister Claire, has
been a constant source of reassurance and comfort. Catherine
Sutton has never failed to listen and offer sympathy. Charlie
Wright was there at the very beginning of this project and has
stayed with it all the way, offering sensible advice and invaluable
computer expertise.

This book was written during my time as a Research Fellow at
the Norwegian Centre for Child Studies at the University of
Trondheim, and as a British Academy Fellow at St. Hugh's Col-
lege, Oxford. I should like to thank the Norwegian Government
and the British Academy for funding me. I should also like to
express my sincere thanks to the William Wyse Fund and Evans
Fund at Cambridge University, for the financial backing which
enabled me to complete my dissertation.

INTRODUCTION

A Personal View

The prostitution of children is not an easy topic to research, to read or to write about. It is a supremely emotive issue, which stands as an affront to accepted notions of appropriate sexuality, to the nature of childhood, and to the responsibilities that adults have towards children. It is unsurprising that so many voices of protest have been raised against it in recent years and that it has become so important an issue for Non-Governmental Organisations (NGOs). It is equally unsurprising that few academics, outside departments of social work or social policy, have shown much interest in it. In some respects, there is little that many people wish to say about it except that it is a deviation, a distortion of adult/child relationships and of accepted sexual norms. There is an understandable squeamishness about inquiring too deeply into the nature of such abuse or in looking too closely at the effects it has on the child or the abuser. It is too disturbing to do anything other than condemn it. Certainly, it is a subject that supposedly dispassionate academics have been reluctant to involve themselves in, not least because it means confronting issues of morality and ethics head-on, which inevitably leads to suggestions and recommendations, becoming 'part of the solution'.

It is not easy to divorce the academic study of child prostitution from its moral context. Issues such as this, or indeed, any form of child abuse, do not exist in a moral vacuum and anybody reading or researching these issues is bound to come to the project with deeply held beliefs about the nature of abuse and strong feelings about those who abuse children. The 'neutrality' or 'detachment' of the participant observer has long been called into question, but it is a problem which becomes particularly acute in research on topics such as this. While applied anthropology has tried to tie the academic discipline of anthropology to concrete problems in the outside world, it has rarely tackled issues as controversial, or as emotive, as child sexual abuse and child prostitution.[1] Instead the field of study has been left to NGOs, activists and others with an explicitly interventionist agenda which relies less on research and more on demands for action. As La Fontaine has written in *Child Sexual Abuse*, those who do study issues such as child abuse from an academic perspective, lay themselves open to charges of 'academic voyeurism [which are] no substitute for more action on behalf of the victims' (1990: 17). These NGOs and their activists have done impressive work in making child prostitution an international concern. Their tireless lobbying and campaigning has lead to greater awareness and to an acceptance that child prostitution, especially that involving Western clients and Asian or African children, is an international problem whose causes, and indeed solutions, cross national boundaries. Their concern for children and their moral stance are explicit and they have little time for academic hand-wringing over dispassionate or neutral research. For them research is valid only as a means to an end. It is a way of knowing more about the children involved in prostitution, so that more effective intervention is possible. In this book, I am often critical of these NGOs although I do admire their activism and their success. It is always easier to criticise their campaigns than to congratulate them on all their achievements, which are considerable.

Child prostitution is quite clearly a moral issue, and whether it is examined by an anthropologist or by a social activist, the underlying moral framework of the researchers needs to be made explicit. NGOs are categorical in their stance: child prostitution is 'a form of slavery', 'an evil' or 'the rape of childhood' (ECPAT Newsletters 1991–1993). Despite the sensationalism of the rhetoric, it is hard to disagree with the morality behind this. There are few people who support child prostitution, or indeed sex between children under the age of consent with adults, who do not have ulterior motives. Various paedophile groups, often claiming the language of children's rights, have argued that children have a right to express their sexuality in whatever way they wish and that if they wish to have sex with an adult, they should be allowed to. It is not worth discussing these arguments in too much depth here when they have been so convincingly demolished by Ennew (1986) and Finkelhor (1979b) who draw atten-

---

1. Although there have been notable exceptions, especially La Fontaine's work on ritual abuse (1994 and 1998) and Ennew's on sexual exploitation (1986).

tion to the enormous power imbalance behind the adult/child relationship and the subsequent impossibility of informed consent being given by a child to have sex with an adult.

My own decision to study child prostitution as an anthropologist is similarly related to a moral stance, which should also be stated explicitly. I have a long standing interest in children's rights and a firm belief in children's importance as social actors. I began to study child prostitution as a form of child labour and as an infringement of children's rights, and I continue to view it as such. Like the NGOs and advocates in the anti-child-prostitution lobby, I also believe that child prostitution is unjustifiable and that men, whether foreign or indigenous, who commercially exploit children sexually are guilty of an enormous misuse of power and a serious transgression of moral laws. I believe that children's rights to their bodily integrity are severely compromised when they work as prostitutes and that, ideally, it is work that no child should have to perform, whatever his or her circumstances.

However, I do not believe that morality is a single, uncontested category which precludes all further discussions. There are other issues and circumstances, such as the economic situation and family background of a child, which inform morality. Economics is integral to morality and issues such as child prostitution must be understood in terms of both. Prostitution is a form of labour, albeit an extremely exploitative and dangerous one where children are concerned, and it is only by viewing it as such that it is possible to understand the children and the decisions they make. Divorced (as some activists would have it) from the labour market, it is positioned as a unique evil, unrelated to economic forces, and linked instead to degeneracy and wickedness. While this may be morally satisfying, it denies and obscures other ways of understanding. Comprehending why prostitution occurs, and explaining the economic and social reasons behind it, does not make the condemnation any less strong. Indeed, morality should be placed in such a context if it is not to degenerate into self-righteousness.

It is in these issues that I am most interested. In writing this book, I have no wish to justify the abuse that children suffer in prostitution or to offer any apologies for men who perpetrate this abuse. However, I am interested in children's rights and children's participation in research, which means taking children seriously as both research subjects and as analysts of their own lives and circumstances. Those who defend sex between adults and children wilfully distort the language of rights and participation (for a critique of this literature, see Scheper-Hughes and Stein 1987). Giving children rights must include the right to protection from harm. It does not include burdening children with responsibilities which they are not ready to handle. A sexual relationship with an adult is predicated on a large power differential which exposes the child to harm and abuses the concept of rights.

Child prostitutes are among the most powerless and least artic- ulate in any society and there is an enormous temptation to speak for them and to interpret what they say, so that it fits in with out- siders' preconceptions. Alternatively, there is a strong tendency not to listen to them at all. Their situation is so dire and they are in such obvious need of help that it becomes unnecessary to hear what they say. Their words can add little to the poignancy and des- peration of their situation. However, even these children have their own views and their own interpretations of their lives and situations and these should not be ignored. An anthropologist or an activist cannot speak for them or be their interpreter; they have their own voices and their own analyses which are equally valid.

It is much easier to hold these beliefs in the abstract than it is to have them confronted and challenged on a daily basis during fieldwork. Conducting this research and writing it up were gru- elling processes whereby many of my assumptions about chil- dren's rights and participation were shown to be problematic. It is simple to claim that children have a right to be heard and believed and much harder to put it into practice when children do not say what they are supposed to say. In common with other researchers and journalists, I went to Thailand with a clear picture of what I expected from a child prostitute. I expected a certain passivity and fatalism and an articulation of their disgust and possibly out- rage at what they had to do. The abuse was obvious and the wickedness inherent in their abusers so apparent that I expected nothing more than to listen and to record stories of exploitation. While I believed that children should be allowed to speak in their own voices and should be able to express what they felt, I did not expect them to say anything more than this. I anticipated that some of the older children might be able to formulate some solu- tions to their plight but I still expected, and in many ways hoped for, an analysis of their situation which reflected and reinforced my own world-view.

The children in the community within which I worked, how- ever, painted an infinitely more complicated picture of their world which challenged any simplistic dichotomies of good and evil, abused and abusers. It proved disturbing and disconcerting that their analyses of their lives were far more nuanced and far more sophisticated than mine. Listening to what they had to say meant jettisoning many of my own beliefs and certainties about child prostitution but also acknowledging the strength of my own feelings about it. It is an emotionally charged issue which I could not view without prejudice. Despite a stated intention not to get involved – to be a dispassionate 'participant observer' in anthropological terminology – I found this impossible, and in many ways undesirable.

The realities of child prostitution are difficult and to stay neutral in such circumstances rides dangerously close to complicity. It is important not to become too blasé about this abuse and not to forget the physical and emotional damage inflicted on a child. There is far too much prurience in discussions of child prostitution; too much furtive enjoyment in breaking the taboo of talking about sex with children. Nevertheless, it must be remembered that a child's body is not made for penetrative sex with an adult and that when this occurs the physical damage is great. It is extremely shocking and very upsetting to see a boy return from a client bleeding after a sexual encounter and it is easy to sympathise with campaigners who do not wish to understand but only to condemn.

The damaging effects of child abuse have only recently been recognised in Western societies and it is hard not to project some of this knowledge onto understandings of child prostitution in Thailand. There is evidence from the West that adult survivors of abuse have a variety of psychological and social problems. The damage inflicted lasts a life-time. Even though Western models of psychology may not be appropriate for Thailand, there is an irresistible tendency to see the future of these children as unremittingly bleak. Their tragedy concerns not only their miserable present but also their ruined future. That children should be condemned to this so that a small number of Western men can enjoy sex with them is terrible. It is something that no amount of research can ameliorate. Dealing with the children who are victims of this abuse on a daily basis is demanding, often draining, and their victimisation is difficult to deal with. Intellectual understanding apart, I found it incredibly painful to see the children suffer. While I understood the wider political-economic forces that allowed this abuse to occur, it was still hard to see children of whom I was fond being abused and to witness the physical damage that was inflicted on them. In those circumstances, I had no desire for impartiality or neutrality, and I felt the role of a detached researcher to be untenable.

Despite this I recognised that conducting this sort of research meant maintaining some distance between the researcher and the informant. It is not enough to empathise with the children or to express horror on their behalf. Research can only be carried out if there is some separation between the researcher and her informants. I, of course, never had to cope with prostitution; the children did. One of the recurrent points of this book is that outrage is not enough and ultimately does little good if it is not accompanied by a more profound understanding. This understanding is only possible if emotions are disentangled from the research and the situation is understood, if not neutrally then objectively. It is impossible to study the situation of child prostitutes without prejudice. I have made little attempt to do so and my own views are clear. However objectivity is more feasible. By maintaining an intellectual, rather than an emotional, distance it is conceivable to see the wider contexts in which these children live and to go beyond simplistic responses. It is always difficult in this kind of research to draw boundaries. It is hard not to become emotionally involved with the children and harder still not to become angry and upset when confronted with the evidence of the abuse which they have suffered. Equally, however, it is difficult to conduct research when one is too intimately involved with the informants and attempting to intervene in their lives. It is impossible to study without changing or intervening, but nevertheless, research does need some distance and the ability to stand back. Often it was not until writing up my field-notes or talking to friends that I became aware of how normal the children's lives seemed to me and how much I accepted the everyday forms of violence to which they were subjected. In order to function in that environment and to understand how the children viewed what they did, it was sometimes necessary to accept prostitution in the way the children did. As ever, there are grave difficulties in this. The boundary between the distance required to conduct research and a lack of empathy for the children is a fine one, but one which it is important not to cross. Further research on child prostitution is necessary. There is still far too little known about the children involved, but research should not be based solely on emotional responses to these children's plight.

Accusations of voyeurism, which are sometimes levelled at researchers who investigate sexual abuse, are easy to understand. Nowhere is this more obvious than in the issue of intervention. All research is a form of intervention and it is naive to assume that the presence of a Western researcher does not change people's attitudes or behaviour. My very presence in the community I studied, and my own attitudes towards what I was studying, were apparent for I made little attempt to hide them. Many of those who work as prostitutes or whose children work as prostitutes are aware of the stigma against them and did not view my dislike or disapproval of their way of life as shocking or unusual. Although they frequently offered explanations as to why they worked as prostitutes, no-one enjoyed it or felt that it was a 'good' way of life. Given different circumstances or better opportunities, many would undoubtedly have left. However, as I argue in later chapters, they had developed survival strategies which enabled them to cope with their lives. These were justifications and ways of understanding that had been worked out over a long period of time and which enabled the community to function. To argue too persuasively against these ways of thinking would mean destroying the ways in which the community kept together and survived.

There is always an unease about how far, and what form, any intervention should take. I specifically promised the community that I would not inform the authorities of the activities that took place in their slum. However it was extremely hard to see Western men visiting the slum to choose which child they wanted to have sex with, or to know that, in a few days time, a man would arrive from Europe and have a child already lined up for him in his apartment. It was at moments like these that I felt I ought to have told the police, in order to have these men arrested or at least warned off. The idea that there was a way of preventing this abuse occurring contrasted painfully with the promises I had given not to inform on members of the community. Similarly, the children constantly stressed the importance of their families to them and expressed great distress at the thought of being separated from them. In such a deprived environment, their love for their families, and duties towards them, were a way of gaining self-esteem and one of the few things of which they could be proud. Despite this, however, I sometimes felt that perhaps the children would be better off without their families. Whatever parents felt about their children, clearly they were inflicting great damage on them. There was no malice in this, there obviously was great love between parents and children but, nevertheless, the children did suffer through poor parenting and deprivation. There were certainly times when I felt that the community should have been broken up, and families separated, if the cycle of prostitution and poverty were ever to be broken.

There are no easy answers to these dilemmas and I have never resolved them fully. I did keep my promise to the community not to alert the police or the welfare authorities but I also agonised about the abuse the children were suffering and my inability to do anything about it. There was also a sense in which there was nothing I could do. In a Western society, there are channels to go through; social workers, state welfare services, the police. In Thailand, the welfare infrastructure is shaky. If families were split up and children sent away, there were few places for them to go, other than prison. The parents, as their children's pimps, would face jail sentences and the provision of care for children with various problems and needs was extremely limited. There were few homes for children with their social and physical difficulties, and care provided by the voluntary sector, while often very good, was patchy and under-funded. Foster care for children such as these would have been equally hard to find and it seemed counterproductive to call for intervention when the problems that these children faced had few practical solutions.

Separating children from their parents and their community may have short-term benefits, but without the intensive and long-term psychological and social counselling and intervention that these children need, it would ultimately be pointless. Instead, it is likely that these children would become more institutionalised and more difficult to help and their problems would simply be shifted to another venue rather than alleviated. There is no criticism of Thailand implied in this. Few societies place much emphasis on children, and children with problems are inevitably low on any social services' list of priorities. The scale of abuse that has been uncovered during investigations of children's homes in North Wales[2] has highlighted this. Even within a relatively wealthy society which claims good legal protection of children and a care infrastructure which should protect the vulnerable, this abuse of children can occur and continue for decades. The children in these homes were 'difficult' cases who were pushed out of sight and mind into these institutions where untrained, badly paid and un-vetted 'carers' abused them. The scandal is not only the depravity of the perpetrators, it is also the scandal of a society which allowed this to happen and which failed to dedicate enough resources and effort into preventing it. In Thailand these problems are multiplied. It is a country which is considerably poorer than Britain, despite the period of economic growth it experienced in the 1970s and 1980s. During this period, little money was invested in welfare or in building social services structures. The current economic collapse of Thailand does not bode well for vulnerable children. It seems most unlikely that resources will be channelled into long-term help and protection for them.

There will be readers of this book who will disagree strongly with this approach and who may feel that whatever promises I

2. See, for example, Millward 1996.

gave and however limited the alternatives, preventing abuse over-rides all other considerations and I should have reported these men to the police. They may feel that academic research should not be placed above the protection of children and that in attempting a long-term research project, I did indeed do this. I share some of these concerns. However, the ethical dilemmas involved in this research, like the research itself, are extremely complex, and there will always be differing views on the nature and purpose of research projects such as this. There are many moral questions that this research posed and I do not feel that I have, or indeed, ever can, resolve all of these entirely. I do believe, however, that children deserve to be understood and that any proposed intervention should be based on their interpretations and understandings. I further believe that the only way to assess these adequately is by intensive research where children's views are respected and listened to.

I am wary of interventions based on claims of the children's best interests when the children themselves are not consulted or even known. While it is possible to imagine the difficulties that child prostitutes face, it is harder to know how they can be helped if there is no base line data or proper research on their situation. Too often child prostitutes are treated as a homogenous category facing identical problems and needing similar help. In this book, I will argue that this way of viewing child prostitutes is theoretically and practically wrong and often damaging for the children. There is a variety of ways in which children become prostitutes and this prostitution takes many forms. Intervention strategies must be tailored accordingly. There are no grand schemes in this book to end all child prostitution. While this may be the ultimate goal, there is a great deal of ground-level research that must be done first. This book is not concerned with the vague goal of raising awareness; the problem of child prostitution is already well enough known although it is still obscurely understood. Child prostitution is a complex problem which will require many forms of intervention. The individual circumstances of the children involved, as well as their own world-views, must be taken into consideration if the problem is to be tackled in any meaningful way.

Academics have often shied away from commenting on emotive and controversial topics because such research frequently carries with it the assumption of recommendations for intervention. When researching children, this dilemma is acute. There are few ethical guidelines on research with children (Morrow and Richards 1996), but there is a basic understanding that research should not do any harm. There is a sense in which research on child prostitution does do harm if it is written only for academics with no attempt to make broader links to social workers or others who could offer practical help. I made no promises to the children I worked with that helping me with my research would provide them with any material advantage, but, nevertheless, I continue to feel a responsibility to them. Part of this responsibility involves admitting the ambiguities and incongruities inherent in their lives and representing them as honestly as possible.

The core of this book, Chapters Three, Four and Five, deal with the children's perceptions of who they are and what they do. I discuss what was important to the children, how they coped with what was happening to them, and what strategies they used for survival. I examine their understandings of prostitution, the stories they told each other and sometimes told me about how they had become prostitutes and how they were seen inside and outside their communities. I analyse their standards and moral codes, the importance of status and hierarchy in their community, and the role of their families in allowing or discouraging them to become prostitutes. As well as the cultural and moral frameworks they had, I also look at their practical choices. I investigate what their other options for earning money were given their background and their surroundings, and what the financial and indeed, legal, penalties would be for giving up prostitution and going to the authorities for medical, psychological, or monetary help. I try to view their prostitution in its social context, as holistically as possible, as an economic, social and moral issue.

These chapters are based on twelve months of fieldwork which I carried out between June 1993 and September 1994. I was based in a small slum community which I have called Baan Nua (North Village in Thai) where the children lived with their families and worked part-time as prostitutes in order to supplement the family income. This slum was on the edge of a town with many tourists and the children's clients were exclusively Europeans. Other than that information, I have deliberately kept the town I worked in anonymous and the region of Thailand within which it is located unidentified. The children that I know are too easily identifiable and I do not wish them to suffer any further intrusion in their lives because of what I have written about them. Some of them no longer live there and some are no longer prostitutes, and I do not want them to be pigeonholed as child prostitutes for the rest of their lives because they have appeared in this book. Also, they were in regular contact with voluntary social workers who took in food, medical care, and started basic education classes. The approach of these social workers was one of co-operation and dialogue with the community, carried out with great humility. It was one which I much admired and which has had numerous good effects. They are some of the few people who have been able to reach out to this community and I do not wish to jeopardise their position. Anthropological convention dictates that all names of informants should be changed, which I have done to protect their privacy as much as I can.

The essence of this book is what children themselves say about prostitution. The children that I know were able to offer a clear analysis of what they were doing and even while they may not fully understand the forces of the wider political economy, they can construct an analysis of their actions which is every bit as valid as that of a researcher or a campaigner. They, too, see a structure and a pattern to their lives. Although many people who write about them give death as the only way out of their situation, the children themselves see it very differently. It is important to remember that some of these children continue to hope, dream, and work their way out of the poverty and desperation in which they find themselves. They do not see themselves defined only by prostitution and remain committed to their families, their communities and their society. Those who are labelled as prostitutes by others, define themselves as dutiful daughters, sisters, or grandchildren, who should be admired rather than pitied or patronised.

The children in Baan Nua challenged many of my own notions of what it is to be a child or a prostitute as well as my ideas about sexuality and exploitation. I did not always agree with what they told me, and I did not share their sometimes fatalistic acceptance of what, to me, was unconscionable abuse, but I do recognise their realities as valid and important. The discourses on child prostitutes have been shaped by many people but only occasionally by the children themselves. There is no doubt that these are difficult children who raise some extraordinarily complex ethical issues, but they are also the children that are talked about so much, but rarely talked to. To begin with, therefore, the underlying attitudes towards child prostitutes must be questioned. It may seem self-evident why child prostitution evokes such horror and disgust but these reactions are based on temporally and geographically specific notions of the correct form of childhood which need to be deconstructed. This is a complex issue which I deal with in Chapter Two. There I examine the different notions of childhood found both in the West and in Thailand, analysing the reasons for their existence and for their current understanding.

Chapter One discusses the history of the myths concerning child prostitution. It contextualises the ethnographic material to show that, although there is a tendency to assume that child prostitution is a recent phenomenon which is being discovered and discussed for the first time, it has a history which can illuminate contemporary concerns. Thailand has a history of indigenous child prostitution which can inform current understandings. Other cultures, at certain points in their history, have become equally concerned with the problem and employed many of the same discourses that are utilised in the current discussions. Concern about child prostitution is not specific to any one culture or historical period, nor is it a new phenomenon that has sprung up suddenly. However, despite all the information available, the extent and even the nature of the problem remain obscure. There have been few serious attempts to estimate accurately the extent of child prostitution. Un-sourced random numbers are used as evidence for its escalation into epidemic proportions, but there is little hard evidence of this.

This is why I have placed so much emphasis on stories rather than on statistical or factual 'truth'. As Fentress and Wickham wrote, stories are more than just memories and they can be without particular truth:

> Stories do more than represent particular events: they connect, clarify, and interpret events in a general fashion. Stories provide us with a set of stock explanations which underlie our predispositions to interpret reality in the way that we do ... Memory is not merely retrospective; it is prospective as well. Memory provides a perspective for interpreting our experiences in the present and for foreseeing those that lie ahead.' (1992: 51).

Each group with a vested interest in these children, including the children themselves, need their stories. It is important to look not only at what they are saying but why they are saying it. What I shall do is to suggest reasons why these groups need these particular versions of the truth and why the current campaign against child prostitution has been so successful. In less than fifteen years, it has gone from an issue which very few knew about to near saturation coverage. It has eclipsed the major concerns of the 1980s, such as child labour, or street children, or in some cases subsumed them; street children are interesting now to the extent that they might sell sex.

I conclude this book with some proposals which might enable the debate to move forward and suggest ways in which children can be offered relevant help. It is easy as an academic to sit back and criticise without offering any suggestions for improvement, and my intention is not to censure any particular organisation or individual. However, practical help must come on the back of good research, of which there is currently very little. In its place is sensational reporting, stereotypes, and myths which can ultimately help no-one. Child prostitution has caught the public imagination: as Maggie Black has written, 'There is, for good or bad, a public appetite for information, particularly of the most sensational kind, which confers a special commodity status on the subject of 'child' sex' (Black 1995: 6). There is a desire to help child prostitutes, but this impetus has its dangers as well. It is important not to let that public appetite slide into voyeurism or titillation.

The recommendations that I make in the conclusion may seem rather vague and tentative. Nevertheless I feel that understanding is the key and that interventions must be made on the basis of research. Child prostitution, like other forms of child abuse, is not an easy area to discuss for all the previously elaborated reasons. It is emotionally draining and morally fraught. It is possible to see the root causes of prostitution as the abuse of the vulnerable and innocent by the powerful and degenerate, but this morally satisfying position does not necessarily bring long term solutions. Foreign clients can be prosecuted in their home countries, but a comprehensive solution which takes account of both supply and demand needs to be tackled at a societal as well as an individual level, involving many different approaches. This does not mean doing nothing in the short term, but it does involve a much more nuanced view of child prostitution, which does not make excuses for it, but looks honestly at the causes, the effects and the possible and practical solutions to it. Research on its own is not a panacea to the problem of child prostitution, but it is where intervention must start. As yet, research is patchy and there are important gaps in what is known about the issue. These need to be explored, but detailed, ground-level, research is possible. There are great difficulties which should not be underestimated, but it is possible to know the children's views and to understand their communities. The advocates and the children rarely speak to each other, and there is little sense of partnership between them. Intervention becomes oppression if it is executed without consent by advocates on those for whom they claim to speak. The aim of this book is to understand why each side thinks as it does and to make no definitive judgements on those understandings but to suggest instead common ground and the possibilities for dialogue between them.

Child Prostitution and Anthropology

The subject of child prostitution fits uneasily into academic research. It is problematic as a subject of study, not just for the ethical and practical reasons I have discussed previously, but also for theoretical ones. Although the concept of the disengaged researcher has been questioned, there is still the assumption of impartiality, which is considered compromised when dealing with such issues. Child prostitution generates a certain squeamishness in academic circles, which tend to view such emotive and possibly sensational subjects as inappropriate topics for dispassionate academic research (cf. Hart 1998). There is a feeling that the proper forum for discussion of such ideas is in the media or through NGOs. Nearly all the previous work written on child prostitution has come from these sources, writing to 'raise awareness' of the problem. This work is often poorly researched and sensationalist in tone, and while it gives a good indication of some of the discourses surrounding child prostitution, it is of limited theoretical interest. However, there are academic anthropological precedents for the study of such subjects and these should be explained in more detail.

Although this book concerns a controversial and contemporary subject, its focus is on many of the traditional concerns of anthropology; kinship, community and the ways these are understood and made sense of by the children. The study of kinship is integral to this book and it is an area in which anthropology can claim a long expertise. Kinship is also the idiom through which anthropology has tackled recent societal concerns, especially those related to identity and to the cultural construction of the body, which resonate throughout this book. Cannell (1990), Strathern (1992), Edwards (1993) and Franklin (1997) have all used understandings of kinship to inform their discussions of the 'New Reproductive Technologies' and the impact of these on contemporary society. Through the terminology of kinship, issues which had previously focused on the rights and wrongs of these technologies were transformed into more demanding and challenging discussions that questioned the construction of identity in contemporary Britain.

Issues concerning childhood, prostitution, or sexuality, as well as understandings of the body are clearly related to broader issues of kinship. Anthropologists and sociologists have recently begun to pay more attention to these areas and to claim them as legitimate areas of research. Issues such as incest, once of primary importance to the study of kinship, have been revitalised by anthropologists such as Jean la Fontaine (1987 and 1990), who have looked at power relationships within families and extended previous knowledge of incest to deepen understandings of child sexual abuse. It is through the study of kinship that anthropologists have had most success in bridging the gap between academia and the concerns of the wider society. Issues such as child sexual abuse, assisted conception, and the nature of the modern family, have all been addressed and problematised by anthropologists whose work has broadened and extended previous understandings of these issues.

The issue of childhood is one such example. It is a subject which seems intimately bound up with the history of anthropology and yet only recently have anthropologists and sociologists begun to deconstruct concepts of childhood. Anthropologists have long talked about children, and works of popular anthropology such as Mead's *Coming of Age in Samoa* take children as their central theme, yet they remain largely silent about childhood itself. Childhood is thus constructed as a universal phenomenon; a time of weakness, powerlessness and ignorance. According to Mead, some children may have better or less repressed childhoods than their counterparts in the Western world, but everywhere children are passive objects and receivers of adult practices. Other anthropologists, such as Benedict, and others of the 'Culture and Personality' school, looked at the effects of childrearing on personality traits and saw the child as a *tabula rasa* on which a future personality was written by the cultural practices of his or her upbringing. The emphasis again, however, was on children as future adults or children as the passive recipients of adult care and attention. They were not studied for themselves, and the way childhood was conceptualised cross-culturally was rarely examined. Outside anthropology, children were studied by developmental psychologists looking for stages in their emotional and physical development, or as 'problem children' by social workers, but childhood itself was rarely problematised. Children were commonly referred to as the 'next generation', 'the future of society', or simply 'our future'. They were interesting only for what they would become; childhood was a temporary, and not particularly interesting, stage they had to pass through before they could become 'proper' subjects of research. The nature of childhood itself was not viewed as problematic and its various cultural constructions were rarely analysed.

Children have thus long been effectively marginalised in anthropology, or studied only tangentially. The beginning and end of childhood have been of interest, but the nature of childhood itself, or how it is socially constructed, have been of little concern. Birth practices and ritual cleansing or separation around parturition have always attracted anthropological attention (Hanks 1962, Muecke 1976, Mougne 1978), but except as bit part players in these ceremonies, children have been absent. Equally, initiation ceremonies have been of central concern to anthropology (see for example Lewis 1980, Lutkehaus and Roscoe 1995) but children are usually passive and written out of these ceremonies. It is only when they become adults, and therefore social actors, that they become important. Clearly, all these writers are concerned with specific ritual processes rather than childhood itself, but it is noticeable how childhood is recognised as socially significant only when it comes to an end.

The rise of Western feminism in the 1970s politicised the role of children but, once again, there was little interest in them as subjects for research. Either they were conceptualised as the enemy of women and their needs and demands seen as a barrier to their social advancement (Firestone, for example, wrote that, 'The heart of women's oppression is her childbearing and childrearing role' 1971: 79), or previous paradigms were replicated in which women and children were conceptualised as allies in opposition to patriarchy (c.f. Oakley 1994). Both groups were viewed as powerless, with 'muted voices', but the concurrent assumption that they therefore have the same agenda, or that women's activism obviated the need for children's rights, or that what was beneficial to women was also beneficial for children, is not necessarily true. Children became central to both feminist and anti-feminist arguments, but never as subjects in their own right. Children were part of a woman's experience; their own experiences, views and conceptualisations were never acknowledged.

It was not until the mid 1980s and early 1990s that childhood and children themselves became seen as valid and valuable subjects in their own right. Ennew (1986), Qvortrup (1994), James (1995), and others began to use the notion of 'child-centred' research. This entailed bringing children back from the margins of anthropological and sociological literature, where references to them had previously been found, and placing them at the centre of research projects. This did not mean focusing only on children, or constructing a sub-culture of society where children existed separated from their families and their communities. Rather, it meant that research on children attempted to understand their perspective, their links to their families, and to examine the importance of their relationships, as they saw them. Wider issues of community were not written out by this perspective but the emphasis was shifted. Instead of looking at children only as recipients of culture, or of childrearing practices, children were re-conceptualised as active agents. The roles they played in shaping their society and their social importance to their families were increasingly acknowledged. Not only they were affected by their communities, but they affected their communities in turn.

Child-centred research also involved problematising notions of childhood and rejecting ideas of childhood as being a universal state, albeit with different local manifestations. Increasingly childhood was recognised as a culturally constructed, social phenomenon rather than a stage in developmental psychology or a time of universal dependence and powerlessness. Children could no longer be seen as a homogenous group with views and priorities that depended only on their physical advancement, but they were acknowledged as interesting for, and in, themselves. Childhood, in many ways a liminal stage, became viewed as a separate area for study. It was no longer possible to add children as a sub-category of women's studies as it is clear they need to be understood using very different categories. Unlike 'womanhood', childhood is not a fixed state and children will eventually move out of it. While expectations may be placed on them because of their social age, they will not be permanently defined by these roles in the way that women are always bound by their gender. Nevertheless, it has been too often assumed that because children's roles were impermanent, they were also unimportant. Child-centred research has shown that childhood is a social phenomenon and should be studied as such.

There will always be some resistance, both practically and philosophically, to child-centred research. Anthropologists especially find particular problems when they study children. The study of a social phenomenon or a cultural group implies a process of socialisation that everyone in that group has passed through, and anthropologists tend to assume that adults are the finished product of this socialisation process. Young children are still learning the ways of their society and to draw conclusions simply from their behaviour, without reference to their surroundings, is dangerous. Young children make cultural 'mistakes' and act 'inappropriately' and it is through the reactions of the adults to their mistakes and through the process of correction and guidance, that acceptable behaviour is defined. Even so, anthropology has tended to look at children only in terms of initiation or socialisation, how they *become* adults rather than how they *are* children. La Fontaine writes:

> In general, anthropology has retained an outdated view of children as raw material, unfinished specimens of the social beings whose ideas and behaviour are the proper subject matter for social science.' (1986: 10).

Children do have the capacity to be social actors and they do have their own views and their own worlds. They should not be seen purely in adult terms (Waksler 1991, James and Prout 1995, Morrow 1995) or as 'human becomings'. They are not incompetent adults or half-formed humans, and when talking about an issue that affects them as intimately as prostitution, to ignore their voices is unacceptable. It is important to find a balance between treating children as a subculture within their society, viewing them as individuals in their own right, or seeing them as little adults. Children can act as independent agents, and yet it must be recognised that practically children are constrained because of their age, their physical size and also other people's reactions towards them (James and Prout 1995).

In a similar way to the study of childhood, until recently, issues of sexuality have been either passed over by anthropologists or related to issues such as reproduction or maternity. The sex act itself is viewed as a biological universal, even if it takes different cultural forms (Vance 1991). Studies of how sexualities have been created and imagined, and their links with the wider political economy, have been muted, and it is only very recently that there has been such an explosion of interest in the subject (Hyam 1990, Dollimore 1991). As Vance (1991) has noted, however, there is still a certain fastidiousness in many anthropology departments about examining sexuality and it is often dismissed as an inherently non-academic subject for study, which appeals only to special interest and minority groups in academia. It is noticeable that many studies have looked at constructions of 'alternative' sexualities: either the construction of women's sexualities (Vance 1989), or those of gay men (Weeks 1981). Alternatively other studies have been constrained by discourses on deviancy and criminality, for example in studies of prostitution. Nevertheless work on these 'deviant' or marginal' sexualities have shown that sexual meanings are not fixed and, like notions of childhood, are not biological universals. Vance's sums this up succinctly:

> Because a sexual act does not carry with it a universal social meaning, it follows that the relationship between sexual acts and sexual meanings is not fixed, and it is projected from the observer's time and place at great peril.' (1991: 878).

Based on such theoretical premises, anthropologists have studied sexual meanings in other contexts and other cultural settings. They have found the problems of translation and interpretation, which are apparent in all ethnographic writing, particularly difficult in relation to sexuality. Caplan's *The Cultural Construction of Sexuality* (1987) clearly showed the limitations of Western terminology in relation to understanding other culture's assumptions about sexuality. More problematically, Herdt's work in Melanesia (1984), has shown that even the same acts have very different meanings in various cultural settings. His work has questioned Western notions of what is, or is not, a sexual act.

The work of other anthropologists such as Fordham's work on Thailand (1993, 1995, 1996) or Parker's work on Brazil (1991) has celebrated the sexual cultures in these places and attempted to understand sexuality as a part of a wider political and economic culture. They have also tried to break down distinctions between 'deviant' and 'normal' sexualities, especially in regards to prostitution. Prostitution has proved a difficult area of sexual behaviour to deal with. It has been condemned as male exploitation by feminist writers or cast as a bio-medical issue which views it as a vector of disease. In Western societies, it is still greatly stigmatised so that researchers are forced to deal with issues of deviancy and social rejection. Both Fordham and Parker, however, have managed to move beyond this deviance paradigm. By normalising prostitution and viewing it as part of wider patterns of male social identity, they have shown the importance of studying sexuality for the insights it provides into other aspects of society. Indeed, as Herdt and Leap have written about sexual behaviour and anthropology, 'more than ever, anthropology is challenged now to define and examine basic concepts of culture and ontology, with regard to what is normative and valued, illicit or stigmatised, idealised and private in the lives of people ... across cultures' (1991: 168). I should like the study of child prostitution to be part of this project. Rather than being academic voyeurism, I believe that it does give an insight into basic concepts of culture and ontology. Children play a central role in forming and articulating these concepts.

CHAPTER 1

HISTORY AND CONTEXT

Myths and Stereotypes

It is, perhaps, a truism that activists in the West need child prostitutes in developing countries far more than child prostitutes need the activists; they fulfil a special need and function in Western iconography. At some level, there is an agreement about what is expected of child prostitutes and how they will be portrayed. The child prostitute has taken on such iconic status that each child's suffering is no longer seen as the suffering of an individual but has become a stereotype of martyrdom. The assumptions behind this have not been examined, and yet it seems obvious to ask; why is the picture received through the media or through the case studies of the NGOs so uniform, with such repetitive ingredients? In his work on street children Hecht notes the particular agenda that many researchers have, whatever their background, and he describes 'a loosely agreed upon recipe. The staple ingredients include a definition of the "problem", a pinch of history about street children, a sprig of statistics about the numbers of street children, and a final shake in the form of suggestions for policy makers (1994: 4).' With slightly different ingredients, the same is true for child prostitutes.

At the very outset then, the stereotypes of child prostitutes that are received must be recognised and challenged. Journalists know what child prostitutes should look like, so they find HIV-positive children, rescued from brothels, who can be recognised as 'the real thing'. The children in their turn know what is expected of them, what they need to do or say to get sympathy and they play the role as best they can. Both sides are telling the stories that are expected of them, while never recognising that the narratives which they present as truth, are only partial. Any examination of child prostitution must be an analysis of the discourses surrounding child prostitutes and the stories and mythology that influence views of them. What stories do the children tell each other and themselves? What do they tell an anthropologist, a journalist, an advocate, or others who demand their stories? What stories do these people then tell others?

I will give just two examples here of the myth, before going on to argue that the stories these articles tell fulfil the needs of the campaigners and advocates, not those of the children. Child prostitutes can suffer enormously through their work but they should not be made to suffer further by being given a pre-arranged script which denies their own history and further reduces their identity. The following two articles appeared within a month of each other during one of several peaks of media interest in the problem of child prostitution and, especially, the issue of child-sex tourists. I have chosen them out of a collection of hundreds, simply because they are so typical. They were no more sensational than usual, neither were they outstandingly well written: they did not radically change anything. Indeed, they are formulaic and are stories that have been told previously. The names of the children have been changed, as have their home towns and even the nationalities of their clientele, but these are old stories with a set pattern and an inevitable consequence. As with folk tales or fairy stories, there is even a certain satisfaction in knowing how they will turn out.

The first is the lead paragraph from the Australian newspaper, *The Sunday Age*, published on 18 April 1993. Although it goes on to give more detail and coverage of the problem, in true journalistic style, it sums up the story in the first paragraph. Under the headline 'Bo, 12, taken to a hotel and forced to have sex,' it tells the girl's harrowing story. It is accompanied by a picture, purportedly of Bo with a younger child, but it makes no attempt to hide her face or shield her identity.

'At 10, Bo was tricked into prostitution after the death of her mother and father and substantially left without family.

For five years in a brothel resort in the southern Thai resort town of Songkhla, Bo endured countless Thai and Western men, including many Australians, whom the brothel owner called 'kangaroos'.

The euphoria of escape has been short-lived. Bo has been diagnosed HIV-positive. She is not expected to celebrate her 25th birthday. She is now 17 or 18.' (Sunday Age 1993: 10).

The second article, entitled 'Impoverished Thai parents sell girls into prostitution,' is by Gayle Reeves and was published in the *Dallas Morning Star* of March 21, 1993. It is a longer article which gives the name and addresses of an organisation at the end of it so its readers can find out more information or send a donation if they wish. Like the previous story, it is based on an interview the child gave the journalist in her home village after returning from a brothel.

> At an age when many American teens are trying to talk Dad out of the car keys, she sits on the floor of a shabby cottage, trying to talk her frail, gaunt father out of sending her back to a brothel. At 17, she has already worked in three brothels, because of the need to help support her ailing parents. In the dim interior of the cottage purchased with her prostitute's wages, her father argues with social workers who want her to live and study at their shelter. The thatched cottage holds a few possessions: a charcoal brazier, a water jug, two battered tin cups and, on the room's one table, a television set. She is their only child, the father says. The brothel agent owns the land on which the house sits, and that day he has threatened to evict them. The father has borrowed money from the agent, with his daughter's work as collateral. What will happen to them if they lose her wages? He does not understand that, soon enough, he may lose her anyway. She has the AIDS virus.' (Reeves 1993).

Bo and the anonymous child in the second article have familiar stories. Abandoned by their parents into brothel life, they are rescued by good outsiders for a brief period of happiness before dying. In countless other articles, the pattern is repeated: betrayal, abuse, rescue, death. There is a neatness and coherence to this story which is compelling; no loose ends and a predictable outcome. The reader is invited to be outraged at the story, and to pity the victims but, ultimately, there is no escape from the plot and nothing that can be done to help these children. Once the story begins, it can only end, unhappily ever after, with the child's death. Anything else is too complex, too difficult to deal with, or too much like 'academic voyeurism'.

Yet there are other stories too, those which the children themselves tell to each other and sometimes to outsiders. They too are constructs, events are structured in a particular order to make particular points and, like the articles above, they are full of omissions and maybe exaggeration but, unlike the journalists or the campaigners, the children are not allowed to tell their own stories or not believed when they do so. There are various ways in which communities and individuals remember, and construct their memories, as Connerton has shown (1989), and yet only one 'true' history is allowed in regards to child prostitutes. The tendency to see children as unknowing or uncomprehending is firmly rooted in both the academic and the NGO worlds. There is an inherent bias in many studies of children that sees them as 'less than' rather than 'different from' adults and therefore their opinions and behaviour are interpreted and analysed by adults as incomplete and incompetent (Waksler 1991). When children speak, especially in relation to sensitive topics like prostitution, they are usually dismissed. They are accorded no authority for their views, and are seldom allowed to decide what is in their own best interest. On an issue like prostitution, it is assumed to be so apparent what the child's best interest is that there is little room for dissent from the child.

The pattern is so well known and so often repeated that it is difficult to remember that there are other routes into prostitution, often less dramatic and more complicated than the previous examples, and that there are ways out of it other than death. In 1993, the same year in which these two articles were published, I went to Thailand to conduct an anthropological study of a community which survived through the prostitution of its children. I was interested in how the community survived, what both the children and the parents thought of prostitution, and how they justified it and rationalised it to themselves. The study of child prostitution seemed to be an area where anthropology could make a key contribution, in that, while economic and demographic studies as well as many speculative articles had been published, no-one had carried out extensive research with the children themselves, studying their home lives and their own perceptions and explanations. There was no context based research or any analysis of the children's experiences and perceptions which only extended fieldwork could provide. In all the literature that I had read on the subject, the voices of the children themselves were noticeably absent.

The study I carried out was based in a tourist resort in Thailand. I worked within a community of people who earned their means of survival through the prostitution of their children. I too had a very clear idea of how I expected a child prostitute to behave or look and although I expected some variation from the usual stereotype, I thought I would recognise the children when I saw them. However, what became clear very quickly was that no-one in this community identified themselves with the images and stereotypes of child prostitutes. What they experienced was not the same as what they read about or were told about. This is not to say that the exploitation they suffered was any less painful or difficult to deal with, only that they responded to it and analysed it in very different ways. Their stories were much less neat than the ones used for campaigning purposes or written up in the newspapers. Here were people whose lives contained messy contradictions, loose ends which were never tied up, and who were still struggling to make sense of their situation.

The stories that they told me reflected this and made it impossible for me to look only at prostitution while ignoring the wider social forces of family, community, economy and globalisation. In December 1993, I met a thirteen-year-old named Daeng who was working as a prostitute. I asked her to tell me her story as she remembered it. Over several days she told me how she had become a prostitute and mentioned the key events in her history, which she felt, explained and influenced her life.

'My mother and father separated soon after I was born. My father supported me financially but I didn't live with him and his new wife. I never saw my mother and I was never given any money by her. Instead, I stayed with a relative of my father, but my father visited regularly. His new wife also came to visit and, although I didn't like her at first, she was always kind to me and always brought things when she came to visit. Even after my stepmother had children of her own, with my father, she continued to treat me the same and was always very fair and I liked her for that. My mother came to visit when I was nine or so and decided that I should go and live with her. But I hadn't seen her for so long, and she seemed like a stranger to me. I didn't want to go with her at all but everyone pressured me to go, so I went with her to where she lived. I liked my grandmother and we became very close but this caused problems and generated hostility from my mother's other relatives. They were suspicious of me and thought I would be left a lot of money by my grandmother when she died, while they would be cut out.

I lived at my grandmother's for another year. When I was ten and living with her, a family friend came to the house one evening while I was asleep and raped me. My grandmother was very kind, looked after me and comforted me and said that it would be a secret between us and that no-one else would ever know. I continued to live with her for a while but the following year, I came to Bangkok with my mother. We tried many jobs, first, delivering goods but that was very hard. Then I worked on a construction site but that was also too difficult, so I left. After that, I got a job in a gas station for another three or four months in Bangkok and then decided to move down to a tourist resort. I had an aunt who worked in a bar down here and she invited me down to work in the same bar. I didn't want to do this so I got a job in a restaurant instead for a few months and then in a shop where I worked until I got fired.

When I was working at this shop, I met a friend called Toi who worked with her mother on a noodle stall nearby. We started to go to discos together which annoyed our parents. I began to have several boyfriends around then. Toi had fallen out with her parents on a number of occasions and kept running away. She had a sister who worked in a nearby brothel and Toi would frequently stay with her. Once when she came back, her mother took her to the doctor who diagnosed three different kinds of sexually transmitted diseases. One night we went to a disco and stayed out all night. The next day when I telephoned work to say that I was ill, they fired me. As I lived at the shop, I had nowhere to go and so Toi decided that she would not go home either. Instead, she and I moved in with Toi's boyfriend who worked as a waiter in a bar. He was twenty-one and already living with another girl who was very jealous of us. Soon enough, I became his lover too and Toi was furious.

Finally, his girlfriend threw us out because she thought we drank too much and had too many boyfriends. We did not know what to do so we went to an entertainment agency which placed us as dancers. We were expected to have sex with customers and we could keep their tips on top of the 2,600 *baht* a month (about £70) that we were earning. How else are we to get money? And anyway, whatever happens in there it's no worse than what I've already done.

What I really wanted to do was to become a nurse, but people like me don't become nurses. All I want now is a well-paid job so that I can go home with my head held up and help my father and stepmother. My father has rheumatism and I want some money for him. I don't care about my mother. I hate her. She never visited me here except one time when she tried to find me in the shop that I had been working in before I got fired. I wasn't there but because I had only just left, my stuff was there. So my mother collected my clothes, my radio and my salary. Then she stole them. She has even written to me and asked me to send money home and I will, but not to her. I'll only send it to my father! For the money though, I'll stay here. I enjoy this place. There is a lot to do here and I have a lot of friends to go to discos with.'

A closer study reveals the variety of forms of prostitution and highlights the danger of privileging one particular image. The constant repetition of the same story containing the same elements ultimately dulls its impact. Certain things are expected of child prostitutes; they should be kidnapped, trafficked, forced into debt-bondage or tricked into prostitution. These are the real victims, the unfortunate ones deserving of sympathy who are fundamentally 'innocent', while others who live at home, work part-time and refuse the pity that would be offered to them if only they fitted, are seen as the 'guilty' ones to be condemned and despised. Holland sums this up eloquently in her book *What is a Child?*

> 'The child who appeals to the viewer, humbly requesting help, has remained the mainstream of aid imagery. But children's actual response to conditions of deprivation may well refuse qualities of childhood which give them their pathos. It is less easy to deal with children who have become fighters, workers or brutalised dwellers on the streets.' (1992: 161).

What cannot be dealt with is treated with great unease, especially when children do develop strategies for fighting back or just for coping.

It is these children, who do survive by any means possible, that are rarely heard about; the children who exist in grey areas. These are often the children on the doorstep, the child prostitutes of Britain who are not the adorable innocents in Thailand or the Philippines, snatched from their families. They are the rejects of society, sent out of care or welfare homes at sixteen, or sexually abused at home but ultimately abandoned by society (Finkelhor 1979a, Sereny 1984, Weisberg 1985, Lowman 1987, Campagna and Poffenberger 1988, Gibsonainyette et al. 1988, Allsebrook and Swift 1989, Widom and Ames 1994, Lee and O'Brien 1995, Snell 1995). Their lives do not have the grand tragedy of abused innocence and they are rarely as 'attractive', either physically or emotionally, as distressed Third World children in rural settings. Their poverty and helplessness are too mundane and too normal to warrant any special consideration. They are, quite simply, not exotic enough. They do not fit neatly into the stereotype that has been created and society responds by ignoring them, being fearful of them and blaming them for their own problems. New laws have been passed throughout the world, promising stiff penalties for men who have sex with anyone under eighteen abroad, but there is no such protection for young people of a similar age in this country. They are covered by adult laws on prostitution and ages of consent, not specific legislation.

Like child prostitutes in Britain, Daeng is positioned in an uncomfortable grey area. She is clearly not a helpless victim but, equally apparently, she is a child who needs support. She does not fit easily into the stereotype of child prostitute and reactions to her story will be very different from reactions to Bo's. It is easy to dismiss her as not 'really' a child prostitute and to place her way down the scale of deserving children, or to emphasis certain events such as the rape and ignore the rest. Yet her account of her life and the events that lead up to her becoming a prostitute are much more complicated and her family life and lack of relationship with her mother are obviously vitally relevant to her. Cases such as Daeng's are common and should add more complexity to analyses of the issue but, often, they are glossed over in place of unequivocal vignettes which need no analysis and admit no ambiguity.

I am not suggesting that other writers are unaware of these difficulties or that the first two stories are necessarily sensationalised and distorted. Different types of child prostitution exist and the kidnapping, debt-bondage and abuse of young girls in brothels has been well documented (Koompraphant n.d., Heyzer 1986, Lee-Wright 1990, Centre for the Protection of Children's Rights 1991, Muecke 1992, Asia Watch 1993). Also, they are written for a particular readership and have distinct functions. There is no space in a newspaper or in campaigns that are trying to raise awareness or money for too much analysis or discussion. Yet the story they tell is presented as the objective truth, often verified not by facts but by the difficulties the journalist or the campaigner had in obtaining the story. The extreme form of prostitution that journalists and NGO workers portray does exist, but it is not the only form. The media coverage of brothel raids, human trafficking and forced debt-bondage causes a hierarchy of child prostitutes. The more innocent, unknowing, and pathetically victimised the better. Yet there are different forms of child prostitution, different motivations for entry into sex work and different ways of interpreting the situation. Those who concentrate on the extreme, ignore the mundane, and run the risk of glamorising and exoticising everyday poverty.

Daeng's story makes uncomfortable reading because it challenges some fundamental ideas of what is appropriate for a child to know or decide. Stories of abuse like Bo's are easier to accept because, disturbing as they are, at least they are working within a paradigm that is familiar to most people. The child is innocent, forced into prostitution and traumatised to the point of death by it. Most importantly, the child is powerless, totally controlled by adults and has been abandoned by her parents, and especially her mother. It upsets no notions of the 'correct' role of either families or children and reinforces ideas that childhood is a universal phenomenon with universal features. It is not the conception or the ideal that is wrong, but the individual circumstances.

NGOs and the Discovery of Child Prostitution

The transformation of child prostitution from a local concern to an internationally discussed and debated issue has been recent and dramatic. Less than a decade ago, there was almost no awareness of the issue and yet now governments are changing laws to deal with the problem. In 1996, there was sufficient concern and interest to hold 'The World Congress Against the Commercial Sexual Exploitation of Children' in Stockholm, attended by government ministers from around the world. Australia has passed a law which would imprison its citizens for up to seventeen years if they are found guilty of sexual offences against children abroad. Norway, Germany, France, Belgium, New Zealand and Sweden have all passed similar laws. In Britain, The Sex Offenders Act was passed in March 1997, which empowered the United Kingdom courts to prosecute people who commit sex offences against children abroad, if they commit a crime which is an offence in both countries. For NGOs, the commercial sexual exploitation of children became one of the most important issues of the 1990s. The Jubilee Action Trust (n.d.), the Michael Sieff Foundation (1996) and Christian Aid (1995), all brought out position papers and reports on the subject and there were numerous newspaper articles concerning the issue in the UK alone.[1] Again, despite all the information, there is little understanding. There are certain questions that have not been answered and many assumptions that must be questioned. For example, is the problem of child prostitution actually new or simply newly discovered?

The history of child prostitution as an international problem is closely linked to the history of certain NGOs which have campaigned so successfully on the issue. The fact that child prostitution is currently such a topical issue is largely due to the tireless campaigning of an NGO called End Child Prostitution in Asian Tourism (ECPAT). As a rough indication of their success, it is instructive to look at the coverage of the issue in the press, especially Thailand's two English language newspapers, the *Nation* and

---

1. See, for example, 'Child Sex Britons Freed with Bribes,' (Drummond and Chant 1994), 'Thais' Uphill Battle Against Sex Slavery,' (Cumming-Bruce 1995), or 'Girls, Girls, Girls,' (Grant 1995), 'Police Link with Thailand to End Trips for Child Sex,' (Tendler and Ford 1994), 'European Widows Exploit Sri Lankan Teenagers for Sex,' (Kennedy 1996a), 'Child Abuse Tourists Boast to Undercover Researchers,' (Kennedy 1996b), 'Vietnamese Children Sold into Sex Slavery,' (Daniel 1996), 'Girls as Young as 12 'Sold for Sex',' (Dutter 1996), 'Lost Children of the Night,' (Rogers 1996), 'Sri Lankan Children for Sale on the Internet,' (West 1996).

the *Bangkok Post*, whose readership is made up of professional Thai middle classes and expatriates. In searching through back issues, I found that child prostitution, although mentioned occasionally, was of minor concern. It merited fewer than a dozen articles between 1983 and 1989, whereas between 1989 and 1995 there have been over 400 articles analysing and describing the stories of these children. In 1989, it was still possible for the Foundation for Children, one of the few indigenous children's rights groups, to bemoan the fact that the interest in child prostitution was so low; these are comments that would be nonsensical today.

> One should keep in mind that outside influence dictates the manner of operation of the organisation; the outside influence also stimulates public interest, as well as the mass media to publicise the issues. For example, sexual abuse or child abduction syndicates received longer public interest than the problems of child prostitution. The publicity of child prostitution would always be curbed at one point, because it involves networks of conspiracy which are nation-wide, and it affects both the economy and the society. Even the government policy indirectly supports the idea of child prostitution. (Foundation for Children 1989: 57).

This lack of interest and low priority for child prostitution changed dramatically, when ECPAT was formed in 1991. It has been by far the most successful of NGOs dealing with the issue in terms of fund raising, media coverage and international support, and it is worth studying its origins in some depth in order to understand its ideology. ECPAT was formed in 1991 as an offshoot of ECTWT (The Ecumenical Coalition on Third World Tourism). This group was founded because 'the churches in the ecumenical movement realised tourism was doing more harm than good to people and communities in the Third World' (Newsletter 1991: 1). Based on much of the anti-tourism literature from the 1970s and 1980s (see for example Turner and Ash 1975, Graburn 1983,[2] Richter 1989) its stance was that tourism

---

2. Graburn is particularly important here as his article, 'Tourism and Prostitution,' has been extremely influential in the debate over tourism. He draws explicit parallels between tourism and prostitution and claims that, in its most extreme form, there is no difference between the two. He wrote:

> 'As host nations, they may have little to sell but their "beauty" which is often desecrated by (sacrificed to) mass tourism. The men of such countries are forced into pimp roles ... At a psychological level [poor] nations are forced into the 'female' role of servitude, of being 'penetrated' for money, often against their will: whereas the outgoing, pleasure seeking "penetrating" tourists of powerful nations are cast in the "male" role (Graburn 1983: 441).

was detrimental to Thailand and should be discouraged as much as possible. Campaigns were launched such as 'International No Golf Day', protesting about the expansion of golf courses for the Japanese and articles denouncing mass tourism were published (Gonzales 1993). Sex tourism and the idea that men were travelling to Thailand with the explicit intention of buying sex from Thai prostitutes was also a great concern to the organisation (ECTWT 1993). Going even further than Graburn, they claimed that tourism was not only indistinguishable from prostitution, but also from sexual violation. Two of ECTWT's leaders wrote 'tourism is the rape of culture, the environment, women and children' (Srisang and Srisang n.d: 11).

The specific issue of child prostitution was not the primary focus of ECTWT's early campaigns but the issue of the commercial sexual abuse of Thai children by foreigners became increasingly more central to it so that in 1991, a dedicated agency, known as ECPAT, was launched to focus on the problem. Although technically separate from ECTWT, it shared many of its founding agency's concerns over tourism and retained much of the original ideology of ECTWT. The overall policy and direction remained the same and as it was still staffed with ECTWT personnel or their spouses; this was not surprising. At its launch, the ECPAT policy was clearly stated, and although its background was excluded and no mention was made of its origins, the similarities between the two organisations remain. The statement read:

> The issue of child prostitution is a symptom of the broader oppression which faces people in developing countries but it may be a starting point for this wider debate. We have deliberately chosen the narrow goal for this campaign because we believe that it can be achieved. We want to end child prostitution as it is related to tourism in the Asian countries of Philippines, Sri Lanka, Taiwan and Thailand. This means that we are not dealing with child prostitution or child abuse in its broadest context but only that which is generated by the presence of foreign tourism. Nor are we dealing with the wider issue of prostitution but only that which relates to younger children under the age of sixteen. (Newsletter 1991: 1).

This mission was later modified so that child prostitution referred to anyone under eighteen, but this definition has remained central to ECPAT's campaign over the last ten years. The role of the foreign tourist in exploiting and abusing Thai children has been the central campaigning point of their work during this time, and they have been phenomenally successful in pushing the issue to centre-stage. Indeed, they have been so successful that child prostitution has come to be defined almost entirely as the commercial sexual exploitation of children by foreigners. There is good evidence in India about the trafficking and abuse of Nepalese girls in Bombay (see for example Mukherji 1986, Rozario 1988, Patkar 1991, Sleightholme and Sinha 1997), with estimates of hundreds of thousands of children involved, yet this situation has not created nearly the same worldwide concern.

The plight of these children has not had the same international impact because once again these children fall into ambiguous categories that many people would rather not examine. It is much easier to place the blame firmly on a sexually perverse foreign man abusing innocent children than it is to look at a situation where the sexual abuse of children is endemic and has become normalised and, indeed, institutionalised. This pervasive structural acceptance and support for prostitution was clearly shown on July 16 1993, in a raid on a brothel in Ranong (near the Burmese border in Thailand) where one hundred and forty-eight Burmese women and girls were rescued. They said they had been forced or tricked into the brothels, largely with the collusion of the Thai police and border guards. After a raid on the brothel, they were arrested by the Thai police as illegal immigrants and kept in appalling conditions for months. No clients were charged and the police chief of the town excused it on the grounds that:

> In my opinion it is disgraceful to let Burmese men frequent Thai prostitutes. Therefore, I have been flexible in allowing Burmese prostitutes to work here. Most of their clients are Burmese men. (Pol. Lt. Gen. Sudjai Yanrat quoted in *Nation* 1993b).

The US-based human rights group, Asia Watch, who investigated the situation of these women claimed that there was widespread collusion by Thai officials in their trafficking and imprisonment. Therefore, making this an issue of child prostitution only as O'Grady later did in his book *The Rape of the Innocent* (1994) seemed to miss the point. The abuse and exploitation that occurred, compounded by the women and children being jailed as illegal immigrants, was a gross abuse of human rights which was going on in the full knowledge of Thai officials. It did not matter what ages were involved: all the women were beaten, abused and kept against their will, and to protest about child abuse alone removed the situation from its political context.

The distinction between children having foreign clients and those having local ones is rather spurious and highlights the arbitrary nature of the boundaries that have been imposed on the issue. In the case of Nepalese children trafficked into India, or Burmese women and children brought across the border into Thailand, and kept in horrendous conditions in brothels on the border, the exploitation is immense, whatever the colour of their clients' passports. It is extremely unfortunate if children with Western clients are seen as the only legitimate image of child prostitution. There are many routes into prostitution, many forms of exploitation, and many different types of client. Concentration on only one form, and one model, excludes many children. The children of Bombay or the Burmese women trafficked into Thailand must not be excised from an analysis because they have the 'wrong' type of clients. Neither should there be arbitrary cut-off points when they cease to be child prostitutes and so become of no interest at all.

There are, of course, some NGOs and journalists who have studied India's child prostitution in-depth, just as there are relentless campaigners for the Burmese women and children in Thailand. Indeed ECPAT itself has used the Burmese girls' stories (or 'a composite of two actual stories', O'Grady 1994: 129) and estimated statistics from India for publicity purposes, even though neither situation involves Western tourists. The stereotype, however, remains constant. The real child prostitute is the young Asian girl in a brothel, abused, infected with AIDS and discarded by a selfish Westerner. Nepalese and Burmese girls can only be brought into this category by a vague suggestion that some of their clients might be foreigners. There are, however, still too many children outside this stereotype: those who have local clients, those who do not work in brothels, those whose financial or familial circumstances leave them with no other choice. The image given of a child prostitute leaves no room for children who do not fit this model.

The Extent of the Problem

According to much of the information available, child prostitution is growing all the time, increasing at alarming rates and reaching epidemic proportions. More and more children are being drawn into prostitution as Westerners search for ever more extreme sexual thrills or choose younger and younger children believing them to be AIDS free. But is there any evidence for this? Are the numbers of children involved in prostitution increasing? Are clients deliberately searching for younger and younger girls? The answer is, as with so many of the issues surrounding child prostitutes, that it is impossible to know. In the absence of in-depth behavioural studies of child-sex tourists and the lack of any baseline data on numbers, there is absolutely no evidence for any of these assumptions, although some may be based on more reasonable premises than others.

There have been a great many estimates (or 'guestimates' in NGO jargon) as to the exact number of child prostitutes in Thailand. The estimates vary from 2,000, (police figure quoted in Guest 1993), to 800,000 (figure given by the Centre for the Protection of Children's Rights quoted in Guest 1993), with many other numbers in-between (The Ministry of Public Health's estimate is 15,000, according to Guest 1993). There is, however, no exact figure and none of these above figures explains in adequate detail the methods of calculation that were employed to arrive at them. To enable estimates to be repeated, and to see if the problem really is growing, it is important to know the sample group, the location, and the time scale of the data collected, in order to make comparisons. In the meantime, propaganda has taken over from reliable estimates.

> The cause of the increase of prostitution is tourists. Third World countries of Asia promote their tourism industry to earn foreign currencies. One of the tourist attractions is sexual service. Data given by the National Statistical Office show that the number of tourists who visited Thailand has risen from 1 million in 1973 to 2 million in 1981, and from 4 million in 1988 to 5 million in 1990. Correspondingly, the number of prostitutes in the country has risen dramatically. A survey conducted by the Department of Police in 1964 showed that there were 400,000 prostitutes. The number has gone up to 500,000–700,000 in 1980. (ECPAT n.d: 3).

In reality, this statistic shows no such 'corresponding' rise in the number of prostitutes. It shows that prostitution has risen by at least 25% in the period 1964–1990 (although 500,000 to 700,000 leaves a worryingly large margin of error and is still un-sourced) while tourism has risen by 400% in the non-comparable period 1973 to 1990.

This misuse of statistics is illogical, unethical, and unnecessary. It is possible to make informed guesses about the scale of the problem and admit that they need further testing. At Mahidol University, Guest made an estimate of the number of child prostitutes using recognised statistical methods, clearly naming his sample groups and giving sources for all his statistics as well as giving the dates that these samples groups were researched. He openly admits that this number is only an estimation, but by using his projections he estimated that, in 1993, there were 200,000 sex workers in Thailand of whom 36,000 were children. He may be wrong, but at least his methods are open to examination. Anyone following him can make the same calculation with the same methods, and arrive at an informed consideration as to the increase, or decrease, in scale of the problem. Likewise, Truong (1990) looks at the police arrest figures and examines the percentages of children included in these. She found that in 1978, 2.5% of the charges against prostitutes related to child prostitutes under fifteen years of age. In 1979, this figure increased to 2.8%, in 1980 to 5.05%, and in 1981 to 6.3%. She is careful not to draw any conclusion about the increase in actual numbers of child prostitutes, however. There are many explanations for this rise, such as increased police vigilance, or willingness to charge, rather than caution, children. There is clearly a rise in the percentage of children being arrested for prostitution, but unless total numbers are known as well as percentages, such figures neither prove nor disprove any rise in themselves; much more careful analysis and contextualisation are needed. What happened, for example, in the years 1979–1980, that caused such a large rise in the percentage of children arrested for prostitution? The concern over numbers is quite understandable. There is a need to know the real extent of the problem, but the complexities and ambiguities of the situation are too often concealed under the obsession with 'increasing' numbers. As Ennew and others have written:

> International interest in children gained momentum in the United Nations International Year of the Child (1979) and was given further impetus through the adoption and entering into force of the United Nations Convention on the Rights of the Child (1989/90), yet, in the space of nearly two decades, little has changed in terms of the way research is carried out and used by child welfare and advocacy organisations, despite considerable advances in theories of childhood and methods of researching children's issues within the academic community. What this amounts to is that the numbers provided for all groups of children in need of special care and protection have tended to remain the same, based on guestimates rather than research. Whereas guestimates have their place in the early stages of research, provided that they are based on sound reasoning, the role they should play is that of baseline hypotheses, to be proved or disproved so that the true scale of a problem can be understood and children protected using programmes grounded in a real understanding of their situation. In the case of child sexual exploitation, however, guestimates have become fact, partly because they have become inscribed in rhetorical discourses aimed to raise awareness. The objective appears to be to heighten public

and policy interest in the issue by stressing the scale of the problem. Yet this is neither ethically acceptable nor logical.' (Ennew et
al. 1996: 24).

There is a great need for a reasonable working figure (if not
an exact number) in order to meet planning needs of both the
NGOs and the government, but such a figure is usually not
available or is lost under the claims of a crisis of epidemic proportions (Sachs 1994). Although the same figures are repeated
year after year, the numbers are always said to be growing. In
fact, no-one knows if the numbers are growing or not, but it is
always assumed that they are, and any figure, no matter how
outrageous, must be prefaced by 'at least'. Similarly, certain
phrases are used and repeated which add to the uncritical repetition of inaccurate statistics; 'children as young as' which might
refer to a group of women, or older children containing one or
two exceptionally young children or 'up to 20 times a night'
which again is presented as typical although it does not mention
the average number of clients or the type of sex work the children have to perform (Ennew et al. 1996). In journalism, it is
common to draw attention to the price paid for sex which is
often described as equivalent to 'a loaf of bread' or 'a box of
matches' with no indication if this is the buying power of that
money in Western or Thai terms, and making the unconscious
implication that it is the small amount of money paid, not the
abuse itself, that is so demeaning.

Numbers, of course, are vital to any campaign. They bring an
urgency and immediacy to it which is vital in gaining support.
They are also a necessary part of the same narratives of child
prostitution where the patterns of kidnapping, abuse, rescue and
death are endlessly rearranged and repeated. Large numbers
emphasise the fact that these children are not individual
tragedies but part of an epidemic which makes all children vulnerable. Statistics negate the need for long term research on the
children because they re-position the problem of abuse as one of
scale not intensity. Vague claims of millions of abused children
leave the fundamental question unanswered of when, in fact,
does child prostitution become a problem. When one child is
brutally and callously sexually exploited? When one hundred
are? Or only when there are one million child prostitutes? Taking the highest possible figure turns the situation into an epic
tragedy, given added poignancy by the standard image of abused
innocence. Such a view of the situation cannot allow room for
the thousands of other children who become statistics without

becoming stereotypes. Individual child prostitutes, with all their ambiguities, do not matter in these statistics, for they are just numbers. They are only transitory, their stories briefly illuminated, for a moment, in the spotlight of this edition's 'human interest' angle before being forgotten. It is paradoxical, that with all the emphasis on heartbreaking personal tragedy in the media, what really matters is numbers. If the numbers of child prostitutes were, in fact, decreasing every year, would the tragedy be any less? For individual children still working as prostitutes, probably not, but for the media and the campaigners against child prostitution, it is harder to say.

Statistics and numbers do give an urgency to any campaign and it is not surprising that ECPAT or Christian Aid, for example, place so much emphasis on these figures. When a problem exists and threatens to grow exponentially if unchecked, an urgent response is needed. By emphasising the huge scale of the problem, both the need for action and the need for the existence of campaigning groups are justified, especially in the face of official disbelief. Equally, numbers suggest thorough and responsible research has been done, and that the campaigning groups know the full extent of the problem. Statistics give research an authenticity that case studies cannot give. Yet this obsession with statistics, while benefiting the campaigners and the activists, does little for the children themselves who once again are overwhelmed and marginalised through rhetoric. In 1983, long before the current wave of concern over child prostitution, the United Nations Special Rapporteur on the Suppression of the Traffic in Persons and the Exploitation of the Prostitution of Others warned: 'The important point is not the scale of the problem but its degree of seriousness as a violation of the fundamental rights of the human person' (Fernand-Laurent 1983: 14). It is a great pity this counsel has not been taken more seriously.

Many activists might respond to these criticisms by claiming that it does not matter how many children are involved: the violation done to one is as bad as the abuse of thousands. This is quite reasonable, and there is a sense in which numbers do not matter, but why then is there this fixation with 'ever-growing' numbers? Why is there so little academic or intellectual rigour in the production of these statistics? It often seems that, in the scramble to prove that there are yet more children at risk than previously thought, individual children who are already involved in prostitution are overlooked. Ultimately, numbers can tell us nothing about the lives of the children themselves . To claim there are a million child prostitutes in Asia tells us very little. It does not elucidate who these children are, how they came to be prostitutes, what gender they are, or their ethnicity or nationality.

These carefully rounded figures must be treated with a great deal of caution. Although one million child prostitutes in Asia is now an accepted figure by NGOs worldwide, it has little basis in fact or in research (Black 1994). It is based on a statement made by The Norwegian Government to the Council of Europe which read: 'Every year, one million children are kidnapped, bought, or in other ways forced to enter the sex market' (Black 1994: 12). No source was given for this figure, nor was there any indication of how it was calculated. Indeed, this random use of numbers was quite unnecessary given that Redd Barna (the Norwegian branch of Save the Children), had, in 1989, the same year in which this statement was made, published a full report on what was known of the nature and extent of child prostitution. This report had been funded by NORAD (Norwegian Agency for International Development) but deliberately gave no numbers and statistics and acknowledged the difficult nature of defining and counting child prostitutes. It also emphasised the unreliability of many of the sources for these numbers (Narvesen 1989: 24). However, the Norwegian government appeared to ignore its own research. Its estimation has taken on a life of its own and it is now a commonly quoted statistic. At the World Congress against The Commercial Sexual Exploitation of Children in Stockholm in 1996, which I attended, it was the statistic that almost all the NGOs used, although often changed subtly to 'more than one million child prostitutes'. It should be noted however that the figure of 'one million children' appears to be a motif in most claims about child abuse, especially those concerning the 'discovery' of a particular aspect of abuse.[3] De Mause's seminal, if somewhat over-stated, argument, made in *The History of Childhood*, was based partly on his acceptance of the figure of one million abused children in America (1976: 4). It is part of the same mythology and stereotyping that informs so many of the representations of children's lives.

The difficulty with these figures becomes clearer when further questions are raised. If one million new children every year become prostitutes, what happens to the children from the previous years? Perhaps they all contract AIDS and die, and a new one million children are needed to take their place, perhaps they

---

3. A report commissioned by the NSPCC and published in October 1996, called *Childhood Matters* also claimed that more than one million children in Britain are either sexually, physically or emotionally abused each year (National Commission of Inquiry into the Prevention of Child Abuse 1996:1).

simply leave prostitution, or perhaps they really do contribute to the alleged rise in numbers. One ECPAT brochure claimed 'tourists create a demand for more than one million 'fresh' child prostitutes every year (Murray 1998: 55). It is yet another area where research is non-existent but clearly vital. There is a great need for some adequate baseline data. If one million children a year are becoming prostitutes, when did this actually begin? It is irresponsible to use words like 'increasing' or 'growing at epidemic proportions' if base levels are unknown.

This concern with numbers obscures many important aspects of the problem, most notably that of definition. There can never be accurate statistics on child prostitution, because the numbers are always fluctuating. Child prostitution is not a matter of counting the children in brothels throughout Asia, or counting the children who have tourists as clients, even if either were possible. If there is a straightforward model of abduction, imprisonment in a brothel, escape and death, then child prostitution is easy to define. These children have literally no life after prostitution, and therefore their entire identity and life is bound up with it. They can be counted, categorised, and defined, entirely by prostitution and there are no grey areas. However, there are other children, as I will argue in later chapters, who categorically refuse to use the word 'prostitute' about themselves and refuse to become a prostitution statistic. They exist in just one of many ambiguous categories. The child who sells sex once or twice, under particular circumstances, is not necessarily a child prostitute, and certainly may not want to be classified as one for years to come. There are other children who work only part-time as prostitutes; when they are not working, are they still prostitutes? There are other children who do not die of AIDS or abuse. Once they have left brothels or bars, are they too classified as child prostitutes for ever?

Unfortunately, there are no accurate data on the extent or the nature of child prostitution in Thailand, and any sources that claim to have this information should be treated with caution. There is no information as to whom the majority of the clients are and why they should prefer sex with a child to sex with an adult. It is not known if they even distinguish in this way between their sexual partners. No-one knows how many child prostitutes there are, or how many there have ever been, or how often they work. Similarly, nobody knows what happens to them after prostitution, except for those who contract AIDS. Again, there are no figures to show how many do contract it. This is why this book is not, and cannot be, about facts, because they are always contested and there is nothing which is undisputed. It can only be about the stories that children tell to adults and to each other, and those that adults tell to each other. ECPAT, Christian Aid, or any other NGO, are not being dishonest in what they say: clearly their stories have meaning to them and fulfil a particular purpose. Yet it must be remembered that they need their belief in one million child prostitutes far more than individual child prostitutes need to be included in this imaginary fellowship.

History and Myth

The elements of mythology and stereotype that recur in the telling of life-stories of child prostitutes exist also in the counting of their numbers and are mirrored exactly in the stories concerning the root causes of their plight. The image of a 'typical' child's life has been repeated so that little variation is allowed, and that life has been diminished so that he or she is simply one of a million. The social, political, economic and even historical contexts that allowed child prostitution to flourish have also been reduced to a single issue: the problem of the foreigner. In 1991, this was summarised most succinctly by The Foundation for Women, a Thai NGO, in their report on prostitution in Thailand for the UN. It began:

> Although prostitution as an organised business in Thailand only started in the 1930s with the import of Chinese prostitutes into the country to cater for Chinese immigrants, prostitution became a big problem in the 1960s with the presence of the United States military bases during the Vietnam war. It was taken over by local demand, and spurred on by the promotion of tourism. (United Nations 1991: 45).

For the media and for NGOs, the easiest and most accepted way of dealing with child prostitutes has been to claim that children who currently work as prostitutes are the victims of foreign paedophiles, who come to Thailand because their sexual preferences are considered perverse and illegal in their own countries. When there is historical evidence for child prostitution, this too is blamed on outsiders, usually the Chinese. This view is only partially true. Despite protestations from NGO groups, such as The Foundation for Women, there are certain factors which provided the right conditions for the alleged explosion of child prostitution in the 1980s and 1990s. These go some way to explaining why child prostitution has such a high profile in Thailand but not in other countries with equally high levels of tourism or foreign involvement.[4]

Child prostitution has a longer history in Thailand than many NGOs would wish to admit. There is some evidence that children under the age of eighteen (as children are currently defined) have worked in the brothels of Thailand in the past, and that they have even had foreign clients for some time. As a social problem, child prostitution did not emerge out of a vacuum in the 1930s or even the 1960s; it has a much longer history, which can contextualise the current situation. Both Thai and Western historians have noted the long history of indigenous prostitution in Thailand. Although they do not distinguish between adult and child prostitution, there is some evidence that child prostitution has long cultural and historical precedents in Thailand. Both feminist writers such as Hantrakul (1983), and social historians such as Boonchalaksi and Guest (1994), have found evidence of prostitution as far back as the Ayudhaya period (1350–1767) when it was legal and taxed by the government. However, it is important to note that Western and Thai conceptualisations of prostitution, especially during this period, were very different. Women who could be referred to in Western terminology as prostitutes, might, in Thai terms be known as slave wives (*mia klang todd*). These were poor women, paid by a richer man and who, because their sexuality was controlled exclusively by him, were honoured with the title of wife (Reynolds 1977).

It was not until 1805, when the elaborate law known as The Law of Three Seals was passed, that the legal category of prosti-

---

4. There is a tendency to equate the imbalance of male to female visitors to Thailand as evidence of the scale of sex tourism. However, as Ireland writes:

> 'Statistics prove a degree of circumstantial evidence concerning the scale of sex tourism, but to equate these proportions directly with the numbers of sex tourists is too simplistic … To accept unquestioningly that Thailand's 65% male tourists figures reflects the extent of the sex tourism to that country would suggest that Indonesia, Malaysia and Singapore have a similar scale of sex tourism, an argument which appears to have no foundation.
>
> Male Tourists as a Proportion of Total Visitors
> | | |
> |---|---|
> | Indonesia | 69% |
> | Malaysia | 64% |
> | Philippines | 80% |
> | Singapore | 62% |
> | Thailand | 65% |
>
> We must bear in mind that tourism statistics include travel for business, itself heavily male dominated. Whilst such business travellers may equally become involved in the use of prostitutes and/or children for sex it is not possible, without further evidence, to conclude how many of them do.' (Ireland 1993: 48).

tute was first introduced into Thailand. This law set out a complex coding of women, ranking them according to their male protectors, and also dividing them into categories of those who gave sexual services to only one man and those that did not (Reynolds 1977, Turton 1980, Truong 1990). For the first time, prostitution became a legal category to describe and stigmatise women who did not belong to any man. This had major implications for prostitutes and their role in society, and also the way that they became viewed as outsiders. A new phrase for women who sold sex, *ying nakorn sopheni* (prostitute), came into use for the first time, and women who exchanged sex for money could now be stigmatised and prosecuted. Women who had previously belonged to an ambiguous, if accepted, category of women now became criminals.

> The incorporation of the category of prostitute into the legal framework in 1805 formalised the social position of women who sold their bodies. This required a definition of their status and an ideological justification. This definition rested upon a combination of what was formerly regarded as a result of a religious offence (prostitution) with what was formerly regarded as a private crime (adultery). Henceforth, the legal definition of prostitution in the Three Seals Law conflated the private with the public, the religious with the secular. (Truong 1990: 148).

In 1905, the King of Thailand passed anti-slavery laws, which technically freed women from one sort of bondage, only to push them into another sort through poverty. Many newly freed slave wives simply became prostitutes with brothel owners and pimps becoming their new masters. The old laws on taxation of prostitutes were superseded by new laws on venereal disease as the numbers of prostitutes increased and the government needed to control their activities (Hantrakul 1983). Prostitution remained taxed and regulated by the government until the 1960s, when it was outlawed as part of a wider plan to rid the country of 'undesirables' such as beggars and prostitutes. There are no statistics to show how many of the prostitutes, now officially called *sopheni*, were children or indeed under the age of eighteen before 1905, but it would be reasonable to believe that the prostitution of younger women and girls from poor families was common. Based on the results of his studies in the 1950s, Fox, in his submission to the Department of Public Welfare, claimed that 90% of prostitutes were between fifteen and twenty and he found evidence of some as young as thirteen (Fox 1960).

Under the new Penal Code of 1908, the seduction of minors under twelve was criminalised and abduction of those under ten was made punishable by law. However, for children between the ages of ten and fourteen, the penalties did not apply if the child had consented to the abduction. Thus prostitution was legal for ten-year-olds with their consent (Truong 1990). The increase in the number of recorded prostitutes after this date, and the continued system of licensing brothels and keeping prostitutes off the streets, must have involved those who would now be considered children. Indeed, until 1930, prostitution and pimping for girls aged over fourteen was not considered illegal (League of Nations 1933). For poor families, now freed from slavery but having to fend for themselves, the temptation to sell their daughters, or at least encourage them to enter prostitution in order to boost the family income, must have been strong. In 1937 a girl of fifteen who had been sold by her family came to public notoriety and caused an outcry in the Thai press. She had been tricked into a brothel by her elder sister, yet even after realising that she had been tricked she stayed there claiming that she wanted to help her mother (Landon 1939: 163).

It is extremely unlikely, therefore, that child prostitution is a new phenomenon that is an element of the industrialisation of the 1960s, or even of the waves of Chinese immigration in the 1920s and 1930s. Although there were more registered Chinese brothels in Bangkok than there were Thai or other ones in the 1920s,[5] Boonchalaksi and Guest (1994) suggest that many Thai prostitutes simply took Chinese names and worked in Chinese-run brothels and that brothels catered for all nationalities. There are even accounts of Russian and European women working in the brothels of Bangkok in the 1930s (League of Nations 1933), which has interesting parallels in contemporary Thailand, where there is some evidence of prostitution by Russian women.[6] While Thai

5. In *The Report of the Council by the Commission into the Traffic in Women and Children in the East*, commissioned by the League of Nations in 1933, the Thai delegation claimed that in 1928 there were 203 licensed brothels in Bangkok, of which 167 were Chinese, 30 were Siamese and 5 were Annamite. They also claimed that the numbers of prostitutes was decreasing, so that in 1930, the number of licensed brothels in Bangkok had fallen to 161 of which 126 were Chinese, 22 were Siamese and 3 were Annamite (League of Nations 1933). They also stated that 40% of prostitutes were under 20. However, even the official delegation notes that these numbers should be read with caution and there were many more unlicensed prostitutes. Officially, there were 200 Chinese and 100 Siamese unlicensed 'sly' prostitutes and around 700 registered ones, but the commission had to acknowledge that, 'One official witness estimated that there are many times this number in Bangkok, perhaps as many as 2,000' (League of Nations 1933: 314).

6. See, for example, 'Russian Women Face Prostitution Charges,' (*Bangkok Post* 1994a), 'Foreign Flesh in Thai Sex Trade,' (Jinakul 1994), or 'Government Can't Keep Russian Women out of the Sex Trade,' (*Nation* 1994a).

feminist groups may attribute such prostitution of both women and children to outside influences and claim that Thai men and women were not involved, there is not enough evidence to support this. It is impossible to know who the clients were, but with the outlawing of polygamy in 1935 the opportunities for Thai men to keep many wives was legally ended. While the rich could still afford to keep minor wives[7] (*mia noi*) for men with less money, a prostitute could serve their sexual needs. In such a situation, it would seem extremely unlikely that Thai men did not participate in prostitution. The League of Nations reports that 'The customers of Chinese prostitutes are exclusively Chinese whereas the Siamese and Annamite women receive men of any race' (1933: 313). Indeed, Hantrakul sees prostitution as being embedded in the structure and lifestyle of the Thai nobility, spreading to other classes with the increased supply of women after the abolition of The Law of Three Seals (Hantrakul 1983). When women who were formerly slaves became 'free' prostitutes, having a large number of sexual partners was cheaper and more accessible for more men, and therefore a demand for prostitution of both women and girls increased and was institutionalised.

The demand for prostitutes was so widespread that by 1949 Bangkok already had a reputation as a place for readily available sex. This reputation need not have been based on the number of brothels that Thailand had, or on any knowledge of actual prostitution practices in Thailand. Orientalist stereotypes about the sensuality and availability of Thai and 'Oriental' women meant that Thailand's reputation, especially in the West, had always included elements of erotic fantasy. In 1949, a book called *Dream Lover: The Book for Men Only*, was published in Bangkok which appealed explicitly to the foreigner seeking sex. In rather distorted English, *Dream Lover* described to the foreigner where and how he could get the services that he had heard rumours about. Written under the pseudonym of Black Shadow, it panders to the sexual stereotypes that the foreigner had of Thailand and speaks of Thailand's attractions in terms of the sexuality of its women.

> It has for a long time been known that BANGKOK is not only the seat of all Ministries, all the big Administrations, and the centre of the intellectual, industrial and commercial life of the country, but also the land of absorbing interest – of sweet romance enriched with paradise. (1949: 1).

7. Minor wives are women who stay exclusively with one man although they are not legally married to him as he already has a major/legal wife (*mia luang*). Although officially not sanctioned or encouraged, it is still common in Thailand.

Despite its florid and contorted language, Black Shadow makes no secret that the purpose of his book is about the availability of commercial sex, guiding the uninitiated foreigner through the back street brothels of Bangkok.

> Now, my dear travellers, the time is reached to the aim of this book to guide you to roam the places of sweet romance – of Bangkok night rendezvous – to the rooms of those young showy Nightingales of the night. Every one keeps waiting and is ready, however, to be the best of your night companion – of your partner, to accompany you and guide you into and through the land of Aden – the place of bliss. By her your dream will become true. With sweet hours of her accompaniment, it will certainly be of the best to your disquieting sexuality. To men the women are sweet paradise …
>
> Before going through with this service, I must first draw your attentions concerning some points of view. As it appears to be somewhat forbidden, however, many of these places are not publicly known so far as these feminine youth – these women of the night and their dwellings are concerned of their actual existence. So, by this book, success is impossible without your common sense and the service of your car drivers in locating them out by close examination.' (1949: 1).

While Black Shadow does not give definite ages on the prostitutes in the brothels that he mentions, he does hint that there are some young girls available in certain brothels. He makes a clear distinction between the more expensive women who 'as you may see and be caught with surprise, are very charming and elegant indeed' (1949: 24) and the others who are 'young girls who are ready to lay their fanciful services to the visitors' (1949: 30). There are also more direct hints that some of the girls are much younger and possibly still virgins. 'The housewife has many beautiful young women who are very smart and charming ready to lay service to their visitors. Besides, there are some being regarded as very special waiting for agreeable terms' (1949: 21). In another house, there are Chinese girls who are 'very fresh, young and gay' (1949: 26).

There is so little documented evidence about child prostitution that a book like *Dream Lover* is extremely useful in its hints and suggestions about the situation in pre-1960s Thailand. That child prostitution existed, especially among those under eighteen (as child prostitution is defined today), appears obvious and that it was institutionalised and taxed as part of a wider acceptance of prostitution seems equally indisputable. However, in the 1960s, Thai prostitution undoubtedly changed and the campaigners against child prostitution are correct in placing some of the origins of its current manifestations in the 1960s and in the influx of large numbers of foreigners.

It is during the Vietnam war that ECPAT and other NGOs start their own history; placing there the origins of Thailand's child and adult prostitution problem. Certainly, at this point prostitution changed dramatically, partly because of the large foreign military presence, but also because Thailand was undergoing rapid social change. By the end of the 1960s, the traditional social fabric of Thailand had changed beyond recognition. The mode of production was changing, and industrialisation was pursued as the primary goal so that agriculture was largely ignored (Tantiwiramanond and Pandey 1989). Coupled with this was the threat of an over-spill of the wars in Indochina into Thailand, and the consequent stationing of large numbers of American troops in parts of the country that had rarely seen foreigners before. The bases at Khon Kaen and the ports in Chonburi brought in thousands of American servicemen, swelled by the numbers of men on temporary 'R and R' (Rest and Recreation). Large numbers of Thais were needed to act as support staff at these bases, as cleaners, servants or translators to the military, and as happened in Vietnam and, to a lesser extent Laos, many local women were soon working as prostitutes. Indeed, often the roles were combined: following the old Thai system, women who stayed with just one man, even if it were just for a few weeks, were not considered prostitutes, but were called *mia chao* (hired wives).

At the end of the 1960s, with the Vietnam War spilling over into Thailand's neighbour Cambodia, the Thais recognised the necessity of accommodating the Americans. They allowed the Unites States not only to station troops in Thailand but, more importantly, allowed American servicemen to use Thailand as an 'R and R' station. Given the huge numbers of young men with large amounts of money to spend, the foreign sex industry quickly became organised with bars and brothels set up, for the first time, explicitly catering to foreign men. Based around Western music and Western food, the girls were encouraged to learn English and to attend exclusively to foreign men. Many women became very mobile, leaving their home provinces and moving to Pattaya or Bangkok in order to find the most lucrative work among the Americans (Malee 1986). To many young women whose families were losing out in Thailand's programme of industrialisation, sex work became an easily available form of work. The social effects of the Americans were compounded by the economic effects as the American presence unleashed a vast amount of money into previously poor communities. In the Northeast especially, the US military presence had a huge effect on the local economy, leading to inflated wages for locals. Men and women who had previously been farmers now had a range of skills and resources. They had come into contact with people from widely different cultural backgrounds and had been paid wages that gave them a much higher income than they had previously enjoyed or aspired to. There was little enthusiasm at the end of the war for returning to work as a subsistence farmer.

The reputation of Thailand as a sex paradise, previously discreetly cloaked in the language of romance and exoticism for the favoured few, became a byword for cheap, blatant, commercially available sex. Equally, the previous pattern of prostitution for Thai men, whereby sex was merely part of a ritualised feasting and testing of masculinity (Fordham 1993) was transformed by the outsiders into a space where sex was an end in itself, a private fantasy secured by money. Yet, prostitution never entirely lost its Thai aspect, and as Cohen writes, it was 'incompletely commercialised' (Cohen 1982: 411). It retained its character of ambiguity, in that women did often stay with one man for some time. Some women married their customers, and it was very common for a man to view a woman as a girlfriend rather than as a prostitute.

By 1975, the majority of the troops had gone, leaving behind the infrastructure of the sex industry and also an illusion and stereotype of beautiful, pliant and docile Oriental women, who offered much more than paid sex. Here was a society where dreams of romance, every bit as fanciful as those described by Black Shadow, could be fulfilled at a small price. With the Communist take-over in Laos and Vietnam, and the suppression of prostitution by the Communist authorities, the only country left in southeast Asia where these fantasies could still be satisfied was Thailand. That these fantasies were fuelled by men and drew on Orientalist stereotypes was never questioned, and in time, they became self-fulfilling. Thai women and children had to be docile and subservient because that was what was expected of them. Some servicemen did not give up the dream and simply stayed on in Thailand, especially in places like Pattaya and Bangkok, running bars. One of the major red-light districts in Bangkok is a lane called Soi Cowboy, named after an American who bought and operated many bars there at the end of the war.[8] What was previously a dis-

8. There are laws in Thailand that restrict foreign ownership of bars and other property in Thailand but these are regularly flouted by using a front man for a purchase, or in the case of some of the US servicemen, staying on after the war, buying in the name of the Thai women whom they had married.

creet, but accepted pastime, for Thai men, suddenly became an
overt and vulgar way of attracting money into the country.

Tourism has been phenomenally successful in Thailand, and it
is now its highest source of foreign currency revenue (Lewis and
Kapur 1990). Thailand is a beautiful country, which is easy to
travel to from Europe. It has spectacular and ancient monuments
and tourist attractions and it is cheap for foreigners. There are
many reasons to go to Thailand other than to buy sex, but it
would be naive to assume that the images brought back by sol-
diers, journalists and others from the Vietnam War, which idealised Thailand as a haven for cheap, available sex, did not affect
the tourist industry. As tourism became more important to the
Thai economy, the role of prostitutes within that wider economy
also became more important. In an extraordinary and widely
quoted statement by the Deputy Prime Minister of Thailand in
November 1980, the existence of the sex industry was justified
and acknowledged as the main tourist attraction.

> I ask all governors to consider the natural scenery in your provinces,
> with some forms of entertainment that some of you might consider
> disgusting and shameful because they are forms of sexual entertain-
> ment that attract tourists … we must do this because we have to
> consider the jobs that will be created. (Ennew 1986: 99).

What is unknown, however, is the link between adult and
child prostitution. Even those who may support prostitution as a
necessary, job-creating evil, would not necessarily condone child
prostitution. It is an unasked, and maybe unanswerable question,
but does the existence of adult prostitutes necessarily lead to the
existence of large numbers of child prostitutes? ECPAT, among
others, would claim that it does. They claim that children are
desired as the ultimate sexual perversion by jaded Westerners
who have tried everything else (O'Grady 1992b: 82). In many
ways, their analysis seems reasonable; it would be naive to think
that children are unaffected by the sex industry or that their bodies are immune from being commercialised like any other commodity. They sell their bodies simply because they can and
because prostitution is, and always will be, an industry that lays a
premium on youth. As Ennew has pointed out 'an old prostitute
is a redundant prostitute' (Ennew 1986: 11). In a job that requires
beauty, which is often synonymous with youth, prostitutes will
invariably be young, and if children are defined as anyone under
the age of eighteen, then rates of child prostitution will always be
high. Other children in the tourist industry will also be affected.

Even if their work is not sexual, in places such as Pattaya or Patpong,[9] their labour is ultimately connected to the tourist trade,
which in these areas is largely indistinguishable from the sex
trade (Wahnschafft 1982, Black 1995). Their labour is crucial to
keep the resort running, and their dependence on the tourist
industry is total. The mayor of Pattaya, for example, said in a
newspaper interview, 'Every morsel eaten by Pattaya's population
of 200,000 is provided by tourists' (*Pattaya Mail* 1993: 1).

However, this is only guesswork, one of the many myths surrounding child prostitution. As ever, there is no evidence and no-
one knows the process (or indeed if there is one) by which the
presence of adult prostitutes leads to a rise in the numbers of commercially sexually exploited children. Indeed as Ennew wrote,

> It is my contention that what actually happens when children are
> sexually exploited or abused is frequently obscured by sensational
> accounts of the problem – by the repetition of shocking and poorly
> documented facts which reproduce the logic of the equation per-
> missiveness = satiation = perversion. (Ennew 1986: 8).

Black, in her analysis of the tourist industry, goes even further.
While admitting the links between tourism, adult prostitution and
child prostitution, she states categorically

> A sober analysis of the evidence does not bear out the claim that
> tourism is 'the main factor in the explosion in numbers of children
> recruited, enticed, and brought into prostitution,' as reliable com-
> mentators recently pointed out … What can be stated on the basis
> of the available – inadequate – information is that demand for
> commercial sex among visitors, including those from neighbouring
> Asian countries, exerts pressures in the market generally, drawing
> in young newcomers at the cheaper end. (Black 1995: 21).

Research on issues such as child prostitution can never be
definitive. Concepts such as childhood, sexuality and prostitution
are notoriously hard to define cross-culturally even though they
are often treated as unproblematic. Yet when definitions change,
the problem also changes and again, questions as to who is or is
not a child prostitute are contested. As long as the only image of
a child prostitute in the public arena is that of a tragic martyred
child, the debate cannot move on or be widened to embrace the
full moral complexity of the issues.

Admitting ambiguities is difficult and raises many uncomfortable questions. Any attempt to offer alternative explanations
invokes the suspicion of extreme moral relativism or facile

9. The main red-light centres catering for foreign tourists.

appeals to cultural difference and for some people there is little difference between exploring complexities and offering justifications for abuse. It is seen as one area where there are universal absolutes which must be enforced internationally. Article 34 of the United Nations Convention on the Rights of the Child is unequivocal. It states: 'States Parties undertake to protect the child from all forms of sexual exploitation and sexual abuse.' There is no room here for moral ambiguity or relativism. Thai children may become prostitutes for different reasons than British or American children do, and their explanations and justifications for doing so may be different, but nevertheless, both groups are sexually exploited. Explanations which rely only on cultural difference lead to harmful hierarchies which rank the relative sufferings of children according to their culture. Cultural difference should not be used as a justification for harm to children. As Ennew puts it 'while cultural context must be respected, it is important to note that culture is not a 'trump card' in international human rights.' (Ennew 1998: 8).

Stating that the situation is more complicated than it first appears is not a sign of moral relativism or equivocation. Indeed, simple moral absolutes are extremely limiting. They can only lead to witch-hunts of individual parents, children or clients, while leaving the larger structures that support and encourage child prostitution untouched. As long as there are absolute standards of morality imposed on children which admit no ambiguities, and say they must be wholly good and their parents wholly bad, then, once again, the voices of the powerless are marginalised. It should not be necessary to rely on stereotypes and simplified case histories to know about the causes and effects of child prostitution. It is possible to recognise that they are exploited, impoverished and abused while celebrating their resilience and strategies for survival. It should not be necessary for children to be consistent or straightforward in order to be taken seriously and given help. Indignation and horror serve no purpose unless they are focused, and the constant repetition of harrowing and tragic life-histories must be handled with care if they are not to spill over into voyeurism. The public desire is for stories which emphasise the degradation and abuse of children, not the mundane aspects of their lives or even the areas of their lives away from prostitution. Far too often, when understanding is substituted for sensationalism and moral outrage, the imagery of child prostitution becomes extremely prurient and serves no purpose at all (Murray 1998).

So far, the analysis has concerned what other people have said about child prostitutes and the ideologies they have used to explain and describe their situation. These theories have focused on the epidemic nature of the problem, said to be increasing all the time, becoming ever more grave, and with all children being under continual threat from foreign tourists. The world of the child prostitute has been summed up and stereotyped to the extent that the causes of their plight are as apparently well known as their life-histories. Children are terrorised and abused by Western tourists who have replaced the American servicemen of the 1960s as their clientele. They have been placed in a framework of East/West exploitation and are seen as an unfortunate, if inevitable, side effect of mass tourism. Yet the children themselves have rarely been heard. What do they say about their lives, their prostitution and their clients? In Chapters Three, Four and Five, I will examine the issues that the children themselves identify as important when they discuss their lives. They have very different models and ways of understanding their lives than the activists do, partly because they have less knowledge of the wider political economy that shapes their lives, but also because they do not recognise themselves in the stereotypes that they are presented with. Now that there is such great awareness of the problem of child prostitution, there must be deeper understanding, so that children who do not fit the previous model can be brought into the analysis. Before these children are introduced, however, it is important to lay out the theoretical frameworks that will inform this book, and to deconstruct the notions of childhood, sexuality and innocence.

CHAPTER 2

CULTURAL CONSTRUCTIONS OF CHILDHOOD

A History of Childhood in the West

During this century, childhood has come to be regarded as an unchanging and ubiquitous rite of passage through which everyone must go. It is assumed to have certain universal features such as innocence, dependence and happiness which are the 'natural' state for all children, regardless of culture or geography. Yet, it is obvious that these 'natural' standards are nothing of the sort and that childhood is socially and ideologically constructed. 'Adulthood is always a matter of social definition rather than physical maturity' (La Fontaine 1986: 19). There are no universal standards for childhood, except for those imposed by the industrialised West and the United Nations. Children become adults at different times and in different ways throughout the world.

The difference between children and adults is such a fluid and comparative issue that there can be endless debates about when a child becomes an adult. The United Nations has attempted to formulate a definitive view of the child based on the age of political majority, but that has proved very unsatisfactory and quite unsuitable for many cultures. Other countries have tried to introduce national legislation based on legal or political considerations, but even that has proved difficult to enforce. Historians, sociologists, and anthropologists have all sought to prove that views of childhood are constrained by history, culture, and politics but there has been a marked reluctance to accept these theories on a legislative level. It always seems easier to view childhood as a fixed category that has remained constant throughout history or, if that is impossible, then to view it as a triumph of progress and civilization, so that modern children are protected longer and better cared for than their predecessors.

Article One of the United Nations Convention on the Rights of the Child states that a child is 'every human being below the age of eighteen years unless, under the law applicable to the child, majority is reached earlier' (1990: 4). Certain Western women's groups are trying to take the definition of a child even further and have suggested that 'child' be applied to anyone not yet fully physically and sexually mature, even though in many cases this process is not completed until twenty years old (Black 1994: 13). The impracticality of this is obvious; even in Western, industrialised societies, eighteen is not a definitive boundary of childhood when it is accepted and enshrined in law that a person under this age can marry, fight for their country, and earn a wage. Applied to developing countries, or newly industrialised countries, such as Thailand, it becomes untenable. Such extended childhoods are a luxury of twenty-first-century, Western thinking. It is ridiculous in most Third World contexts to demand that a child stay economically inactive until he or she is eighteen. In *For Her Own Good*, Ehrenreich and English write:

> Today, a fourteen-year-old who can tie his or her shoes is impressive. In colonial [American] times, four-year-old girls knitted stockings and mittens and could produce intricate embroidery: at age six they spun wool. A good, industrious little girl was called "Mrs." instead of "Miss" in appreciation of her contribution to the family economy: she was not, strictly speaking, a child. (1979: 186)

To define a child simply by age is to ignore the complex role of the child within the family, where status and role depend on more than dates of birth.

Concepts such as 'the child' take no account of the heterogeneous nature of childhood. Children are viewed and treated very differently cross-culturally and even within a culture, there are great variations on how children are viewed, depending on gender or position in the family. As Ennew has pointed out, the diversity of children's experience has been downgraded to such an extent that it has become possible to speak of that 'strange, ungendered isolate, the child' (quoted in Oakley 1994: 21). Yet a firstborn child is dealt with differently from a third-born and boys are usually socialised very distinctly from girls. The child 'is spoken of 'as a singular being, ... as a representative of a category whose social roles were to be accounted for in terms of categori-

cal forms of behaviour rather than in term of individual actions'
(James and Prout 1995: 19). Mead and Wolfenstein in *Childhood
in Contemporary Cultures* in 1955, summarise this approach to children very well. They claim that, universally, children are 'pygmies
among giants, ignorant among the knowledgeable, wordless
among the articulate … And to the adults, children everywhere
represent something weak and helpless, in need of protection,
supervision, training, models, skills, beliefs, education' (1955: 7).

The evolution of childhood has been well documented by sociologists (Ariès 1962, Engels 1977, Sommerville 1982) and historians (Pollock 1983, Macfarlane 1987). Despite the inevitable
controversies, most commentators are in broad agreement that the
interest in children has fluctuated at various historical moments
and that it reached its height in the mid-nineteenth century. The
twenty-first-century Western family may be conceptualised differently from the ideal Victorian type, but, nevertheless, it owes its
genesis to the Victorian reformers, who placed the ideal of an
enclosed, nuclear family at the centre of society. This influence is
shown not just in the hierarchical structures of the family, of the
father being the head of the household with his wife, children and
servants beneath him but also in the concept of the 'family wage'
(Walkowitz 1983, Ennew 1986). Taking their cue from the upper
and middle classes, the newly formed trade unions in Britain
fought for a family wage so that the man as breadwinner could
support and keep his wife and children in seclusion in the home,
based on ideologies of the inherently weak nature of women and
children. Both groups were seen as enfeebled, needing the protection of men, whether on an individual basis as their means of support or on a wider level in the form of national legislators, who
would look after the interests of those too helpless to work or
defend themselves. Allied to this view was the beginning of the cult
of childhood, a view that children were living in a mythical age of
innocence when they were free of corruption and should be spared
the unpleasantness of the outside world (Firestone 1971). The
world became separated into two parts; the world of male, paid
employment, only to be undertaken by the strong and empowered,
and the world of women and children which was a world of imma-
turity and disenfranchisement. Ennew writes:

> At the turn of the century, child labour reforms had been so effective
> that work had become part of the conceptualisation of male adult-
> hood, and play essentially linked with childhood. Work, of course,
> refers to paid employment. Women's work became housework and
> children's work was transformed into schooling. (1986: 16)

Similar thinking has spilled over into the international NGOs' efforts to give development aid for children in the Third World. The myth of a 'golden childhood' is perceived as universal and can tolerate no discrepancies wherever the children are. Seeing pictures of starving, ragged children is an affront to deeply held beliefs about the nature of the world. In efforts to help developing countries, children are one of the top priorities. Firestone examines the reasoning behind this myth and suggests:

> It is clear that the myth of childhood happiness flourishes so widely not because it satisfies the needs of children but because it satisfies the needs of adults. In a culture of alienated people, the belief that everyone has at least one good period in their life, free of care and drudgery dies hard. And obviously you can't expect it in your old age. So, it must be you've already had it. This accounts for the fog of sentimentality surrounding any discussion of childhood or children. Everyone is living out some private dream on their behalf.' (1971: 93)

As religious beliefs decline, it is perhaps not surprising that the horror is intensified. That there is no time, either in life or in the afterlife, that a person can be happy, is indeed terrible. As Firestone says, for 'a culture of alienated people', this is a terrifying prospect, and so the myth of childhood and the perfect family is clung to with great insistence.

As the UN and other international bodies push for a universal view of childhood, the realities of children's lives within the various cultures that they come from have become increasingly overlooked. To say that a child crosses the barrier to adulthood at the arbitrary age of eighteen is to ignore the complex rituals and rites of passage that are part of the life-cycle of many people. Likewise, the removal of children from the world of work because they are under eighteen fails to take into account the economic and social necessity of Third World children to work. It also reinforces Western dichotomies of work and play which are associated with adulthood and childhood respectively, whereas in other societies, children may not necessarily be seen exclusively as 'players', nor adults as 'workers'. (Mead 1962).

Too often, those campaigning against child labour see it only in its most narrow concept of paid labour employment (Archavanitkul and Havanon 1990). Rarely are protests raised against children working for members of their own families or their own villages as unpaid manual labour and yet this too can be harmful or dangerous (Rodgers and Standing 1981). A report by Chulalongkorn University in Bangkok went so far as to claim that:

It is customary for children in Thai families to always do some work for the family. This custom is particularly applicable to poor families, urban and rural alike. Children working in this fashion do not create an alarming problem. But once they step outside their household territory, they are no longer protected by their families.'(Banpasirichote and Pongsapich 1992: 21).

Once again, idealised views of how childhood should be, colour reality. There is a widespread tendency to assume that children are not exploited within their families, it only occurs with the interference of outsiders or when the family is no longer functioning 'properly' (La Fontaine 1990).

Thus notions of what is a 'correct' childhood, and what is a correct path of development, become political, with a contrast set up between the sheltered and privileged life of 'developed children' and the miserable and pitiful situation of those who are forced to work in a contradiction of their 'natural' role as children. Often emotive pictures of working children are used to make the implicit contrast between the developed West (or native middle classes) with their educational and social structures and the brutal and backward lives of the 'undeveloped' who have yet to share civilized values.

The wide eyes of the needy dark-skinned child look reproachfully out from the news pages and from those advertisements that solicit rather than seduce. The ragged child who is not ashamed to plead so dominates the available imagery of Africa, Latin America and the Indian subcontinent that the whole of that vast area beyond Western culture seems in itself to be a place of distress and childish subservience. (Holland 1992: 150).

The West, or the Westernised elites in other countries, are therefore given the 'right' to intervene in the social structure of the Third World poor, and thus definitions of childhood change from culturally conditioned and locally understood concepts into universal moral imperatives which demand and justify interference. 'Childhood becomes a valuable commodity in the power structures of relationships between developed and developing countries'(Ennew 1986: 23).

Childhood in Thailand

Childhood in Thailand is very different from Western models, although recently Western notions of the 'special' status of the child have begun to gain acceptance among the educated middle class and the government. Despite objections to certain parts of the UN Convention, particularly with those dealing with nationality, the Thai government ratified it on March 27 1992. However, the legal definition of childhood, at an international level, has little in common with either national laws or cultural customs. Under the Thai legal system, there are discrepancies in the boundaries between adulthood and childhood. Suffrage is universal at age eighteen while education is compulsory only up to age twelve (usually six years of primary education from the ages of six – twelve). Children are not, however, legally allowed to work full time until they are fourteen, although they can work part-time from the age of twelve (Banpasirichote and Pongsapich 1992). Marriage is governed by the 1976 Civil and Commercial Code (Book 5) which stipulates the minimum age for marriage is seventeen for both men and women (Morgan 1985). What is striking however, is the almost universal lack of knowledge about these age limits by everyone I interviewed, whatever their class or education. Middle class Thais often did not know the legal marriage ages and among poorer people with less education, they simply did not believe it. Having been married long before seventeen in most cases, there was widespread incredulity that the government had any say at all in dictating a minimum age for marriages.

Therefore, to discuss childhood in Thailand, legal categories and definitions have to be regarded as largely irrelevant. Also, different areas of the country have very different traditions regarding childbirth and childhood, and there is no way to discuss 'traditional' Thai childhood without specifying which area of Thailand is being referred to or without problematising the very notion of what is traditional. The Muslims of the South are obviously very different from the Central Thais who in turn are sharply differentiated from the northern Thais (*khon muang*) and the northeastern people from Isan.[1] The families in Baan Nua were of mixed origin, some people identified themselves as Northerners while others saw themselves as people from Isan.

---

1. Although the Northern Thais are slightly different linguistically from the Central Thais, the differences are not as marked as with those people from the Isan. The area known as the Isan covers the north-eastern part of Thailand, including Nakorn Ratchasima, Udon Thani and Khon Kaen. People from the Isan are both linguistically and ethnically different from the central Thais. They speak Lao, appear much darker skinned to the Central Thais, and are often considered backward and stupid. Many jokes are made about them and they are pitied as illiterate peasants. The Isan is also the poorest area of Thailand and earnings there are less than a quarter of what they are in Bangkok (Eliot 1978: 130).

There is, in rural Thailand, no concept of any golden age of childhood, nor are children seen as being in an enviable state. If anything, children are pitied because of their lack of power and the fact that they are everybody's *nong* (younger sibling/inferior). Children are tolerated when they make mistakes or behave badly or inappropriately and their lack of responsibility is sometimes envied. However, children are at the bottom of the social hierarchy which is a position that few people would willingly put themselves in. I sometimes asked people if they would like to be a child again and among the older people whose rural roots were stronger, there was universal agreement that they would not. One of my informants, Saew, used to laugh with me about this saying:

> When I was young, it was always, 'fetch this', 'do that' from my older brothers and sisters. I was everyone's servant and everyone would tease me. Now I am old no-one can do that to me but I can do that to other people.

The other important family dynamic is that, in many areas of rural Thailand, children are seen as an investment which will quickly pay returns because children can work on a farm from an early age. They can contribute to the household economy when young and support elderly parents later on. It is usually the youngest daughter who looks after her parents in their old age and in return she inherits the house (Piker 1975, Blanc-Szanton 1985). Van Esterik claims that this expectation of return is explicit and in direct contrast to Western notions of parental sacrifice for children.

> In rural contexts, women express the idea that one raises a child in expectation of explicit returns. A daughter repays the debt to her mother by remaining in the parental household to care for her parents in old age, while a son ordains as a Buddhist monk to pay his mother back for her breast milk. (1996: 27).

Historically, raising children has not been dependent on parenting them. Often children were not brought up by their biological parents if there were other childless families around or if the parents were too poor to have another child or felt incapable of looking after it (Goody and Tambiah 1973, cf. Carsten 1991).[2]

2. Amongst other groups in Thailand, the propensity to adopt children from other ethnic groups, including Thai, seems to be quite common. Kandre comments that 10% of married Yao of both sexes were born into different ethnic groups (Kandre 1976), a finding supported by Miles who claims that over 80% of those adopted in the Yao village that he studied were originally from different ethnic groups (Miles 1972). The fact that these children were then all described as Yao suggests something of the fluidity in relationships and kinship patterns that characterise the people living in the area.

Continuing up to the present, boys are often sent away, at a very young age, to a monastery to live and learn in a system that provides education for the child as well as merit for the parents.[3] Literature on the subject is scarce but almost all of my informants talked about knowing at least one person who was brought up calling people mother and father who were not his or her natural parents. However, there are some suggestions that there are also great risks in fostering a child and van Esterik quotes a Thai proverb: '*Ao luk khao ma liang, ao miang khao ma om* [which] means raising another's child, is like keeping another's wad of fermented tea in your mouth.' (1996: 26).

Anthropologists who worked in Thailand in the 1960s wrote of elaborate birth rituals and ritual head shaving ceremonies at adolescence (Hanks 1964, Rajadhon 1965, 1987). In the community that I worked in, I saw no such rituals although some of the older people I spoke to remember similar rites of passage in their natal villages. The most important markers of adulthood for boys for ordination in the monastery, while for girls it was motherhood. Before these events a person is still considered 'unripe' (*mai suk*) and unready for marriage and social responsibilities. A boy is considered fully adult or ripe (*suk*) and ready for marriage and fatherhood only after he has become a monk (Keyes 1986). For girls, maturity is conferred during the ritual period after childbirth, which is:

> ... one of a series of rites of the life-cycle which marked the course of an individual from birth to death. The others were the cutting of the umbilical cord, first head shaving, top-knot tonsure, ordination (for men), marriage and cremation. Through the consecrated fire[4] a woman formally achieved full maturity: she became *suk* (cooked, ripe, mature). Maturity did not come just by bearing a child.' (Hanks 1964: 71).

The birth of children is fundamental to both men and women's adult status. Land is often given to a couple at the birth of their first child, rather than on marriage, as it is parenthood and not marriage that is a sign of the couple's maturity (Hanks 1964, cf.

3. Making merit is a fundamental concern in Thai Buddhism. Buddhists believe in a series of lives and rebirths are a source of constant concern. A rebirth in a better position can be earned through constant acts of merit-making which include giving alms to monks, building temples and other acts of piety.
4. For a short time after a birth, a woman will 'lie by the fire' (Mougne 1978) or 'lie cool' (Muecke 1976) in order to give herself time to recover from the birth. It is also a period of adaptation to her new role as a mother within the village.

Carsten 1991). As ownership of land is vital for prestige and social standing (Potter 1976), parenthood gives the couple new responsibilities and a new status within their village, another sign of their full adulthood.

Elements of this continued in Baan Nua and which I will discuss in greater detail in Chapter Seven. While there is no land to distribute and marriages are rare, motherhood remains the primary marker of adulthood for women, and while few boys join the monastic life, its importance as an ideal did not diminish. In this community, however, other factors such as money and status are also important in defining maturity. Sexual experience and money are seen as being closely related to the adult world and forbidden to children. They are two of the key issues which, in the West and in urban, middle class Thailand, define and separate childhood from adulthood. Yet within Baan Nua, maturity is viewed in a very different way. Sex and work are still linked to adulthood but there is no age boundary. A girl could be an adult at eleven by having a child and taking care of it, or still be considered immature at twenty because she did not take care of her offspring. This ability to look after people, whether emotionally or financially, is very important. Therefore earning income, to the people of Baan Nua, is a sign of maturity. One child in Baan Nua was working to support five family members and she was considered an adult, even though she was ten years old. In the same way, when her elder brother was working he was considered the head of the family because he was bringing in a large enough income to support it. Even work itself, by giving someone a title and a role, can confer maturity and adulthood on the young. A girl from a neighbouring slum put this clearly when she was given a job at a voluntary centre in the city. The pay was bad, the job was fairly low status but it was the first job that she had ever had and she said "before I was a child, now I am an adult".

As Thailand has transformed, alternative views of childhood have become muted. One of the first indications of this was the formation of a National Children's Day on January 9 in the rule of Field Marshal Sarit.[5] Up until this point children were not accorded any special status but in keeping with the 'modern' image that Sarit wanted to present, a day especially for children was instigated. However, this had a political subtext because, as

---

5. Again, no-one seemed to know exactly when this first appeared, including the National Youth Bureau and the Office of the Prime Minister when I contacted them to find out. The nearest indication I got from friends was that it was during the 1957–62 period when Field Marshal Sarit Thanaratat was in power.

Wyatt points out, Sarit saw the nation as a family and the people as his children.

> Sarit attempted to redefine democracy to mean the responsiveness of the government and bureaucracy and the king to the people's needs and aspirations. The new, active responsiveness of government was to be asserted in a highly paternalistic manner. The society's leaders were to act toward members of society as a father toward his children, solicitous of their welfare and stern in maintaining discipline. (1984: 281).

Childhood had become politicised, the role of children to their parents was modelled on the same duties and responsibilities that a person had to the state and the state elite was projected as the family writ large. Kinship was used as a metaphor for the state structure and the king was cast in terms of the benevolent head of a large family of people. The use of kinship names to designate social relations reinforced the idea of the nation as family (Piker 1979). The emphasis was traditional – duty, respect, obedience and gratitude – but its expression was modern. Just as an individual had to celebrate obedience to the state, so a child was now institutionalised as someone who had to celebrate his or her position of dependence. The patterns of control and dependence that were present in the family were now reflected in the state. The family with its prescribed roles for fathers, mothers and children had entered the political arena and the image of the family was seen as an image of the nation with the dependent, helpless but obedient child being the model for the good citizen.

What Constitutes a Good Childhood?

This change in the official view of childhood has obviously affected the middle classes and those who live in the urban areas more strongly than those in the rural areas. To talk now about the 'modern' view of childhood, is to talk about the view of policy makers and the educated, urban middle classes. The most obvious indication of this is the acceptance of the international baseline of eighteen years as a definition of a child for all issues of child welfare. Child labour and child prostitution are both defined in Thailand as being concerned with those under eighteen, even if the workers themselves do not see themselves as children. In one debate on age that I witnessed between a group of activists, the discussion was cut short by a leader of an anti-child labour organisation, who said "A child is a child until the age of eighteen – we have that in writing from the United Nations". Yet this was clearly out of keeping not only with the reality for most children but also with the cultural traditions that did not define the end of childhood at any distinct age.

The shift of emphasis which happened in the West is also occurring in Thailand. To those who can afford it, a child is a luxury that has to be provided for up to the end of higher education, often twenty-two if they complete university. Families are inevitably smaller as the children drain resources from the family, without contributing in return as they did in the past. Children are now dependent for much longer and removed from responsibility for a much greater time. So much so, that on Children's Day in 1994, Prime Minister Chuan Leekpai claimed that childhood was the most perfect state to be in because it was the only time in a person's life when they were really free (*Bangkok Sunday Post* 1993a). No mention was made of the powerlessness of childhood, of the weak and vulnerable state that until now many people had viewed it to be. Indeed, his speech can be seen as celebrating that impotence and implying that freedom can only come with powerlessness which has obvious parallels to the role of the citizen. Dependency and control are once again ideologically linked.

His speech emphasised that the cult of the happy, innocent childhood had finally come to Thailand. Most people, however, could see no discontinuity. So often, I was told that Thais loved children and looked after them better than those in other countries. It was certainly true that children, especially very young ones, were welcomed anywhere and treated with a great deal of tolerance, and yet the idealisation of childhood innocence and freedom was confined to those with exposure to Western ideas and concepts. The love of children was there in all classes but the traditional pity for the powerlessness of the child that I found in the rural areas, had been replaced by envy for the child's freedom among the middle classes.

As childhood is increasingly seen as a time of innocent freedom and release from the pressures of the adult world, the issue of child labour becomes problematic. Work belongs to the adult world and should be forbidden to children (Ennew 1986). Newspaper headlines in Thailand make this very clear claiming 'Childhoods Sacrificed to Labour' (Joshi 1993) or 'Children's Day Means Work as Usual for Go-Go Kids' (Tourn-ngern 1989). The implication is that a working childhood is not a proper childhood as it is corrupted and distorted by paid labour. Equally, Children's Day is a day to celebrate the childishness of children, not their earning potential. The freedom that children are understood to have is a freedom from adulthood and all the trappings of an adult world and it is this which leads to a conflict that confuses child labour with child exploitation.

As the school-leaving age is twelve, inevitably many children have to work at this age, even though they are not legally supposed to until the age of fourteen. Others cannot even afford this primary education and start work much younger. As argued previously, economic necessity and cultural norms sanction this early entry into the work place, and work during childhood is a reality for the majority of children (Schildkrout 1979, Elson 1982, Lai 1982, Ennew and Milne 1989, Fyfe 1989). However, an ideology that states that children's work should be channelled only into education cannot tolerate such a concept even though, as many researchers have pointed out, education is not the solution to all social ills and if schooling itself is conducted in overcrowded, unsanitary buildings it may be just as unhealthy as work (Rodgers and Standing 1981, Boyden and Bequele 1988). Still, paid work and money are not considered to be a legitimate part of a child's life and thus the banning of all child labour for all Thai children under eighteen is viewed as a realistic goal by many activists. The exploitation of child workers in Thailand is intense and as a 1987 World Health Organisation report emphasised, children do have different health risks to adults, even when they are doing the same work. They are more likely to suffer occupational injuries, fatigue, poor judgement and insufficient knowledge of the labour process, often because the machines and technologies are designed by adults (WHO 1987). However, paid labour is not the same as exploitation (Ennew and Milne 1989, Morrow 1995) and earning their own money is not inherently corrupting to children. Rather the exploitation comes from the very low wages, poor working conditions, and lack of control over their labour.

The children of the urban middle classes are growing up in a society where their status and role are very different from those of their parents at a similar age. What is necessary for their 'good' childhood is closely linked to their standard of living and the material benefits that their parents' income can bestow on them. The most important aspect of this seems to be education. Sending children to the 'right' private school and affording a private tutor in order to coach the child through university entrance exams are considered necessities. Although higher education has expanded in recent years and the opportunities for study are greater, the system is still highly stratified, with Chulalongkorn University remaining the most prestigious and sought after university. As entrance there becomes based more on merit than connections, and is no longer reserved for the children of the aristocracy, there is a great incentive for parents to push their children into applying. The pursuit of the best education becomes another way of gaining social status and prestige so education becomes an economic and social asset. Among most of my middle class friends and informants, however, education in their children's future is not considered an investment in their own lives, which would be repaid in full by the child after he or she had finished education. Instead, the best education that money can buy is considered a 'right' that every child should have. The expense of having children has become much greater but the expectation of repayment is now smaller. Obviously the hope of support has not entirely vanished, but it is not seen as inevitable and it certainly is not something that can be counted on.

In the poorer families that I know, especially among the first generation migrants from rural areas, the relationship between parents and children is based on relationships of reciprocity. Parents have given children life and in return are looked after until death. While the external forms of this relationship have changed, so that the family farm may not exist any more and the children must become factory workers or take other unskilled jobs, the motivation of the children has remained the same. In a seminal study of masseuses in Thailand, Phongpaichit (1982) showed that daughters who left their rural homes were not running away or discarding the principles of support and repayment but were fulfilling them as best they could in a changed environment.

The shift in family dynamics among the middle classes is also reflected in the shape and space of modern households. As families become smaller (Sittitrai et al. 1992), the importance of each family member having his or her own space has increased. Advertising increasingly shows children sleeping in separate rooms from their parents and from each other. The freedom of the child, that is so idealised, is physical as much as emotional and the new found autonomy and separateness of the child from his or her parents is reflected in their living arrangements. The Thai poster advertising the UN Year of the Family (1994) is a prime example of this. The poster shows two children living in a large, traditional Thai house with their parents and grandparents, surrounded by orchards and grass. The implication is clear; freedom rests on space and wealth and the happiness of the children is paramount. To show this poster to the informants in Baan Nua produced a very different reaction. They thought it would be frightening to live in such a big house and when asked if they would like their own bedrooms, replied that they would not because they were scared of ghosts, did not want to be alone and would prefer to have their parents nearby .

Childhood and State Intervention

In the case of child prostitution, already there have been calls for specific penalties for parents who allow their children to become prostitutes. Dr. Saisuree Chutikul, the Secretary-General of the National Youth Bureau, has stated that parents whose children become prostitutes should lose all their parental rights and even be actively discouraged from having children in the first place.[6] Likewise, NGOs working in the North have already begun to advocate and implement the removal of 'at risk' hill tribe children from their villages to raise them in a Thai-speaking community away from the traditions of their families (DEP n.d.). Although these hill tribe children are seen as being at risk of becoming prostitutes, there is also the subtext that they are at risk of being brought up as non-Thais. The onus for eradicating child prostitution has been placed on the individual families but the threat of punitive state intervention hangs over the families if they fail to comply. Notions of a correct family life have become centralised, standardised, and also subject to government regulation. Parents who do not act 'properly', according to these guidelines, will then be penalised and the state will take over the job of looking after the children.

The control of the family is fundamental to the creation of the nation state of Thailand. The children most likely to be removed from their families are those children who are from the marginal groups such as the hill tribes or the very poor, underclass, elements. By removing them to a place where they can be inculcated with the three virtues of a Thai citizen – respect for the 'monarchy, military, and monastery', the government also ensures a better integrated and hence less volatile next generation. By promoting obedience to the government as a form of merit-making, acquiescence to government intervention in the family is given religious sanction (Jacobs 1971).

Even among the ethnic Thais, the government's policy of state control of the family is pervasive. In 1994, Prime Minister Chuan Leekpai claimed that he would end child labour and child prosti-

---

6. She wrote: 'We should insist that people are not to have any children if they are not ready, economically and spiritually, to raise them properly (Chutikul 1992: 5)

tution problems by making education compulsory for another three years until the age of fifteen. Although there have been studies which suggest that prostitutes do not have as much education as the rest of the population (Podhisita et al. 1993), the thinking behind keeping children in school for another three years seems more concerned with lengthening the period of state control. There have been no suggestions as to how to improve the quality of the education they receive, just panic that so many children are leaving schools and becoming prostitutes so quickly. By keeping them in school for longer, it is hoped that this will keep them out of prostitution for a few more years.

The proposal to extend compulsory education was met with angry protests from parents who could not afford to keep their children economically inactive for another three years. They were losing labour needed for their own land as well as giving money to the schools to educate their children. In one school in the North, children were asked to come back at weekends to plant vegetables to sell in order to raise money for the upkeep of the school, even though this deprived their parents of yet another day's labour and was greatly resented by them.[7] As children increasingly become an unproductive financial burden to their parents, an unexpected pregnancy becomes an unwanted encumbrance. No longer does it mean more hands to help but means more mouths to feed.

Already the influence of the media and the government has begun to trickle down. The threat of state intervention hangs over the poorest and those who do not live up to the standards the government has set them. Those who send their children to work, those who are not, in Dr. Chutikul's words, spiritually ready to have children and those who are not raising their children as good Thai citizens, are already being targeted. Inevitably, therefore, ideas of a good childhood are changing as the twin influences of government threats and images of middle class affluence are gradually adopted and internalised. The following chapters emphasise the local nature of 'child prostitution' and 'child abuse', demonstrating how different communities understand what is an acceptable treatment of children and what is not. I will argue that the children who became prostitutes in Thailand must be understood in their own terms, and that consequently they must be viewed as both individuals and as members of a family and a distinct community. A brief examination of the cultural, social, and temporal constructions of childhood already points to

7. Leif Jonsson, University of Singapore, personal communication.

a dangerous lack of dialectic between local experience and global expectation. There is a Western teleology present in narratives of child prostitution in which the Western view of childhood is imposed as 'normal' on other cultures and which has a tendency to misinterpret, and sometimes even to demonise, their attitudes to children.

Anthropology has traditionally been associated with a relativistic understanding of moral issues, a position which is increasingly problematic in a period of globalisation. The creation of an international community, sharing the language of human rights and the values of liberalism, considerably complicates the way anthropologists now have to think about the specific cultures with which they have engaged. Local understandings of culture, which anthropologists have hitherto emphasised, no longer seem to do justice to the demands of an increasingly global culture. Contentious issues such as child prostitution raise important concerns as to whether a universal morality can exist, and, if so, what form it can take. The local knowledge of the anthropologist now has to engage with this universalising instinct. The following three chapters will help to problematise this new perspective, not least by emphasising how local variations and traditions challenge any simplistic reduction of local phenomena to universal facts.

CHAPTER 3

THE CHILD PROSTITUTES OF BAAN NUA

Data Collection

Before setting out for Thailand, I had done a great deal of background reading on child prostitution, mostly from newspapers and from NGO reports. I was fascinated by the repetition of the same stories, with the same details that recurred constantly. What also interested me was the gaps and silences in these stories. Despite all the media horror stories that I had read concerning child prostitutes, what struck me most from reading newspaper stories was just how resilient the children seemed to be. They were rarely allowed to speak, unless it was to express sorrow at what had happened to them, but their ways of surviving appeared impressive. Occasionally stories would be told of children running away, persuading a client to help them escape or even of returning back to their villages and getting married.[1] This information, however, was rare and usually understated. Instead, the stories most usually emphasised the children's utter passivity: they were sold into prostitution, rescued by a charitable organisation and died of AIDS. The children's own agency, the strategies that they had developed for survival and the active roles they played in shaping their own lives, were almost totally overlooked. Although the campaigns against child prostitution were conducted in their name, the children's opinions were strangely

1. In the example of Bo, given in Chapter 1, for example, Bo is rescued by one of her Thai clients who wants to marry her and helps her escape from the brothel. Black makes a similar point about child prostitutes in the Philippines – many children leave prostitution to marry one of their customers (Black 1994).

absent. Indeed, this was never questioned, because, as Waksler writes, 'The absence of children's explanations is rarely missed because its very existence is not recognised' (1991: 62).

I went to Thailand in June 1993 to study child prostitution because I felt that the image that I had of child prostitutes needed to be problematised and questioned. I wanted to look at whether these children had developed survival strategies, how they made sense of, and how they explained, their lifestyles, or if they were indeed the passive victims of fate represented in media iconography. Child prostitution was not an easy research topic. First, the Thai government was not issuing research visas to anyone studying prostitution (Odzer 1990, Gilkes 1993) and therefore I had to conduct this research on a visitor's visa, leaving the country every three months to have it renewed. Second, shortly before I arrived, the Prime Minister at the time, Chuan Leekpai, announced a crackdown on child prostitution which had made brothels, clients, and the children themselves fearful. Therefore it was not easy to gain access to working children who were willing and free to talk.

I also arrived in Thailand at a period of intense media interest in prostitution. The summer of 1993 saw three major events which were given a great deal of media coverage in the Thai press. First, *Time* magazine published a special report on the sex trade which featured on its cover a picture of a young Thai prostitute (Hornblower 1993). As Thailand was only one of the countries mentioned in the report, there was a good deal of anger that a Thai woman should have been used to represent the worldwide issue of prostitution. A week later, a new edition of Longman's Dictionary was published in Britain which described Bangkok as 'the capital city of Thailand. It is famous for its temples and other beautiful buildings, and is also often mentioned as a place where there are a lot of prostitutes' (*Nation* 1993a). This description caused great offence and led to protests outside Longman's as well as outrage in newspaper editorials in both the Thai and English language press in the country.[2] Lastly, an US-based human rights group, Asia Watch, published a report on the trafficking of women and children from Burma into Thailand, which accused the police and government officials of colluding in the forced transportation of women into Thai brothels; reports which were unconvincingly denied by the officials involved (Asia Watch 1993). The pressure of these three events led to media calls for

2. Reactions in Thailand to this dictionary can be seen, for example, in, 'Government Will Try to Educate Longman' (*Nation* 1993a) or 'Silver Lining in Longman's Stormy Cloud' (Sakborn 1993).

government action and a crackdown on prostitution. In July 1993, Mr. Leekpai's government proposed tough new anti-prostitution laws. This heightened media interest made research extremely difficult, as people became increasingly afraid of the government's response. Police action was threatened against the brothels, making it impossible to talk to people directly concerned with running or working in a brothel.

I therefore had to talk to children who did not work in brothels. Despite the image that all child prostitutes are kept caged in brothels, this is not the case. There are different forms of prostitution for both women and children, and there are different ways in which children become involved in prostitution. Although some activists claim that all child prostitution is involuntary (Ireland 1993) and therefore in one category, I believe that there are distinctions. There are three main types of child prostitution in Thailand. First that involving trafficked children, kidnapped against their will, usually from neighbouring countries (Centre for the Protection of Children's Rights 1991, Asia Watch 1993). Second, that involving children sold or debt-bonded by their parents (Heyzer 1986, ISIS 1990, Lee-Wright 1990, Koompraphant n.d., Muecke 1992), and third, that involving 'free children' who live with their parents and work on a part-time basis. Increasingly, there is also a group of street children who have run away from home and live on the streets and who survive through prostitution, which may constitute a sub-group of 'free children' (Graham Fordham, Griffith University, personal communication, 1995). My work involved children who lived with their parents in a slum community, and who worked part-time in prostitution.

I initially made contact with the children through a small NGO that had spent many years working in a slum area of the city and whose members were well trusted. They ran a small programme in the slum village which I have called Baan Nua, providing meals, health care, advice and basic education, and it was through this group that I was able to get to know children who worked in the sex industry as well as the community they came from. I admired the NGO's work enormously, based as it was on the premise that informing the police or using the authorities to intervene was counterproductive. They expected no overnight miracles and no quick solutions, but through their long term involvement in the slum they were able to make a difference to the lives of the children there and to give them options other than prostitution. The sensitivity of their work, and the long term nature of it, proscribes me from naming them, and I have no wish to jeopardise their success. I have used pseudonyms for this village and for all its inhabitants, and I have not named the city in which it is located. I do not want the children to endure any harassment as a result of my writing.

There were fourteen households in Baan Nua, composed of six families, members of which, over a period of approximately fifteen years, have married, had children and settled in new households of their own. The slum was located on a piece of land for which the people paid rent to a local landowner. He supplied them with electricity, but they had no running water. There was one tiny shop in Baan Nua and the central shopping area of the city was about two miles away. Most of the inhabitants have lived near the city for some time although all are migrants from the North or Northeast. Baan Nua is a Thai-speaking village (Central Thai), but this was often the second language for many people who claim either Lao (northeastern), northern Thai, or Khmer (Cambodian) as their native tongue. All of these households contained some children who worked as prostitutes, and child prostitution was the main source of income in the slum. There was a certain amount of adult prostitution also, but it was mostly the children who worked.

The number of people who live in Baan Nua fluctuated between seventy-five and one hundred people depending on the time of the year or the number of people imprisoned. The high level of gambling, drug selling and other forms of illicit business in the village meant that people were regularly arrested and sent to prison so that I never met some of the people who were considered to be integral parts of the village. During the rainy season (May to September) there were more men in the village than usual, as this was the time when construction jobs were scarce and work was harder to find. At other times of the year, such as in March when the heat was at its worst, some of the villagers temporarily moved away, returning to their relatives or travelling upcountry. As this was also when the tourist season was at its lowest, work and money were harder to find, and some people depended on relatives to help them through these times.

During my time in the field, I talked to sixty-five children from several communities, not all of whom worked as prostitutes. Although I concentrated on the children who were already working in some part of the sex industry, there were certain children who either did not work at all or who worked in other jobs. The core group of my informants, however, were twenty-five children who lived in or around Baan Nua. There were forty-eight children under fifteen who lived in the village itself, and the others came regularly to the Baan Nua to visit friends there. They lived in two villages that were about a quarter of a mile away from Baan Nua, and were linked not only by the friendship of the children but also through the NGO which ran similar social projects in these two villages, educating and caring for their children at the same day centre as the children from Baan Nua. The children in Baan Nua shared many of the same clients that the other children did, and because there was so much interaction between them and the children from the two neighbouring slums, they were included in my sample group.

The children that I knew best and concerning whom I have the most information were largely self-selected. Those that gave me most of my information were usually older and more articulate, and they also had a longer history of prostitution. They were also the children that I had the best personal relationships with, and who were therefore prepared to trust me. In this respect it is instructive to note, that although both male and female prostitution occurred in the village, the boys were considerably less willing to talk to me about it than were the girls.

I talked to many of the younger children, but that proved very difficult as often they did not have the vocabulary to discuss what they did and they had often started prostitution only recently. The longer life-histories that I collected, therefore, are all from children in the older age groups who found it easier to talk to me, and who had a clearer understanding of what they were doing. The younger children are very important to my analysis, but because they were often unable to articulate what they did, their voices do not occupy the same space in this study as those of their older siblings and neighbours. However, their voices are there in other, more indirect ways. There was a definite 'career cycle' of prostitution and it was possible to see a distinct pattern in the life-histories of the older ones. The younger children may not have been able to articulate their feelings or explain their situation, but in the context of their surroundings and of the lives of their older siblings and neighbours,

Table 3.1. *Age of the Children (September 1994)*

Age of Children	Number	Percent
0–6 months	2	3.08%
7–12 months	0	0%
1–3 Years	4	6.15%
4–6 Years	22	33.85%
7–9 Years	12	18.46%
10–12 Years	13	20%
13–15 Years	12	18.46%
Total	65	100%

it was possible to analyse their current experiences and to assume that their future would follow patterns of a typical 'career cycle.'

As I was associated with a group that the villagers trusted, it was relatively easy for me to gain acceptance into this community and to find out the extent of the child prostitution that occurred there. However, there was a confusion about my role, and what I was doing there, which made research problematic and which made writing about them even more fraught. I was closely associated with the NGO and many people thought I was working for them. I tried to explain my project, but this was hard when they had little understanding of what a university or a doctorate were. Although they knew I was studying and writing a book, I felt they sometimes blurred my role, so that they saw me as another social worker and sometimes told me things as a social worker but not as a researcher. This was yet another impossible dilemma to resolve, but it further explains why I am so insistent on keeping their identities secret.

The people in Baan Nua were very uncomfortable with questionnaires or formal interviews. They did not like me asking too many direct questions, especially about issues such as prostitution. When I attempted such interviews, people would often refuse to talk or would just walk away. Much more productive were informal methods of research, simply sitting around in the slum chatting to people or eating with them. People who did not like formal questions would respond positively to prompting on other issues. There was little entertainment for the women in the village, except drinking or gambling, and so to talk to a stranger, even one who did not always understand them, seemed a welcome break from the monotony of everyday life. I would go to the village with a Thai translator who was also working for the NGO and, as the people in the community liked her, they would often insist that we sat down and talked.

The main problem with this was the level of alcohol use in Baan Nua. Often I would arrive at about ten in the morning to find most of the women insensibly drunk. Sometimes they would just be asleep, at other times they would be tearful and aggressive, running wildly round the slum and threatening anyone who came near. The men also would often try to sell me the mixed-race children in the village when they were drunk. One man in particular, who always seemed hostile to me, would become particularly abusive when drunk and would attempt to sell me his grand-daughter who was half-European. At times like these, I felt my presence aggravated the tensions in the slum and I would simply leave, returning with some trepidation the next day to find that everything was forgotten and that there were no hard feelings.

The threat of violence, however, was never far away and my most productive times were when the children attended a rudimentary school. At the time of my arrival, the NGO had started a new project to collect the children from Baan Nua and other slum villages and bring them to a centre in town for a few hours a day in order to teach them, feed them, and also to remove them from the drink and glue sniffing that otherwise took up their afternoons. I would drive to the villages in the morning to pick up the children and return them there in the afternoon. Having dropped off the children, there would be a chance to talk to their parents and find out what problems had come up in the day, or just to sit around talking. Often some of the mothers would want to come into the school as well and would then wait for their children there all day. At these times, I was able to talk for a long time with them, discussing their lives, their families and their neighbours. People in the village were never very comfortable discussing feelings or their worries, but they were happy to talk about their lives and their children in terms of events or anecdotes. One of my chief informants, Saew, gave me most of my information this way. When I visited her at home, she was invariably drunk and incoherent, often dishevelled and taunted by the children who laughed at her, but at the school she was extremely gentle and charming, and full of stories.

Life-histories and case studies, therefore, were rarely collected at any one sitting. I would build them up in my notes over the course of my time in the community, checking facts and incidents when I could with other people. When there are life-histories in the text, therefore, it is important to note that they were usually told over a period of time, the major incidents being presented in a certain way to emphasise particular points. Telling their stories in hindsight, both children and adults were able to restructure and reconstruct the events that shaped their lives, just as I have edited and presented their stories in this context. There may well have been other events that were left out by my informants, but it was impossible to know. Rarely is there a set of uncontested facts; people constantly edit and recreate incidents from their own lives, and the life-histories I have presented in this book suggest a coherence and articulacy that the children themselves did not always show. The importance of children as social actors is central to this book and, as far as possible, I have used the children's own words. Often, however, stories were told on different occasions and came from more than one source, and I have not wanted to attribute quotes to the children that they did not say, even when they seem an integral part of their life story.

Child Prostitution in Baan Nua

The sensationalism promoted by sections of the media and the ideology of the anti-child-prostitution lobby obscures much of the reality of prostitution. For the majority of those involved, it is not about kidnapping or virginity being bought for high sums, but it is about the scarcity of choice and opportunity for those who are poor and vulnerable. In none of the cases that I studied is there any of the straightforward greed and wickedness that informs the stereotypes of child prostitutes and their families in so many stories about them in the media. There is certainly apathy on the part of the parents, but what is most apparent from these cases is the dearth of opportunities available to these children: prostitution becomes the easiest way out of short term difficulties, and it is then extremely difficult to leave. The children in Baan Nua are only a small part of the problem of child prostitution in Thailand. I am using a small sample group, and I make no claims that these children are typical of all child prostitutes in Thailand. However, these children do challenge the uniformity of the view that is presented of child prostitutes in Thailand, and they problematise stereotypes of children's passivity and helplessness.

Indeed passivity and helplessness are noticeably absent in Baan Nua. Nor are other familiar elements from the media portrayal evident. None of the children are formally organised or attached to any particular bar or hotel. Neither have any of the children ever worked in brothels or been debt-bonded. Instead, recruitment into prostitution is usually by word of mouth from other children. Their clients are men who have known the village for some time and who come back on a regular basis, sometimes bringing friends with them. Although the children are vague about dates, it appeared that, in one case, a man had been coming to the village for over ten years. Usually, the children stay in the village and live with their families, but sometimes they stay out overnight with clients. In a few cases, the older children stay for a period of a month or two with visiting men, but they frequently return to the village during the day when they are not wanted by their clients.

The prostitution set-up is very different for the boys and the girls. There is often an assumption that child prostitution refers only to girls, but in Baan Nua the incidence of boys prostituting themselves is also high. Clients for the girls are usually found on the recommendation of men who have been to the slum previously, who know the people well, and who recommend friends. Sometimes, the girls do solicit for clients in town, but this is seen as a desperate tactic, to be used only when times are especially tough. When one child from the community was bought by a client in this way, she was beaten up and seriously injured, and ever since the children have been wary about soliciting strangers. For boys, the situation is different. They do not have regular clients as their sisters do; they have to find them themselves and, in consequence, their livelihood is more precarious. In one case, a woman from the slum finds clients for her son in the town, but the rest wait at certain places in the city where they know that they can be picked up by paedophiles. However, after the Prime Minister, Chuan Leekpai, ordered a crackdown on underage sex in 1993, it became more risky to undertake such open hustling and they became more discreet.

Dealing with the clients of the children was the hardest part of my research. I met them in the village on a number of occasions, but it was from the children themselves that I gained most of my information. As far as possible, I tried to verify the facts that the children told me, but none of the men involved was prepared to talk to me about the children or to answer questions about his activities. The stories of these clients therefore were not given to me directly, but came second-hand from the children. However, as it was the children's viewpoints and the children's perceptions that I was most interested in, this source of second-hand information seemed valid.

One of the mainstays of the mythology and demonology of child prostitution in Thailand is that of the 'child-sex package tourist', who buys his sex as part of a package tour from the West, using an underground network of organised paedophile groups. While this does occur and there are certain organisations and networks[3] which do tell people how and where to find children,

---

3. Books like the Spartacus handbook, published in Amsterdam, did provide names and addresses of children in Thailand for paedophiles. However, such books are illegal, the publisher of Spartacus is now dead, and evidence of organised, wide spread information exchange about child prostitution is limited. However, although I am sceptical about claims of a world-wide paedophile conspiracy, there are certainly smaller groups and networks which can provide access to child prostitution. For obvious reasons, many are secretive and the information is limited to members only, but some are more open, especially in their use of the internet. By simply typing in 'child prostitution,' I was able to find comments such as the following:

> 'hotel girls are usually younger than most other 'available' girls in Bangkok, 14 and 15 year olds being rather common. They are in effect 'owned' by the hotel, which means that you can treat them more or less any way you want – and many men do. Hotels like this should be like paradise for those of us who are into S&M ... ' (www.worldsexguide.org Accessed on July 14th, 2001).

the majority of the clients of the Baan Nua children did not fall into this category. These clients, especially those concerned with buying sex from pre-pubescent children, are either long term residents or very frequent visitors who have connections in the city to help them if they do get into trouble. They usually are well settled in Thailand, have built up businesses and are very hard to identify as clients. Often they have integrated themselves into the family of the child they are abusing, thus gaining the loyalty of the parents and making it very difficult for the child to speak to any outsiders about it.

The closest to a paedophile network that I came across, involved the regular clients of the children who arranged visits for other men interested in sex with children. One client, an Italian in his mid-thirties called Julio, is a regular visitor to the slum and both a client and a pimp of the children. He comes to Thailand twice a year, and stays for a couple of months, during which time he buys sex from the children. He also takes some of the younger girls from Baan Nua to tourist spots around the town. He videos them playing and takes the tapes back to Italy to show friends and/or other men interested in having sex with them. When these men visit Thailand, he arranges them to meet and have sex with the girl they have picked out from the video.

The clients that I heard the children talk about came to buy sex in a number of ways, and their relationships to the children were very different from one another. Some Westerners came on the recommendation of friends, bought anonymous sex from the children, and then left Thailand without any sort of relationship developing, while others, such as Julio, had become involved in continuing and more ambiguous relationships. Although they were still buying sex with children, and still exploiting their structural power in terms of their gender, race and class, their relationship to those children was more complex. While it still involved pressure on the children, in that they had to be available for sex whenever the men wanted it, it also meant that the children had some claim on the men and could ask for financial help when they needed it. As I will explore in the final section of this chapter, the children made very clear distinctions between the types of clients that they had and the relationships they had with them.

There were five children in Baan Nua whom I was particularly close to, and whose life-stories illustrate many of the complexities I have discussed previously. I have presented them without comment, but I will analyse them in more depth in the following sections. What is clear from these stories is that these children are living in extraordinarily difficult circumstances, making choices that, ideally, no-one should have to make. In many ways, they are typical of the children in Baan Nua: living in desperate circumstances, but still struggling to improve their lives within tight constraints, they remain dutiful children and they try to retain their self-esteem. As ever, it is easy to claim that this is all false, that they are simply exploited and deluded, but this goes against everything that they told me, and everything that they clung to.

Sompot and Fon

Sompot and Fon are the son and daughter of Pen, one of the earliest settlers in Baan Nua and herself a former prostitute. Sompot is the younger of the two at around eight, and Fon is about six years older. Sompot started prostitution only recently, while Fon claims she has worked for over three years. They both live in Baan Nua with their mother and three other siblings. Their sister, Tik, lives next door with her second husband and her son by another man from Baan Nua. Pen has separated from her husband, a chicken farmer in the Northeast, but despite the separation he comes to the village regularly to see her and his children. He takes a lot of interest in the children, and comes every couple of months to bring presents for them, although they tend to see him as one father figure among many. There have been a series of father figures in their lives since their father left, and despite their affection for their father, neither Sompot or Fon regard him as a particularly close relative.

Pen worked as a prostitute until fairly recently but, as she has become older, she has found it more difficult to find clients and currently she does not sell sex. She began to find foreign clients for Fon several years ago and started to pimp for Sompot a year or so later. She would go onto the streets and try to find foreign men who wanted sex with either of her children, and then send the children to their apartment or hotel room. However, more recently, she has started to send them out to find men themselves, and they often hang around the tourist bars, trying to find customers. She prefers that they only go away for an hour or two, and while she lets men keep the children all night if they want to, it makes her uneasy, and she would rather they did not.

Sompot and Fon clearly love their mother, and they have resisted all attempts to take them away from her. Their father and his family are still in contact with the children, and have come to the slum on a number of occasions and taken them to their home village. On one occasion, at the height of the hot season, when the diseases which had been festering in the slum finally broke out and caused terrible skin and stomach problems for the children, their father came to Baan Nua and begged Sompot and Fon to come back and live with him but, as always, they refused to go. On another occasion, their paternal grandparents came and took them back to their village, but they immediately ran away again. When asked why, their response was that this rural village was "no fun" and "there are no discos or karaoke bars to go to". Sompot also claimed that "he missed his mother too much".

Lek

Lek was introduced to commercial sex at the age of three by Ta, her eight-year-old neighbour, in Baan Nua. She was taken by Ta to meet James, a British businessman who lived in the city. Lek cannot remember meeting him but remembers watching as Ta was paid to masturbate him. A few weeks later Lek did the same and continued to do so until she began, at the age of six, to have intercourse with him. In return for this, James gave money to Lek's family, which enabled her to go to school for a brief period. She has been a prostitute ever since, averaging around twenty men a year, although her most regular source of income is still James. She refuses to call him a client or a customer, referring to him instead as a boyfriend. She also refuses to see him as an exploiter; she says "he is so good to me, how can you say he's bad?"

When I met her, Lek was twelve and pregnant by another of her foreign customers. By this time, she was both a prostitute and a pimp, finding children younger than herself to take to James. She gave birth prematurely in March 1994 to a daughter, a *luuk khrung* (mixed-race child) called Oy. She wanted her mother to return to her home town and raise the baby there, away from Baan Nua, but her mother refused to go. Lek debated putting the child into an orphanage, but eventually decided against it, returning to prostitution as a means of supporting the child. There was no money in the family for the medical expenses of the birth, and so she turned to her cousin Nuk's client, a sixty-year-old Australian called Paul, for help. Paul paid all her medical expenses, and in return she traded sex after she gave birth. Six weeks after the birth, she was back at work both as a prostitute and a pimp for others, leaving the baby in the care of her mother.

Kung and Nuk

Kung and Nuk lived in Baan Nua with their father, Prasert, and their brother, Em. Kung started to work in prostitution at eleven and at fourteen had a child by one of her clients. After the birth, she continued to work as a prostitute but she married her Thai boyfriend, Aey, and lived in Baan Nua with him and with Moo, her daughter. Kung had been the main breadwinner for her family until she was arrested for prostitution at the age of sixteen. She could not pay the fine on her arrest and was sent to prison. At this point, Nuk accepted an offer from Paul, who is also a regular buyer of sex in Baan Nua and who later became Lek's client. When I knew Nuk, she had been with Paul for two years and had struck a deal with him so that she agreed not to have sex with other men; he, in return, would give her an allowance. She lived with Paul in an apartment in the centre of town, but as he spoke only a little Thai and she spoke no English, she got very lonely and would return to Baan Nua and spend the day with her father and brother-in-law.

Nuk had a very serious addiction to glue and once, after a heavy bout of sniffing, she collapsed and became paralysed. No-one knew what was the matter with her and, when she was taken to the free public hospital, they injected her with a remedy for influenza and sent her home. She and Paul quarrelled continually about her addiction and she complained that he constantly scolded her. He threw her out of his house regularly because she would not give up glue sniffing, and she would then move back into Baan Nua. During one of these trips back to Baan Nua, Nuk began an affair with Aey (her brother-in-law) and eventually, after Paul had thrown her out for good, she moved in with Aey.

After another heavy session of glue sniffing, Nuk collapsed again and was taken to hospital. The other children went to fetch Paul, believing that he had obligations towards her, but he refused to help, saying that all she needed was vitamins. She had a great deal of difficulty breathing and had to be put on a drip. She was eventually diagnosed as having tuberculosis, but, as no-one could afford to pay for long term treatment, she discharged herself. Paul refused to give her any money, as she had broken the deal, and Aey, although he tried to look after her said, "it is better if she dies". Paul then tried to pay Tik, Pen's oldest daughter, to move in with him, but backed out when he discovered that she was twenty (she looks no older than fourteen) and that she already has a child. With Lek's family desperate for money to pay for a new baby, Lek's mother, Saew, approached Paul and offered him Lek, a deal which he accepted. Without medication, Nuk lived only another five months; she died on August 19 1994. She said that she wanted to die, claiming that she had little reason to continue living when those around her thought her death would be for the best, and when she could no longer earn money from Paul.

Kinship and Reciprocity

One of the most difficult and problematic issues to deal with is the role that parents play in the prostitution of their children. In newspaper reports, the two methods of dealing with this involvement are either to deny it and to claim that the parents are tricked into letting their children become prostitutes, or to portray the parents as wicked people unfit for parenthood, heroin addicts or prostitutes, who sell their children out of greed. The issue of parental, and especially maternal, complicity in allowing prostitution to occur is extraordinarily difficult to deal with and, as a consequence, it is often ignored. In a community such as Baan Nua, however, it cannot be overlooked. The children continue to live with their parents, their parents continue to use the money that the children earn: it is clear that prostitution takes place with full parental knowledge and consent.

It would, perhaps, be easiest to claim that these children have been so abused and brutalised by their parents that they continue to prostitute themselves because they know of no other way of life. The children, however, give very different reasons for doing what they do. They claim that they become and remain prostitutes out of duty and love to their parents, that they have a moral debt to their parents for bearing and raising them; a duty known in Thai as *bun khun*. This is the debt of gratitude that children owe to their parents, and especially their mothers, for their existence:

> According to the Thai Buddhist moral scale, parents are entitled to be "moral creditors" (*phu mii phra khun*) because of their presumably self-sacrificing labour of bearing and rearing children ... while children are moral debtors. (Tantiwiramanond and Pandey 1987: 134).

Again, it may be easy to dispute this reasoning as an outsider, but the sense of duty they have to their families is overwhelming, and is used by them to inform and contextualise what they do. The duties of kin towards one another are used by the children who work as prostitutes as a way of explaining and condoning what they do, and it is through the obligations that kinship entails that the public vice of prostitution is turned into the private virtue of support for the family.

The concepts of gratitude and obedience towards parents are pervasive in Thai society (Mulder 1979, Tantiwiramanond and Pandey 1987, Vichit-Vadakan 1990, Havanon and Chairut 1985, Komin 1991). It is the duty of children to support their parents as soon as they are able, and to repay the care that has been given to them. In a traditional rural setting, this meant working on the family farm, or more recently, working in a factory in a nearby town, and sending money home (Ford and Saiprasert 1993). The children in Baan Nua have a similar obligation towards their families, and they feel that it is their duty to support their parents financially. However, with no family land to farm and limited options available to uneducated children from the slums, there are few ways to earn enough income to support a family. In these circumstances, prostitution is the only job which brings in enough money, and many children turn to prostitution as a way of fulfilling these obligations.

The family of Saew and Siphon, my chief informants in the village, is a good example of how the expected duties of kin are turned into ways of encouraging and justifying child prostitution. Their story is not one of betrayal of family responsibilities or of abandonment of children by parents into prostitution. Rather, it is about the sacrifices that children are expected to make for their families and the sense of duty towards kin which is encouraged by the community.

Saew and Siphon

When I first met Saew in 1993, she claimed to be about forty. She was born and raised near Buriram in the Northeast of Thailand (the Isan region), where her family are rice farmers and where she still has relatives. At twelve, she married Siphon, to whom she is still married, and gave birth to thirteen children of whom seven survived infancy, and only four were still alive when I met her. The land that she farmed in the Isan, the poorest region in Thailand, became increasingly inadequate to support her family, and so her two eldest children left Buriram and went to a tourist resort to sell chewing-gum and other sweets in the streets. As they appeared to be making a reasonable living, she and Siphon, along with the rest of their children, followed and lived in a squatter community there. Saew started to work as a rubbish collector, going round the streets and picking up waste to sort out for re-sale. Although this was not lucrative, she earned enough money doing this to rent a small piece of land in Baan Nua and build a small house there. She continued to scavenge rubbish until she was hit by a car from which she never fully recovered. She could not walk properly or push her cart, and so she gave up this work. Her children tried to continue street-vending, but when it did not bring in enough money the family started to rely more and more on the earnings of their youngest daughter, Lek, who was working as a prostitute.

Lek claims that at no time did her mother demand that she become a prostitute, she just felt that she had to help. Saew also specifically rejects the idea that she asked her daughter to do so. She says that she knew nothing about it until it was too late, and simply did not know how to stop it once she found out. It is impossible to know what pressure, if any, was applied to Lek, but her sense of obligation and filial duty are particularly strong and all the money that she earns is immediately given over to her mother. Lek is insistent that the work she does helps to fulfil her obligations, and she feels she is duty-bound to support her family. Lek's elder brother, Pring, seventeen, is also involved in the sex industry. He works as a boxer and part-time prostitute in one of the bars, but because he often gets hurt in the ring, he is regularly out of work. Saew and Siphon's eldest son, Tam, also lives with them in Baan Nua. He was married to Tik, Pen's eldest daughter, and they had a son called Bok. After they split up, Bok was given to Saew to raise and Tam gave up work and started to drink heavily. He now also lives off Lek's income. Lek is the only reliable wage-earner in the family and her money supports six people: her parents, her brother, herself and Oy, and her nephew Bok. When I asked her if she resented this burden, she just shrugged and said "it's only my body but this is my family". Although Lek is angry with her mother for refusing to look after Oy in Buriram, and is vociferous in expressing the belief that her mother favours her grandson Bok above Oy and Lek, Lek expresses no resentment of her family living off her money.

In another family in the village, the role that obligations and duty play in regard to prostitution is also evident. Malee is bringing up six children on her own after her husband was sent to prison. Four of these children are hers and her husband's, and the other two are the daughters of her husband's sister, who has abandoned them. The two nieces are raised alongside her natural children, and she claims that she treats all the children in the same way. However, some of the villagers (and indeed Malee herself on occasion) seem to think that the debt the nieces owe to her is greater than that which they would owe to their natural mother, because Malee has taken them in and looked after them, even though they are not her own blood relations. Therefore, it is these nieces who are expected to work as prostitutes to repay their adoptive mother for the care that she has given them. Her own children do not prostitute themselves, and although Malee always denies discriminating between her nieces and her daughters, it is very clear that the nieces are expected to repay their 'mother' much sooner, and to a greater degree, than their cousins. When I asked other women in Baan Nua about this arrangement, no-one thought it unusual. Indeed, the general consensus on Malee is that she is a very good mother to all six children.

In Baan Nua, it seems that it is the mother's influence which is the deciding factor. Indeed, there seems to be no other discernible patterns. Education, for instance, has no effect, and some of the children who still sporadically attend state-run schools are prostitutes when they return home after school. Sometimes children are sent out only when there is economic necessity, while in other families children work whenever they can. In other families one member supports the rest through prostitution, while in others everyone works. In Baan Nua, however, it is the mother who makes the decision about who works as a prostitute and who does not. The children themselves may feel that they 'choose' to become prostitutes, but it is their mother's influence or encouragement that is the driving force behind this choice. I never heard of children becoming prostitutes against their mother's wishes. Questions about why certain children were chosen are always met with shrugs or denials, or statements such as "whoever the men [the foreign clients] ask for, they get" (Malee). Twelve-year-old Kob, for example, can earn a great deal of money as a prostitute and her mother thinks it unnecessary to send the other children out to work regularly. However, when a client did ask for Kob's younger sister, she was immediately sent. It appears that the mothers allow their children to be prostitutes whenever it is profitable for them to do so. As far as I know, Malee has never been offered a very high price for her own children (rather than her nieces), and I do not know how she would reacte if she were. She says that she would never let them "go out with foreigners" and I never found out anything to the contrary. However, the fact that her nieces work regularly as prostitutes and also that she herself had done so in the past, did cause speculation in the village (and in my own mind) that one day her children might become prostitutes.

For many outsiders, the complicity of mothers in their children's prostitution is regarded as the ultimate betrayal of family relationships and an abdication of the parental role of protection and care. To the people of Baan Nua, however, there is no such feeling. The responsibilities of parents towards children are seen very differently; no-one in Baan Nua believes that they are harming their children by allowing them to work as prostitutes. Life is difficult for all of them and children, just like their parents, have to do the best they can. When I asked Pen, Sompot's mother, why she sold him, she looked at me blankly and replied "It's just for one hour. What harm can happen to him in one hour?"

Reciprocity, Friends and Clients

The Western clients who visit the children in Baan Nua have obvious financial and structural power. Yet despite this, the children have been able to manipulate these men to such an extent, that, in certain cases, the men have been made to enter into some sort of reciprocal arrangement with the community, with responsibilities and obligations. Julio, for example, through his connections with Kob's family, is now seen as someone who can help the community and as someone with whom ties of reciprocity can be set up. Saew's family have also managed to form an arrangement with Julio whereby Saew's daughter, Lek, has sex with him and finds him other children, for which he regularly gives her family money. These two families are very protective of him, and the children are very loyal and will not hear criticism of him. During the Christmas period in 1993, I watched them in school making Christmas cards for their friends and families. Kob, her eleven-year-old sister Yit, and Lek, all asked me how to write "Thank you Julio" and "We love you, Julio" in English on their cards. I asked them why they loved him to which Kob replied, "He is young, handsome and rich, and one day he will take us away and buy us nice things". Kob's mother, Sai, frequently sends requests for money, and the fact that he has always responded enables her to see him as a friend or even as fictive kin. His social role in her family's life, and the money that he sends, enables them to survive, allowing her to see her daughter's client as a form of kin. She believes that one day Julio will marry Kob and install her and her family in a large house, just as 'good' kin would if they became successful. Sai genuinely believes that this is his plan, and thus justifies sending Kob to him, saying "when we are rich, she will not regret anything. Now, things are not so good, but one day, they will be good for us". In Sai's view, he is like kin because he fulfils the kinship role of reciprocity.

In a similar way, another client has fulfilled the same role for Saew's family. He has also managed to indebt the villagers to him and, in return for his money, he is protected and defended. James is a British business man who has been settled in Thailand for many years and was Lek's first client. He is about forty and is married, but has a preference for young girls. When Lek was seven, a friend of hers, from another slum in the city told her parents that James had propositioned her and tried to pay her for sex. This child's parents went to the police and reported James, and they gave the police Lek's name. The police asked Saew and Siphon to press charges, but they refused to do this. Instead, they gave a character reference for him, saying what a good man he was, how much he had helped them, and how he was giving Lek a scholarship to put her through school. With no witnesses and with such firm denials, the police were helpless and could not press charges. James was released without charge and continued to live in the city.

James has been a regular in Baan Nua for so long now that nobody refers to the fact that he buys sex from the children. He is always euphemistically referred to as a friend or, by the children themselves, as a boyfriend. Lek always justifies this description of him by telling me how he gave her money all though her pregnancy, and how he continues to support her and her family. Even though she is not his only sexual partner, she still talks of him as 'my boyfriend'. In return for his continued protection and financial support, Lek pimps for other children from Baan Nua and makes sure he has a regular supply of girls when he wants them. Like Julio, he has built up a series of relationships in the village that confer mutual obligations on either side. Although he is in a much more powerful position and can simply stop paying money when it suits him, as Paul, Nuk's client did, the families of the children that he pays view him as fictive kin with responsibilities and ties to them.

Silvia, Henri and Maria

In contrast to these men, there is another set of clients who have a very different relationship to the children. They have managed to avoid many of the ties and obligations that are expected of them and, in consequence, are disliked and distrusted in a way that Julio and James are not. Silvia and Henri are a Spanish couple who have adopted a young Thai child called Porn. They live in Thailand for most of the year with a young Spanish woman called Maria, who is also Henri's lover. They fund this lifestyle by dealing in heroin. The three adults regularly have sex together and, although Porn is not expected to participate, she is encouraged to watch. As Maria speaks fluent Thai, she acts as a go-between in buying both drugs and children, and while I never found out when or how they got to know the Baan Nua children, they often pay Fon (Pen's daughter) for sex. Maria picks her up from Baan Nua and takes her to the flat where she has sex with Henri. Silvia sometimes participates, but Fon says that Maria does not, except to pay her at the end of the sessions. Neither Silvia nor Henri have ever been to Baan Nua, however, and they have never met the children's families. All negotiations therefore are carried out between the children and Maria, which leads to a level of distrust in the village because the parents are excluded from the bargaining process. None of these people will give money to the families of the children, and they do not respond to requests for money. For Henri, sex with the children involves financial obligations for services performed only, and Maria, as his pimp, refuses to give into any extra demands for money. There is no continuing relationship between prostitutes and clients, even though they use Fon regularly and tip her well, but this relationship has not been extended within the slum in the way it has been with James and Julio. As a consequence, Henri, Silvia and Maria are not liked in Baan Nua, and Pen is not always happy about Fon going there. She never forbids her but she remains very uncomfortable with the situation. However, Fon earns good money and Pen is not going to forgo that income, whatever her reservations. There are, however, none of the ties of reciprocity and duty which make relations between James, Julio, and the villagers comparatively easy. Henri and Silvia are viewed very negatively in the slum, because they refuse to participate in the social obligations that the community see as vital to building relationships. They cannot be seen in kinship, or even in friendship, terms, which creates unease among the children and parents. For them, without reciprocity and without mutual obligations, there can be no relationship.

The emphasis on supporting the family, and the 'private virtue' of doing so, which the children aspire to, cannot be underestimated. To talk about choice in this environment is not easy, as choice becomes intermingled with duty and obligations. Even the clients become embroiled in this system of reciprocity. They have infinitely greater choices than the children, and it would be impossible to ignore the larger political and economic factors that enable them to walk into the slum and buy sex with the children whenever they wish. However, it is also obvious that by constructing prostitution as a form of reciprocity, the children can see prostitution as something other than the anonymous and obscene selling of sex. As a consequence of this, prostitution no longer has to be seen as the shameful public vice that so many outside their community see it as: it can be explained away in terms of reciprocal arrangements. Although campaigners against child sexual exploitation are quite correct in pointing out the huge power imbalance between child and client that helps to push the child into prostitution, they fail to take into account the children's perceptions and reasons for selling sex.

CHAPTER 4

STRUGGLES AND CONTRADICTIONS

Children as Social Agents

The children in Baan Nua were caught between many contradictions: between social stigma and community sanction, between force and choice, and between prostitution and the failure to give their families economic support. It is difficult for those outside the community to reconcile these. Yet, in one way or another, many of the children did attempt to make their own sense of these difficulties; through claiming that they chose prostitution, that it fulfilled their familial obligations, or that it was a ticket to another life. Although there were flaws in all these arguments, and the children's approach to their world was based on partial knowledge or an unwillingness to see their situation differently, it is important to look at the reasons behind their claims. Their world-view and understanding of their situation deserve serious consideration, even when alternative explanations can be offered.

In studies of adult prostitution, the issue of force versus choice, or voluntary versus involuntary prostitution, are crucial (Day 1994, Delacoste and Alexander 1988, Bell 1987; in contrast to Barry 1984). These debates are notably absent in discussions concerning children. Those, such as Ireland (1993), who do address the issue, claim that there is no need for discussion: all child prostitution is involuntary and therefore forced. He writes:

> Child prostitution is where the person selling or hiring their sexuality is under 18 years of age, although, wherever possible the terms 'child prostitute' and 'child prostitution' have been avoided, as they imply a sense of decision and control on behalf of the child.

All children under the age of 18 who are in prostitution are considered, *de facto*, to be sexually exploited. (1993: 3).

Clearly, however, children like those in Baan Nua are different
from Burmese girls trapped in brothels. They do have greater
mobility, greater power in choosing and rejecting clients and have
the possibility of other options. The Baan Nua children respond to
the conditions around them, and they do try to maximise their
opportunities in the limited environment they come from. While
I do not believe that any child would choose to become a prostitute if they had any other real alternatives in the form of reasonable income, I also believe that, having become prostitutes, the
children do not passively accept exploitation. As far as possible,
the children in Baan Nua are active agents in their own lives,
capable of making decisions and choices about their lives, and
developing strategies for coping. Their choices are extremely limited and their lives are difficult, but there is no quiescent acceptance of this; they are constantly struggling to improve their own
lives and those of their families. They are not always successful,
yet they rarely give up trying.

The children kept in brothels have neither choice nor control
over their own lives. Equally, choices for the children and their
families in Baan Nua are extremely limited. For their parents,
their right to live on their land is tenuous and they can be
evicted at any time; their rights over their children are also
under threat; the income generated by their children fluctuates
and is unstable. I think that it is impossible that the children in
Baan Nua freely choose prostitution or that given other, better
paid, options they would continue as prostitutes. For people
who are poor and powerless, however, prostitution is also one
difficult choice among many. Although many of the children
rationalise prostitution as 'filial duty' and undoubtedly gain satisfaction from being able to support their families and fulfil their
kinship obligations, it is hardly a free choice. Yet having some
sort of control over their circumstances is important. Their self-
image is dependent on their believing that they do have control,
and, given the poverty of the options open to them, that they
have 'chosen' prostitution.

I do not wish to claim that all the other stories of child prostitutes are wrong; that children are not enslaved or trapped in
brothels, or that what they do is anything other than forced and
involuntary. However, there are other children whose lives have
different patterns and who are able to struggle against their circumstances. In Baan Nua, the children I knew are very definitely

in the latter category. The most obvious and immediate way in which they showed their agency is through their deliberate rejection of the terms and labels foisted on them. They refuse to use terms such as prostitute as it does not express who they are or what is important to them. Campaigners against child prostitution may prefer terms like 'children exploited by prostitution', but this phrase is never used by the children. It is, however, common for children or their parents to say that they go out for fun with foreigners (*pay thiaw kap farang*), catch foreigners (*jap farang*), or even have guests (*mii kheek*). After a client has returned three or four times, he is simply known as a friend. I never heard anyone refer to themselves as a child prostitute (*sopheni dek*) or even a business woman – a common slang term for prostitute (*ying borikan*). They are keen to downplay the importance of prostitution in their lives; it is what they do, not who they are. As Lek said, "it's only my body". The children are acutely conscious of the social stigma which surrounds prostitution, and for them to be called a child prostitute is a great insult and deeply hurtful. It is much easier for them, and much less damaging to their pride, to construct an image for themselves which turns their clients into 'friends' and their prostitution into 'going out for fun'.

There are many reasons why the children might do this: their inability to cope with reality, a strategy for survival, or as a form of false consciousness. All these reasons may be true, yet in their rejection of other's terms, the image of passivity breaks down. These children do have their own discourses and their own active ways of survival. They challenge the researcher's preconceived notions, and they are clearly struggling against the stereotype of what a child prostitute should be. In all the stories about them, child prostitutes are not silent because they have nothing to say. They are silent because they have been silenced. However incomplete and contradictory the children's justifications for their lives are, and however little they perceive the wider social relations that they labour under, the child prostitutes in Baan Nua do use what little control they have to make life more bearable. The children have tangible markers of status and hierarchy, and by moving up, or aspiring to move up, within this hierarchy, they claim some sense of control over the world. While child prostitutes are often viewed by outsiders as a homogenous group, forced into involuntary prostitution, they do not see themselves in that way. In Baan Nua, there is a great internal differentiation in the group, and in their classificatory system there is a distinction between those who have no power to refuse or negotiate and those who do. The issue of child pimps therefore is central to an understanding of child prostitution, but it is one that many campaigners would prefer to overlook. In the classic myth of child prostitution, pimps are middle-men or middle-women who procure a child and take her away from her parents either by force, trickery, or financial inducement. It is simply inconceivable that children should pimp for each other and take a cut of the earnings of another child who has become a prostitute. Yet this is exactly what does happen as part of the children's survival strategies (for further evidence of this see International Save the Children Fund 1991).

There is a very definite pattern in child prostitution, of which the children who are prostitutes are keenly aware. The importance of status and place in a hierarchy cannot be underestimated, and it is a constant concern of the children. The more control a child has over the lives of other children, the more status he or she can accrue. Therefore if a child can coerce or persuade other children to visit clients and obtain a cut of the money, he or she gains respect from others. The ambition of most of the children is to have this status and so command the authority for doing this. Kob, whom I shall describe in the case history below, is a prime example of this. Her success in prostitution is not just material, it is social and even moral. By selling sex, she can earn money to support her family and she can also prove her higher social status by having others who are indebted to her.

Kob

Kob is twelve years old and one of the most successful prostitutes in the village. She is considered very beautiful and earns enough money to support her mother, stepfather and seven siblings. Through prostitution, she has even been able to build her parents a new house so that they now live in a waterproof, concrete house, rather than in the leaking tin shacks lived in by the rest of the community. She has one regular client in particular, Julio, who returns to the slum twice a year. He sometimes brings friends with him, who are also interested in buying sex from the children. He sends 3000 *baht* (£80) a month to Kob's mother, Sai, and has also helped out financially on other occasions. When the roof on Kob's family house needed repairing, at a cost of 5000 *baht* (£135), it was Julio who paid for it. Kob's obvious financial success has enabled her to make progress within the hierarchy of prostitution, and she has been able to 'move up' from selling sex into pimping. When Julio's friends come to the slum, it is Kob who decides whether she will have sex with them or if others will. Although she is sometimes specifically requested by the men and feels unable to refuse, she can at least negotiate her price. Frequently, however, she simply finds girls younger than herself to take to foreign men, and this is viewed as progress in Baan Nua. In gaining such respect, she has moved up the career ladder of prostitution and can further prove her status by getting the younger children to do the work that she no longer wants to do. She continues to see clients herself, but, she is no longer in the lowest category of prostitutes in the village because she can send her younger sisters and her neighbours to less desirable clients. She has earned the power to negotiate, despite the power differential between herself and the clients. It may be a limited form of choice and power, but in the harsh conditions within which Kob operates the options she does have are used skilfully and deliberately.

Other children in Baan Nua also act in this way. Lek was first procured at the age of three by her neighbour. At that age she had no power to refuse or negotiate, and for many years she had a very low status in Baan Nua because she was a child who could be forced to do whatever she was told. As she has grown up, however, her status in the community has improved, so that now she too procures younger children and sends them to James. In Lek's case the status she receives in doing so is particularly gratifying. She and her family are especially poor, even by Baan Nua standards, and are often viewed as being at the bottom of the community, and it hurts her that she is looked down upon by so many. Her behaviour after sending children to her former client seems designed to flaunt her new found status. She takes the children to James's house, delivers them to him, and then uses his swimming pool until they have finished. Although not taking a cut of their wages, as she has already been paid by James, the respect she earns in the eyes of the community in being able to do this enhances her self-esteem considerably.

For the rest of the children of Baan Nua, pimping is something that can be worked towards. There is usually an initial period of prostitution where enough money has to be earned for respect and authority to be gained, and it is only after a considerable time, usually about two or three years, that a child can become a pimp. Even then, there is no clear demarcation, and many children continue to do both. Often children can only become pimps when there are other younger children around so that they can enforce the traditional status relationships based on age. The following case study is unusual in that Nong does not fit into this pattern. He has managed to move straight into pimping without an initial period of prostitution, and is much admired by the other children in Baan Nua. He does not actually live in the community, but he knows most of the children there. He lives on the streets most of the time, and comes into contact with them during the day when they are soliciting or selling other goods. Nong first came to the attention of the police when he was arrested and jailed at the age of seven for pimping. I met him a year or so later and asked him how he had started pimping.

Nong

"I was born and brought up in Bangkok. When my mother remarried, I ran away and came here. I lived on the streets for a while and tried to make money by selling chewing-gum and flowers, but it wasn't enough. So, I had learnt a bit of English from the tourists and I decided to become a pimp, fixing up contacts between foreign men and other children. I didn't do very well at first, the police caught me and put me in prison for a month. On my release though, I got lucky. I met a foreigner who employed me to pimp exclusively for him. This man did not have the courage to find women and children himself, so I did it for him. I had to explain his sexual requests to the women and girls that I had fetched from the bars or the streets. I sometimes recruited children from the street also, and some of the younger women who were working in the bars illegally."

Nong is adamant that he has never worked as a prostitute himself, and I once made him cry by asking too repetitively if he had ever been a prostitute. He said "I never went with foreigners, but no one will believe me". His own sense of identity and security are very dependent on that distinction, as he thinks that being a prostitute, especially for a child, is the lowest category for a person to be in. He is insistent in his refusal to be categorised as one. He sees nothing intrinsically immoral or wrong with being a pimp. On the contrary, it reinforces his self-image and confidence because he has, at a young age, been able to command so much power over others. The fact that this includes adults is a source of pride, as he has stepped out of his inferior role and moved up in social rank. Among the other street children in particular, he is regarded with a mixture of awe and envy. He is aware of this, of course, and there is undoubtedly an element of bravado and exaggeration in his story. It is hard to believe, for example, that the police would jail a seven-year-old. Nevertheless, he does pimp for other children, he is unusual in being able to avoid prostitution, and his exploits greatly enhance his status.

Nong's story, however, also illustrates how badly prostitution is thought of, even by those involved in it. It is a job that people would rather avoid and which carries a stigma that people are very aware of, even though their understanding of this exchange is never complete or without contradictions. The people of Baan Nua do not live in a vacuum, and they know that the sex industry is regarded with a mixture of shame and disgust by wider society. They know that they are frequently despised and rarely pitied, but that this is the price of survival. Believing in the values of the broader society – that prostitution is wrong – the children in Baan Nua locate prostitutes at the bottom of their own social scale. However, unlike the wider society, the children and their parents have further split this category so that the lowest level is divided into many layers. Status at this level is relative and is based on numerous things: the types of clients, the actual acts performed, and the degree of autonomy involved. A pimp, with his or her control over other people, and distance from actual prostitution, is inevitably seen as having moved up the social ladder, because it is a movement away from controlled prostitution, which is the lowest form of sex work. For the children, their place in the hierarchy is determined by the number of people they can directly or indirectly control. To many outsiders child pimps are the exceptionally depraved end products of a community where viciousness and licentiousness have taken over. It is inconceivable to many that pimping is seen as a means of self-improvement and an advance in status.

Prostitution and its Alternatives

The association between prostitution, work and economic exchange was not always very clear among the children in Baan Nua, and most of the children had complex and contradictory attitudes towards what they did. The children used the concept of 'work' very loosely, and often used it to cover all forms of income production and economic activity. When I asked children if they worked (*tham ngan*), many would readily say that they 'had guests' or would use other euphemisms which implied the same, yet this clear conflation of prostitution and work was not always very apparent in practice. Although these children include prostitution in the category of work, they also distance themselves from it so that work and economic exchange are not necessarily connected. Clients are sometimes customers who simply buy sex while at other times they are 'like kin', men such as James and Julio have reciprocal obligations with the children and their families which function just like real kin networks, where economic transactions take place which would never be described in economic terms.

Despite recognising the commercial nature of the sex they perform, the children use the terminology of love and romance in order to deny the connection between the money they earn and what they have to do in order to earn it. The children refuse to use the word prostitution, and prefer to construct a view of the world where their customers are guests, boyfriends, or simply friends. One of the ways in which this is made easier for them is that there is no fixed rate for prostitution. The men pay them after sex, but this is given as a 'gift' or a 'tip'. The sums of money they are given as gifts are relatively substantial. As noted above, Julio sends Kob's family 3000 *baht* (£80) a month as well as large one-off payments such as that for mending her parents' roof. James often sends money to Lek when she requests it. These factors enable the girls to deny that they are 'really' prostitutes. Their clients are 'friends' and fictive kin who merely fulfil their obligations whenever the children need it.

Although, as an outsider, it was clear to me that the children 'worked' as prostitutes, it was also clear that there was a great deal of ambiguity about this, and that the children would often attempt to deny the connection between paid sex and work. The jobs listed in the table below are all the result of self-definition. I first asked the children if they worked, and if they replied that they did, I asked them what they did and simply recorded their answers. As the word prostitution is disliked, most children told me they had guests but as this is such a common euphemism for prostitution, I have assumed that everyone who used this phrase was a prostitute. However, not everyone is prepared to admit even this, and there is, therefore, a large overlap between prostitutes and those in other categories, such as those 'supported by foreigners' or boxers who often work at bars where they are bought out at the end of an evening. Also, it is possible that the jobs are not exclusive. Although the typical pattern of informal economic activity would suggest that the children had more than one source of income (Hart 1973), in fact very few children seem to work in several areas. Occasionally Lek and her family beg, and her former sister-in-law, Tik, sometimes attempts to sell garlands of flowers in the streets but on the whole they listed their most regular and lucrative source of income as their work.

It is noticeable that all the children over seven years old work and bring in income to the family, and that the vast majority of these jobs are related to the sex industry in some way. In both the

Table 4.1. *Children's Work by Age*

Work	0–6 Mths	7–1 Mths	1–3 Yrs	4–6 Yrs	7–9 Yrs	10–12 Yrs	13–15 Yrs	Total
Not working	2	0	3	12	0	0	0	17
Have guests (prostitute)	0	0	0	4	7	8	7	26
Supported by foreigner	0	0	0	0	3	2	4	9
Street Vendor/Beggar	0	0	1	3	0	1	0	5
Garbage Collector	0	0	0	3	1	0	0	4
Odd Jobs	0	0	0	0	1	1	0	2
Boxer	0	0	0	0	0	1	1	2
Total	2	0	4	22	12	13	12	65

ten-twelve and the thirteen-fifteen age range, all the children rely on sex with foreigners for their earnings. A similar pattern is evident in the next age range, although one child earns a living through odd jobs which might include temporary construction work or running errands. There are only six children under three, and only one of these works selling chewing-gum on the streets. It is the four to six year-old range that is especially interesting, therefore, as not only are there many children in this range, but the majority of them do not work. Three of the working children beg in the main town, three sort rubbish on the nearby refuse tip, and four of them (two boys and two girls) are already working as prostitutes. However, although there seems to be a group of children who do not work, given the prevailing patterns in the older age groups it does not seem that these children will never work, merely that they are not working yet. It also appears likely that they will work in the sex industry. No child over nine is working as a rubbish collector, which tends to suggest that earnings in prostitution do draw children into the industry as there is almost universal involvement after that age.

The options available to uneducated children, such as collecting rubbish or factory work in sweatshops, are often physically dangerous. Children know that there is a very limited window of opportunity in which they can work in a factory, especially the illegal ones that will employ children with no papers. Such work often damages health permanently and retirement happens at a young age. Phongpaichit claims that textile factories:

> ... had a policy to sack their women around the age of thirty because they knew that the women's absenteeism and inefficiency would soon increase dramatically as a result of lung disease and other products of the bad working conditions. Construction workers suffer in a

similar way, while the demand for such workers as waitresses and beauticians drops off severely with advancing age.' (1982: 8).

The supposedly prestigious and less arduous jobs that are available to young women such as working in a department store require at least Grade Six schooling and the very few training schemes available to slum or street children like those found in Baan Nua are often centred on punitive 'rehabilitation' centres which enforce a feeling of inferiority in the children. Here, they are trained to do menial, service-orientated, jobs such as welding or woodwork for boys or hairdressing for girls. All these are jobs which reinforce their status and position in society as those who are always at the service of others.

Within Baan Nua, selling sex is an accepted part of their lives, and while no child says that sex in this way is pleasurable for them, it is still seen as an easy way to earn money. Many of them have tried other jobs, but those that are available for poor, unskilled, women and children in the town are badly paid and often backbreaking. The rubbish dump is close to where they live, but there is little money to be made there and it involves plenty of risks. The rats, the filth and the smell are all deeply unappealing, and the risk of injury and infections from broken glass or jagged metal is high. Selling food is another option, but there are start-up costs which would involve savings that most people do not have and the financial returns are not as high as in prostitution. In comparison with the jobs available, prostitution is well-paid. In addition to 'one-off' payments which can sometimes be coaxed out of clients, children can earn comparatively large sums. Eight-year-old Sompot, for example, earns between £20 and £80 a month (750 and 3000 *baht*), and Lek is given around £55 (2000 *baht*) a month to find clients for James. Without the school-leaving certificates which are necessary for any sort of office or shop work,[1] and lacking any vocational training, the children's only other option, besides sorting out rubbish, is begging, which is seen as a poor choice as earnings fluctuate greatly. On a good day in the tourist season, children can make up to 500 *baht* (£15), but during the rainy season when there are fewer tourists, they can sometimes come back with nothing. Begging also means running the risk of being arrested by the police or having their money stolen by older street children. Compared to this, or to the 20 *baht* (50p) a day that the younger children earn from scavenging

---

1. Proof that the woman has finished compulsory education up to Grade 6, usually up to the age of twelve.

rubbish, from a purely economic perspective, prostitution is a rational choice.

The paradox of this way of thinking is that no matter how much they work, they never seem to have any savings or anything that would help them improve their lives over the long term. When the children have money, they give it to their parents straight away, who often spend it immediately. Saew's children, for example, always give her the money that they earned, only to see her lose it; she lends it to other people without ever getting it back, or just spends it on drink. Sometimes new houses are built or roofs mended, but often, if money is saved, it is ultimately spent on conspicuous consumption. All the houses in Baan Nua have powerful stereos and many people have motorbikes. However, such things are important in terms of status, and in the constant jostling for position in the social hierarchy that goes on in Baan Nua, such symbols are of ultimate importance.

For many campaigners against child prostitution, a child selling sex is the ultimate horror, and one that must be avoided at all costs, but for the children themselves it is often viewed as yet another hazard to be negotiated in a life full of difficulties and poverty. When faced by disease, stigma, and a deprived environment, all the options are bleak, and some are worse than others. Other jobs have been tried, such as Saew's family collecting rubbish, but they do not bring in enough money to survive. With so few opportunities to change their lives, and with the alternatives to prostitution so limited, it is not surprising that children claim to choose it above other options. They certainly do not like prostitution, it is a job which carries an immense social stigma, and it has serious risks. They would sometimes reproach me when I asked about it, saying "why do you want to talk about such ugly things?", but it is seen as a means to an end. There is a certain satisfaction in being able to fulfil filial obligations. After one of many visits of Julio to Kob, she was able to build her mother a new house. "I built it all by myself" she told me proudly. She has repaid some of the *bun khun* that, as a daughter, she owes her mother, and is able to derive a great deal of satisfaction from doing this.

There is undoubtedly a strong sense of duty which helps the children to explain and understand prostitution yet these stories and explanations are not as straightforward as they might appear. This expectation of reciprocity is often ambiguous, not formalised in any way, and it can be problematic. Both parents and children expect some sort of mutual indebtedness and obligation, but it can be manipulated or misunderstood to the extent that neither side is clear about exactly what they must do. This is particularly true in the case of prostitution where the denial involved is great. I asked Pen, who regularly sends her eight-year-old son to clients, why she allowed him to go. She replied, "I am his mother. If I ask my son to make money for me, he will go. I don't send him, he wants to go for me". Likewise, whenever I asked Malee why her nieces were prostitutes when her own children were not, I was told, "Tam and Noi want to help, I don't ask them". On the other hand, one of the youngest children in my survey told me, "I don't want to go with foreigners, but my grandmother asks me to so I feel I must". Both parents and children are working within the same cultural framework of reciprocity, but it is clear that there is uncertainty on both sides. Both adult and child are aware of the duties that children have: there is a degree of unease about how far a child has to go to fulfil these duties.

I found the children's justifications for prostitution problematic in other ways. Their rationalisations of their work and their motivations for doing it make life easier to cope with, in that they are able to claim a control over their lives even if this may appear illusory to others. It also enables them to reject the wider society before it rejects them. It is easier for them to say that they have tried other jobs and discarded them than to admit that they cannot be employed. They are unable to see the selling of their sexuality in its wider political context, and whatever they say about sex work, they do not have the knowledge to make a fully-informed decision. Although they reject rubbish sorting and factory work as too dangerous, prostitution brings serious physical risks. Apart from the risk of an abusive client, there are the dangers of sexually transmitted diseases, of which AIDS is but one. Any disease, however, to a child with poor health and a weakened immune system, can be devastating. Also, the physical trauma involved when a pre-pubescent child has sex is immense. A child's body is ill suited to penetration by an adult; the damage is painful and the effects long-lasting.

The justifications that they give for working in the sex industry must also be set against their dependence on drugs and alcohol to get them through the day. There is a high level of drug and alcohol use in Baan Nua, with over two- thirds of the children addicted. Towards the end of my time in the community, I conducted a survey of the types of addiction within the sample group of sixty-five children.

I had not specifically asked about gambling or other 'psychological' addictions and it was instructive to note that twelve chil-

Table 4.2. *Levels of Addiction Among the Children*

Type of Addiction	Number	Percent
Gambling	12	18.5%
Glue	10	15.4%
Alcohol	6	9.2%
Drugs	6	9.2%
Smoking	3	4.7%
Mixed	15	23%
None	13	20%
Total	65	100%

dren stated gambling without being prompted in that direction. Whenever I asked why the children took various drugs or why they gambled, my questions were answered with a shrug and the answer they gave was that they took drugs because it was *sanuk* (fun). When I asked why they took certain drugs, there was little consensus other than they took whatever drugs were cheapest and easiest to get hold of. The high level of glue sniffing could be explained by the fact that glue was the most widely available and affordable drug. Some children did admit to wanting to try cocaine or heroin, but none of them could claim with much conviction that they actually had. In many cases, children had been introduced to drugs by their parents as a way of keeping the children quiet while they drank alcohol or gambled in the evening. The effects of sniffing glue made the children listless and lethargic and hence easier to deal with, but it also gave them headaches and induced nausea. Sompot, in particular, hated his mother giving him glue to calm him down, and he would regularly sit quietly in a corner, playing endless computer games with the sound off, in the hope that his mother would not notice him. Again, she believed that he did not mind, and told me, "Children like to play with these things. It is better that he is here with me and I know where he is. Otherwise he would wander off and get lost". Even when not directly introduced to them by their parents, drinking or glue sniffing are what the adults in the slum do and the children simply follow suit. Possibly, if the parents start taking harder drugs, the children will follow, but the price of them may preclude most experimentation.

The children always deny that they take drugs to cope with prostitution, and indeed many claim to have started to use drugs before they began prostitution. They are quick to deny that they turn to drugs to help them cope with the specific stresses concerned with prostitution. However, I feel that this must be seen within the context of other statements that they made. Their addictions are self-identified and possibly not completely accurate, and they are very reluctant to admit that they cannot cope. Once they have entered prostitution, they struggle to justify it and want to be seen as in control of their own lives and able to make informed choices. To admit that they are addicted to certain drugs because they find life too difficult would mean having to deconstruct their carefully built up self-image which many of them are unwilling and possibly unable to do.

Without wishing to deny the children's sense of reality, I believe that the links between prostitution and drug use are strong. Although drugs are so pervasive in the slums and on the streets that all the children have been exposed to them at some point, it is noticeable that all the older children who have been prostitutes for some time are addicted. The thirteen children who claim not to be addicted are younger (all are below nine years old) and will possibly become addicted later. I saw at least two of the thirteen children sniffing glue around Baan Nua on different occasions, and therefore they can be classified as users, even if they do not identity themselves as addicts. In other situations, researchers have noted:

> Drug use is another associated risk of sexual work. Accounts of children who engage in casual sex-for-cash on the street often include the use of solvents (glue sniffing), alcohol, tobacco, and sometimes marijuana and cocaine. This is done to dull pains and block out the difficulties of street life, these difficulties may include prospective pain, fear and self-disgust related to sexual soliciting. (Black 1995: 50).

It would seem obtuse to recognise no link at all between drug use and prostitution. In Baan Nua, it seems a vicious circle. Even if the children are addicted to certain drugs before they start prostitution, the money they earn through sex work enables them to buy more glue or alcohol. This fuels their addiction until prostitution and drug use are mutually reinforced. Prostitution is necessary to pay for their drug use and the drug use is necessary to enable them to stay in prostitution.

The Life-Cycle of Prostitution

Within Baan Nua, child prostitution is not something that has grown out of a vacuum to cater to demand, and it should not be examined in isolation from the history of the village in its various forms. It is illustrative to look back to the older generation of women who live in Baan Nua. In eight of the fourteen house-holds concerned, the children are the second or third generation to have worked as prostitutes. For example, one woman, Dam, was one of the first women to make contact with the Americans on 'R and R'; two of her daughters are in prison for prostitution offences, and her granddaughter, Ning, also brings money into the household in this way.

The role models that children have are almost all prostitution related, their mothers, sisters, aunts, and often their fathers, brothers and uncles, have all worked as prostitutes and any other way of earning money seems inconceivable. Even more impor-tantly, they have seen what happens *after* prostitution when a woman has become too old to work or to be employed by a bar or bought by a customer. Although the dream may be to marry a rich foreigner and be taken away from Baan Nua, there is also a more prosaic version if this fails. One of the main arguments of the anti-child-prostitution lobby is that once a child has been abused in prostitution, there is no point in rehabilitation because the child is too deeply scarred and beyond help. These activists see little point in trying to undo the damage done to a child, because within their ideology what has been permanently deforms and degrades the nature of a child. O'Grady writes, 'When boys and girls have been forced to receive several customers a night seven days a week, they will be so traumatised that very little can be done to help them resume anything like a normal life' (1992a: 1).

In direct contrast to this, the lives of the children of Baan Nua witness that it is possible to continue with a 'normal' life after prostitution. Their relatives go on to marry, and have children, and, while the quality of life in the village may be low, it is possi-ble to find some sort of stability there. Saew, for example, would rather stay in Baan Nua than go back to Buriram and raise her grandchild there. When I asked her why she did not return, she said, "people will look down on me there". For her, as long as there is an accepting community of people in Baan Nua, life is worth living. The children are often deeply pessimistic and would not talk about the future, saying things like "I don't dream any more" (Lek) or "I'm too scared to dream in case I get disappointed" (Daeng). Their mothers were also very fatalistic, "my life is fin-ished for now, but next time I come back, I will come back as a nurse and help people" (Malee). However, this is not the same as viewing their lives as worthless. There is a real hope of regenera-tion in their current life, through a change of luck, such as Kob marrying Julio and removing her family from poverty, or failing that, in coming back in a future life to a happier or higher position.

Despite their lifestyles, which flout much traditional Buddhist morality, especially by drinking or by having multiple sexual partners, their faith in Buddhist philosophy is strong, and a great deal of emphasis is placed on karma and merit-making. While there is pessimism about this life, the future seems very much brighter when viewed over several coming lifetimes. That the children are abused and often unhappy in this lifetime is undeniable, but at the same time there is an absolute and unshakeable belief in reincarnation, and many believe that their next rebirth will occur in more favourable circumstances only if they endure this one and continue to make merit through filial duty and sacrifice for their families. Buddhism remains important in the community, and the fact that they can provide money for the temple, and can lay on a good feast for the monks when they come to the village is also a source of pride. Pen and Saew in particular are deeply religious; they go regularly to the temple, celebrate all the Buddhist festivals, and try to give up alcohol at the Buddhist equivalent of Lent. When Pen's second husband was killed in a motorbike crash, the funeral was a traditional five day affair at the temple. Seven days after his death, the monks came to Baan Nua to bless the house. They returned after a hundred days, and again after a year, to make sure that his spirit had not returned. Sompot, Pen's son, was sent to be ordained straight after his stepfather's death so that he could make merit for his mother and stepfather.

The children also have one other alternative life model of what can happen in this life after prostitution. Dam is an older woman who worked as a prostitute during the Vietnam war, and she is now raising her grandchildren while her daughters are in prison. She has become a greatly respected medium, and is in great demand as a communicator with the spirits. She is seen as someone who can predict the future and who is a healer. When Nuk was paralysed after a bout of glue sniffing, she was taken to the welfare hospital by the others, but they could do nothing for her and sent her home. When Dam was called in to help, she went into a trance and saw an evil spirit which was causing Nuk's paralysis. She cast out this spirit, and the next day, Nuk was able to walk again. The local hospital had always been unpopular because of the perceived rudeness of the nurses, and after this Dam became the healer for most of the village. Even people who had previously braved the hospital for quite serious injuries or illnesses, gave up going there and turned to Dam instead. Dam is one of their own and someone they know and can trust. She is also a direct link back to the village roots of the community where spirit mediums, usually post-menopausal women, wield great power (Tanabe 1991). Dam has become the most powerful person in the village through her spiritual power, and is now the *de facto* head of the village. It is she who negotiated the rent of the land and the installation of a lavatory for the community.

The children, therefore, have another possibility shown to them by Dam's example; they could one day leave prostitution and become a medium. Equally, Dam has shown them that it is possible to leave prostitution and raise a family. They are not condemned to a life where prostitution of some form is their only option and their only way of escape is death. The campaigners against child prostitution claim that a child is always broken and ruined by prostitution, and, unfortunately, in many cases, this may well be true, especially in the era of AIDS. However, the children of Baan Nua do not see life in this way, and the hope of a sudden upsurge in fortune is always there, despite the pessimism of some. Not only is there belief in reincarnation, but there is also hope that life will change and that they will marry out of the slum, or that through becoming a medium, like Dam, they can gain prestige and merit. Dam's example has shown them that there is another end-point and an alternative to the prostitution cycle. Becoming a medium after they have finished raising their families is a way of ending their lives in a virtuous state, and of being guaranteed a better reincarnation next time. Although spirit cults are supposedly quite distinct from Buddhism, many monks also practise animistic rituals and, in the understanding of Dam and others, being a medium is a clear way to gain Buddhist merit. Indeed, as Thitsa notes, 'The only time in Thai society when a monk may be observed kneeling before a woman is during such spirit medium sessions' (1982: 103), and, significantly, the medium and the prostitute are symbolically linked (Muecke 1984).

> If the category of prostitute caricatures sex-role expectations by exceeding them, the category of spirit medium, like that of the nun, exists in an ambiguous area of sex role transformation and denial of sex role stereotypes. (Thitsa 1982: 43).

In becoming a medium, a woman is able to transcend her sex and attain such a high status that even monks bow to her. Ning, especially, is both afraid of and awed by her grandmother's powers. She obeys her in everything, and wants to emulate her. She once said, "one day I will be like my grandmother, not like I am now". For Ning, becoming a medium could remove all the de-merit she has accrued through prostitution. A student of Buddhist scripture and theology might well contradict this belief, but in aspiring to become a medium she sees a way of undoing the past and creating a better future.

CHAPTER 5

Identity and its Difficulties

Status

It is evident that the child prostitutes of Baan Nua challenge many assumptions about how children generally, and child prostitutes in particular, should act. Their stories make uncomfortable reading because they contain none of the elements of helplessness that are expected of children. Issues such as child pimps are particularly hard to deal with as they foreground the children's agency and their attempts to order and make sense of the world, struggles usually only recognised in adults. The image of child prostitutes that has been received from the media and from NGOs locates their identity solely in their abuse. They know little of their life before prostitution, and afterwards, there is nothing to know except that they will die. However, as always, this is true for only some children. Identity in Baan Nua is not formed around abuse, or indeed around prostitution. Children are judged, and judge themselves, on whether they are good to their families, whether they have 'good' clients and on their place in the social hierarchy of their community. This hierarchy is based on the complex and subtle links between identity, social status and sexuality which the children are acutely conscious of and which they actively try to change.

To many, children are seen as having neither sexuality nor status, yet the importance of status is central to these children. One of the most fundamental aspects of status is relative age. There is, in Thai, no such thing as an equal – even twins are separated into older and younger – and status is clearly demarcated into inferior

and superior, even at a very early age. The importance of finding
out exactly how old someone is and hence, whether that person
is a *phi* (older sibling/superior) or *nong* (younger sibling/inferior),
is something that is learned early in Thailand. In many of the
children's games that I observed, this stratification is obvious with
the elder child being the dominant one who was given first choice
of games on offer and would take away the game of another child
if he wanted it without the other child feeling in any way able to
resist or complain. The older children show their status in a multitude of ways; by demanding favours from younger siblings or by
indebting their inferiors by providing services for them. In terms
of prostitution, this relates directly to the issue of child pimps.
Older children can control the sexual services of younger children
and can demand that they have sex with certain clients.

Children lack power because there are few people below them
in status, which is an unenviable position. Even in a community
like Baan Nua, it is important to have someone beneath you so
that you are not at the very bottom. Within the community, Saew
and her family are viewed as being at the bottom of the social
hierarchy, and this is a reason for others to feel that they are better off, and therefore, that they are also better people. I was told
repeatedly by Sai, Kob's mother, for example, that her children
were not allowed to beg as it is only 'bad' people like Saew who
begged. Saew contradicted this, and while downplaying begging,
pointed to the wealth of her children's clients as sign of her family's social worth. In Baan Nua, status is based on hierarchies
rather than conventional structures and measures of rank, and is
continually contested. Saew could claim that because James sent
money to Lek and had a relationship based on reciprocity with
her, she was more important than others in the slum who did not
have such powerful friends. Sai, however, viewed begging as
proof that Saew could not indebt people to her, and therefore
that she held the lowest position in the slum hierarchy.

The subtleties of status, what gives it and what takes away
from it, are extremely important for an understanding of the
complexities and hierarchies of prostitution in Thailand. During
the course of my research I met a group of young women who
were considered to be at risk of becoming prostitutes. They were
sent by the NGO that I worked with for special training in order
to have a skill that would allow them to stay away from prostitution. One of them, a fifteen-year-old called Pom, was sent to learn
dress-making at school and to gain tailoring skills so she could
become self-employed later on. She did well at the school and
enjoyed it, but, on completing the course, refused to go into busi-

ness on her own or help in a dressmaking shop. All she wanted to do was to work in a department store where she would have possibly earned less money but which, she felt, conferred higher status. She told me,

> It would be better to work in a department store because it is cool
> and air-conditioned. The people who come in are dressed in good
> clothes and I'll get a uniform and perhaps some make-up if I work
> there. If I have my own shop, I'll be hot all day and the people will
> be rude and it won't be as good.

While she did not hope ever to attain their status, she hoped that by working with the richer people and being closer to them, some of their higher status would rub off on her. She believed that proximity to status was status-giving in itself.

In a similar way, the children (and women) that I dealt with had almost exclusively Western clients. This is partly because of the large tourist population in the city and partly because they strive to keep their exclusivity. Westerners are considered high status because it is assumed they are rich, and the children claim therefore that working with Westerners is a high status occupation. If a child goes to a high-paying, foreign client, he or she is looked on more favourably by others in the community than a child who has a mean, poor, or Arab client. Even within that hierarchy, however, it is not unusual for the children to compete between themselves for the richest Western client and, again, the assumption is that some of his status could be transferred from client to prostitute. During my time with this community, no children, to the best of my knowledge, actually had Arab or African clients but it was a constant fear for them.[1] While Westerners (*farang*) were generally considered rich and high status, Arabs were considered brutal and Africans sadistic. It was thought that the low standing of an Arab, would reflect badly on the child who was his sexual partner.

Status is endlessly contested by both children and adults in Baan Nua, often through the control of money. In Baan Nua, money is not simply seen as a way of providing necessities but also as a way of gaining power and status. Within the slum, money is of paramount importance. It is understood that who-

---

1. Interestingly, this fear of Arabs is part of the mythology surrounding the clients of child prostitutes and appears in other descriptions of child prostitution. Sereny, in her study of children in London notes, without giving any supporting evidence, that 'Much of the "demand" at least in London, is now from foreigners, many of them Arabs' (Sereny 1984 viii).

ever has money can buy what they want. Money brings power as anyone and anything can be bought with it. It also brings with it moral authority. Money is a symbolic assertion of merit because it is assumed that without merit there would be no ability to get money (Hanks 1962, Mulder 1979, Fordham 1993). Having money is a way of proving to the outside world that you have merit, and it is also a means of compelling others to do what you want. One of the reasons given by the other residents for Saew's poverty and inability to look after money is that she has no merit. If she were a good person, she would be able to keep her money and would not lose it or squander it in the way she does. There is no point in having money if it is not spent conspicuously, and financial success can only be enjoyed if other people could see the results. A seventeen-year-old prostitute who worked outside Baan Nua, once told me:

> During the next few months I am going to work as hard as I can so that when I go home for Songklan[2] this year, I will be ready. I am going to spend every last penny I have on gold jewellery and chains and nice clothes and walk up and down the main street in our village so everyone can see me. And when they have seen me, I am going to say "fuck you" to all of them. Fuck you because look at what I have and look how little they have. How could they possibly ever look down on me when I have so much.'

If she had remained in her natal village, her status, due to her relative youth, would be that of an inferior, but money and material success are ways of improving her standing. Even though she has violated many rules and customs by leaving the village and becoming a prostitute, money is a direct way of restoring and enhancing her position.

Money enables power to be wielded both directly and in more subtle ways. Financial power endows a person with the ability to act as a patron, by which means people are obligated and put into debt to that patron (Hanks 1962). The people of Baan Nua explicitly recognise and acknowledge the link between money and power and acquiesce to the power that money brings. This attitude is shared by everyone in Baan Nua, so that it is common for a woman to tempt a lover into staying with her by buying him a motorbike or a large stereo. Pen, especially, keeps a series of men in this way, even if it means that her children have to work as prostitutes to pay for it. The power of money means that these

---

2. The Thai New Year, when it is traditional for people to return to their home villages and spend time with their families.

young men can be indebted to her, and forced into doing things that they do not necessarily want to do, because Pen has financial power over them. It causes an interesting dynamic in the community: it is the women who have power within the community because they have money and the men are dependent on them for it. While they have little choice in their sexual partners outside the slum, in that they have to take whoever is willing to pay them, within the community they can chose with whom they sleep and can, if necessary, pay for that to happen. The children are brought up in a culture of materialism where money and power are synonymous. Throughout their lives, they have seen that money buys whatever they want, whether that is fulfilment of their filial duties by buying their parents a house, or being able to buy the glue and alcohol which makes life in Baan Nua more bearable. Money places a tangible value on everything. I once heard the children say to their teachers "why should we learn to read and write, we don't get paid for it?"

Interestingly, one of the only psychological studies done on prostitutes claims that one of their most pressing psychological problems is what the author describes as a 'Cinderella' syndrome; that is waiting to be rescued (Green n.d.).[3] In my experience, however, this is not the case. Most women and, indeed most children, try to raise their status through earning enough money so that they never need to be patronised again. Unsurprisingly in a society which promotes 'the value of passivity as the ultimate virtue' (Tantiwiramanond and Pandey 1987: 135), elements of waiting to be rescued are there, but they are not the only hope of many children who try hard to improve their status and take charge of their position in the social hierarchy. Although the ultimate hope for some children may be a foreigner who marries them and takes them away from Baan Nua, few children wait passively to be rescued. On a daily basis, they are actively involved in trying to prove and change their status, and consequently to assert their identity.

Sexuality and Identity

It is common in the Western world to view sexuality as something that belongs to the private, enclosed world of the family. Prostitution is a deviant sexuality because, by definition, it is public

---

3. This survey should be treated with some care, however, as its author has an explicit Christian evangelical agenda and runs a conversion centre in Bangkok.

and not in its proper place. However, this distinction is blurred in Thailand and the link between sexuality and social status is not an easy one. Equally, although sexuality and sexual activity are extremely important in determining status, especially for women, there is not always a direct correlation between the two and status can be determined by other means. Determining status involves a dialogue between the self and society: it is continuous because status is flexible. Prostitutes, women normally despised because of their perceived immorality, can and do achieve high status through other means and even children can have a degree of control and flexibility.

Sexuality in Thailand cannot be viewed independently of public morality which in turn is dependent on interpretations of Theravada Buddhism and other religious teachings. While there is an obvious difference between scriptural and individual readings of concepts such as morality (Keyes 1984b), there are understandings of sexuality which have a wide consensus. This consensus comes from the central Thai moral discourse, which is displayed in its official and legal forms, and now, through the spread of the mass media, is being impressed on the populace as a whole. This discourse claims Buddhist teaching as its source and thus promotes its own version of 'proper' sexuality. In the North, for example, female chastity is controlled by girls' parents through sanctions deriving from ancestor spirits. Sexual misdemeanours are punished by the spirits in the form of illnesses of descent group members (Muecke 1981, 1984, Tanabe 1991). However, views on chastity are changing, and it is now being presented as a 'Thai' ideal, based on Theravada Buddhism (Thitsa 1980) even if this ideal is crumbling in contemporary Thailand. One problem is that despite equating sexual purity for women with Buddhist teachings, the scriptural basis for it is shaky. As Goonatilake points out:

> In Buddhism, there is nothing uniquely wicked about sexual offences or lapses. This is evident from the fact that the third precept of abstinence of sexual misconduct is on exactly the same footing as the other four precepts, namely abstinence from the following: taking life, taking what is not given, false speech and taking intoxicating drinks. The seriousness of the offence of sexual misconduct is neither more nor less than that of the other four and thus neither guilt nor shame is given to it. (1993: 36).

This interpretation of Buddhist morality has largely been taken as referring to men. Sexual misdemeanours certainly do not carry the same moral weight for men in Thailand as they do in the West (ten Brummelhuis 1993, Fordham 1993, Saengtienchai

1995). Nevertheless, there is a great difference in beliefs concerning the sexuality and sexual needs of men and women and, in consequence, their sexual roles within the family (Soonthorndhada 1995). That a woman should be virgin before marriage and afterwards should stay with her marriage partner is the ideal, yet there are no such prohibitions on a man (Heyzer 1986, Mills 1990, Catholic Commission for Health 1993, Walker and Ehrlich 1994, Saengtienchai 1995). A Royal Proclamation in The Law of Three Seals, for example, laid down in 1805, states 'a good woman should not let more than one man gain access to her body' (Hantrakul 1983: 3). For men, sex is an appetite, and tellingly, it is said in Thai that men need different flavours (*rotchat*) of women and must obtain these as best they can, usually through prostitution (Fordham 1993, Saengtienchai 1995).

For women, the situation is very difficult, and sexuality and sexual enjoyment are not things that a 'decent' woman can admit to (Soonthorndhada 1995). Female sexuality, whether actual or potential (in the case of younger girls) is strictly controlled. All females are expected to conform to certain norms of behaviour and sexual modesty, and even in Baan Nua, girls as young as two are told to sit appropriately and modestly. In law, adultery by a woman is grounds for divorce, although adultery by a man is considered so normal that a wife must prove that he maintained another woman as well as having sex with her (Parakh n.d.). A Thai woman should be pure until marriage and faithful thereafter, her primary role being a mother not a wife (Mulder 1979). Even a very Westernised Thai woman once told me how lucky she was to find a husband at thirty-three because "I had two boyfriends [i.e. sexual partners] before I met my husband. Even though he is very modern, it was hard for him to accept, and, if his friends knew, he would lose face." Her husband openly had at least two *mia noi* (minor wives) but it was his wife who was expected to feel dutiful and grateful for his consenting to make her his legal wife (*mia luang*).

The two basic roles for women are prescribed as 'mother or mistress' (Keyes 1984a), the former who nurtures but is passive and asexual and the latter who is sexual and active. While women's sexual needs are often disregarded and denied, they are also feared, and there is a tradition of dread and misogyny against rural Thai women. King Mongkut referred to women as viewing monks as 'fattened hogs' (Kirsch 1985) that they could seduce and marry, while van Esterik writes 'In general terms women are viewed as "oversexed" and actively seeking sexual satisfaction, even to the point of tempting or seducing monks (1982: 76). It is only through motherhood that a woman's sexuality can be brought under control. The primary factor of a woman's virtue lies in her reserving herself for one man. Therefore, there is a vast difference in status between a *mia noi* (minor wife) and a prostitute. The former is virtuous because of her exclusivity, she has sex with only one man and is therefore rewarded with the title of wife. As Hantrakul writes,

> Of course, in modern Thailand today, a wife is less than a matter of acquisition by money or love than that of sexual monopoly. Even prostitutes who normally were and still are the wives of no men by definition become *mia chao* (wife for hire), carrying the honourable title of wives when they are temporarily engaged in sexual ties with only one man – who could be seasonal tourists or GIs on R and R as well as expatriates. (1993: 7).

One of the traditional justifications for prostitution is the differing sexual natures of men and women. Reynolds (1977) translates a text known as *A Defence of Polygamy*, written by a nineteenth century Thai courtier called Kham Bunnag. The author claims that a large number of wives or concubines is necessary, so that a man, with his overwhelming sexual needs, does not have to force himself on his wife if she is menstruating or pregnant, thereby causing demerit to himself. He goes on to write that although women are passive in sexual relations they are also jealous and ruthless. He claims that a women would kill her husbands if she had more than one, whereas a man would treat all his spouses fairly. While polygamy has been abolished, the ideology of male sexual needs that lies behind it still exists (Saengtienchai 1995). Sittitrai et al. (1991) calculated that 22% of urban men and 9% of rural men visited prostitutes in the last twelve months while Soonthorndhada (1994) claims that 45% of males had their first sexual contact with a prostitute. The Thai government estimates that over 90% of Thai men have at one time or another visited prostitutes (ECPAT 1991). Work by Fordham suggests that visiting prostitutes, drinking and feasting, are all part of social rituals that help to reinforce and construct male identity (Fordham 1995). In the religious injunction on sexual morality, laid down in the Buddha's five precepts, sexual misconduct is often interpreted to refer only to adultery which is defined as sexual violation of a woman without her parents' consent or having sexual relations with another man's wife. No reference at all is made to prostitution, as prostitutes, it is assumed, are no-one's wife.

These differing standards have huge implications for any study of prostitution in Thailand (Thitsa 1980, Muecke 1992). Although the level of prostitution is beginning to cause embarrassment to the government on an international level and the arrival of sex tourists is resented by many, prostitution is still seen as a necessary institution to meet Thai men's sexual needs which might otherwise erupt into rape. One study of sexual networking found that almost all the men in its sample group, married or single, thought sex with prostitutes was normal and acceptable (Havanon et al. 1992). Comments such as 'without prostitutes, many women and girls would have been raped' or 'because of prostitutes, men have somewhere to vent their sexual energy, thus sparing decent women' are common, both in the newspapers and in every day speech (quotes taken from Chuenprasaeng 1993: 8). The need for men to indulge their sexual appetites is considered to be so strong that rape and taking sex by force would be the result of any clamp down on prostitution. One Police Chief warned that 'The rate of rapes and other sex related crimes might sky rocket if these men find no place to satisfy their sexual desires' (Brody 1995: 2). One of the words for male orgasm, *taek*, literally means to burst but it carries with it connotations of release and unstoppable force.

Prostitution therefore has an ambiguous position and the sex industry is often defended by women whose relation to it is ambivalent (Saengtienchai 1995). While there is contempt for individual prostitutes, there is also an understanding that they are necessary and Phongpaichit claims that they are viewed with a mixture of 'sympathy and distaste' (1982: 47). Views that sex workers ease the strain on other women account for the acceptance of prostitution in many areas. There is also an unspoken assumption that men will go to prostitutes for certain sexual acts that wives find unpleasant and in return men will not expect their wives to perform these acts. Fordham writes that:

> ... both men and women claim that sex in the domestic and extra-domestic sphere is quite different, and this probably underlies the ease with which women permit male participation in the commercial sex sector. In the domestic sphere sex has a highly pragmatic nature, and is clearly viewed as part of a long term marital exchange relationship rather than one which satisfies fundamental human appetites.' (1995: 31).

The Thai wife is often expected to remain sexually passive. Her sexual role is limited to bearing children and therefore sex is for reproductive rather than recreational purposes. Although some prostitutes also pride themselves on doing very little, it is more common for a men to request different positions and different 'flavours' in the form of many women. While ideally, prostitutes are supposed to be active sexual partners, they are still cast in a dependent role. Men demand sexual activity from prostitutes just as they expect sexual passivity from their wives, and they pay for both. As Fordham notes: 'it is in sex with prostitutes where gender relations most nearly approach Northern Thai male views of ideal male-female relations: dominant men and highly submissive females.' (Fordham 1996: 12).

The role of the prostitute is therefore one that many women depend on, even as they stigmatise and reject individual women (Saengtienchai 1995). One woman who I knew in Bangkok summed up the ambiguity very clearly:

> Every Friday night, he would come home absolutely drunk with what was left of his pay packet and want sex. I put up with that for a long time but after I had a third child, that was enough. I look after the money in the house, so when he would come back like that I would give him enough money to *pay thiaw* (go out for fun, to a brothel) with his friends and then he wouldn't pester me any more. He had fun with the dirty women, I had peace and because all my friends did the same, we could meet in peace.

Sexuality is part of a complicated system of exchange where women, often very blatantly, barter sex for material advantage. Even women who are not prostitutes view jewellery or money given to them by boyfriends as proof of their worth. In one survey looking at prostitution, 60% of the men interviewed admitted giving money or gifts to non-commercial partners in the last year (Havanon et al. 1992: 16), suggesting that payment or reward for sex is not solely a feature of prostitution (de Zalduondo 1991: 229). The woman who can convince a male partner to spend a lot of money on her, is considered clever rather than mercenary and it is taken as a sign of the strength of his affection.

The same is true for prostitutes and a client who pays over the odds, tips well, or comes back regularly can be classed as a boyfriend. Generosity towards a woman is taken as proof of affection and it is therefore difficult even for the women themselves to separate clients from boyfriends, as the category is so ambiguous. Cohen, in his study of Thai bar girls and Western men, shows very clearly the confusion inherent in these relationships and describes the 'incomplete commercialisation' of these relationships (1982: 411). The Thai woman believes that if a man cares about her enough, he will be prepared to support her financially while the Western man clings to his ideal that sex is about love and this removes his obligation to pay her.

While it may be too gross to say that in Thailand love can be 'bought' with money, it can certainly be 'earned' with it at least in relationships with open-ended prostitutes (*sic*), and probably also in other realms of Thai society, whose attitudes these girls reflect, in a perhaps exaggerated manner. (Cohen 1987:226).

In Western eyes both sex and money should be given on a voluntary basis, but to many Thai women, who know the value of their sexuality, this is not the case. As ten Brummelhuis writes, 'The extreme contrast between the world of marriage and paid sex is very much part of a Western discourse. The open linkage of money with marriage is not strange to most non-Western societies' (1993:14).[4]

Although prostitution is not subject to the religious disapprobation that it is in Christian or Islamic societies, it is still not viewed as a socially acceptable profession. Despite understandings of why women become prostitutes and a tradition of judging them on their motivations rather than their actions, there is still a stigma attached to women who work as prostitutes. Prostitution is a violation of society's sexual norms for women and there is a deep reluctance, especially among NGO activists, to view entry into prostitution as an anything other than a coerced decision. Although many women become prostitutes after working in other jobs and finding that the wages are too low to live on or finding that they hate the long hours of factory work, this is rarely publicly admitted. No-one is willing to acknowledge that prostitution may be a purely financial choice and while few people view it as a good job, there is a chance of escape from home or from poverty which is irresistible to some women (Fawcett et al. 1984). One woman, typical of many of the women that I know, was interviewed for a book of love letters from Western men to bar girls. She answered the question 'Why did you start working as a bar girl?' saying

4. Indeed it seems to be very common that monetary recompense is used as an indication of personal worth outside the West. Watson describes how marital disputes and separations in the City of the Dead in Cairo are settled by a man giving his estranged wife gifts which are viewed by both the woman and the community as 'a token of her worth' (1994: 36): in the same society Wikan (1980) discusses the giving of money and gifts by a man to his wife as signs of his respect for her. La Fontaine makes the same point in writing about prostitutes in Kinshasa:

> A girl expects her lover to present her with the most expensive presents he can afford in order to show his appreciation of her. Indeed she may break off the relationship is she thinks he is not being generous enough, not necessarily for purely mercenary motives, but because he is not demonstrating the esteem and love he professes to have for her. (1974: 98).

First time because I with Thai boyfriend and have one baby. I
working 70 *baht* one day, work 12 hour, making belt, making ear-
ring, making lighter, making anything for a company in Bangkok,
I come Patpong because I hear good money. I can make home better. I want to live better.' (Walker and Ehrlich 1994: 52).

It is assumed by activist groups that given the option many
women would rather leave prostitution and go back to menial but
'respectable' jobs, such as food selling or hairdressing. The failure
rates of 'rehabilitation' programmes which give training in these
skills are notoriously high, as sex workers vote with their feet and
refuse to accept the huge drop in wages that they would incur.
Although prostitution is an unstable job with large fluctuations in
earnings, it can pay more than many other jobs available to
unskilled, uneducated rural women (Truong 1982, 1986). Phongpaichit found that masseuses could earn between 25,000 *baht* if
they worked in a good hotel and 500 *baht* in a seedy brothel
(Phongpaichit 1982). She concluded that income from prostitution 'was about 25 times as large as the median level to be
expected in other occupations' (Phongpaichit 1982: 8). Likewise
DaGrossa (1980) found that the women in the brothels of Chiang
Mai earned around 3000 *baht* a month and all but one earned
over the government's minimum wage level of 1500 *baht*. When
even working in a department store requires a school-leaving cer-
tificate or higher, the options available to women who wish to
leave prostitution are scarce, especially as sex workers may have
missed out on formal education (Podhisita et al. 1993). As there
is a high level of entrance and departure into sex work, prostitution is rarely seen as a long term plan. Many women do dream of
leaving and starting their own businesses or settling back into
their communities when they have earned enough money to
become 'respectable'. ten Brummelhuis points out

> ... the gap between marriage and prostitution is not unbridgeable.
> Expressing this more positively: certain cultural notions enable a
> woman to act as a prostitute without having to enter into a deep
> identity crisis, without a feeling of spoiling her life, or being a bad
> daughter and/or bad mother. (1993: 13).

Prostitution may also be viewed as the duty of women as family members. As wives and daughters they have a duty to sacrifice
themselves for their family, whether this is by becoming the *mia
noi* of a richer, older man or working as a prostitute or in a sweatshop. Interestingly, the one section of society most tolerant of

prostitution, at least in its refusal to condemn it, is the Buddhist clergy. Muecke discusses the opinions of various monks that she interviewed about prostitutes:

> ... some monks denied that merit could be made through prostitution, most opined that the karmic outcome depended upon the prostitutes "intention" in prostituting herself. If she did so solely to help others or to make merit and not for pleasure, they found it plausible (but not likely) that her merit would be sufficiently great to counterbalance the demerit of prostituting herself.' (1992: 894).

Once again, the motivation is considered more important than the action. As long as prostitution (either male or female) is entered into for a moral purpose, such as to help the family, the immorality of the act loses its significance. Other writers have been explicit in linking prostitution with the low social role that women occupy in institutional Buddhism (Kirsch 1975, 1982, Thitsa 1980). The most important source of merit-making open to a man is to join the monastery but there is no comparable institution for women. Nuns are not shown the same respect (Beesey n.d., van Esterik 1982, Thitsa 1982, cf. Grimshaw 1992) and women are seen as pollutants to monks and the temple (Kirsch 1982, Tanabe 1991). With the belief that a woman has to be reborn as a male if she is to reach the ultimate goal of nirvana still common, women are perceived as spiritually inferior to men (Thitsa 1980). This inferiority combined with the promotion of female sacrifice as an ideal, helps give some motivation to the dutiful daughter becoming a prostitute to help her family. Thitsa writes. 'With the low value attached to the female body and the female spirit by Buddhism, she has been sufficiently degraded already to enter prostitution' (1980: 20).

Many of the women and children in Baan Nua manage to combine prostitution with a sincere belief in Buddhism and are devout supporters of the monks and local monasteries. They are either unaware of their place in the Buddhism system or claim not to care about its implications. They are respectful to the monks, never touch them, and talk in a polite manner that I never heard them use in other situations. The traditional tolerance shown towards prostitutes and the belief that their motivations and circumstances are important in determining merit means that many people like Saew and Pen see no contradiction in their lives between how they survive and what they believe. Prostitution is only a temporary stage in their life which is insignificant given the overall numbers of lives they will have. Pen, in particular, sees no discrepancy between Sompot being a prostitute most of the year and taking time out to be a novice for a week. In doing this, she believes, he is cleansing himself and making merit for her. Just as prostitution can be classed as a moral act by Sompot because he is repaying the obligation to his mother by bringing her wealth, so entering the monastic life brings them both spiritual merit.

Despite their justifications and the lack of any strict religious stigma against prostitution, however, there is a level at which sexuality and sexual experience do reflect something 'inalienable' that is outside the role of conventional exchange patterns and sexuality. The sexual act possesses something beyond monetary value. Although many of the children survive by colluding with the ideology 'it's only my body', many develop other forms of expressing sexuality, quite separate and distinct from the paid sex which they perform. The most obvious one is the high incidence of lesbianism or lesbian activities among the pubescent girls both inside and outside Baan Nua.[5] This orientation is not necessarily long term or even fixed, and it is certainly not part of any organised 'gay scene'. Rather, it seems as if this experimentation with lesbianism is an attempt by the children to carve out an independent sexuality away from paid sex with foreign men. Within Baan Nua it occurred among the girls who most regularly worked as prostitutes and a particularly intense relationship formed between Kob and Fon. They insisted on always sleeping in the same bed and were quite open in their sexual behaviour. It was ignored absolutely by the other people in Baan Nua and did burn out fairly quickly so that, while they remained friends, the sexual side of the relationship ended. Daeng (the child whose history was outlined in Chapter One) also began to have a relationship with a girl in a similar position for about six months after being paid for sex for the first time. After being hospitalised for five days with a severe uterine infection, Daeng was transferred to a private rehabilitation centre for 'problem' girls where she soon became very attached to a fellow patient called Noy. When another girl was assigned to share their room, Noy attempted to seduce her. Daeng became very jealous and threatened to kill herself. Nobody took the threats very seriously until, one day, she poured petrol over herself and lit a match, badly burning her stomach and arms. Noy was then removed from the centre and Daeng continued to threaten suicide if Noy did not come back, which never happened. Eventually Daeng discharged herself and went back to living in the city with other friends.

5. I was unable to find similar patterns among the boys who worked as prostitutes, as they were considerably less open about homosexual experiences

In neither of these cases did they identify themselves as lesbians or attempt to make any links to a wider gay community. There is an organised gay movement in Thailand, but it is small scale and largely confined to Bangkok and other major cities (Jackson 1989). Its language and ideology are based on similar Western movements so that it sits slightly uncomfortably with notions of sexuality in Thailand, where sexual acts between members of the same sex do not necessarily constitute a gay identity (Jackson 1989). In this world, lesbians are known as *tom* (short for tomboy if they are perceived to be masculine) or *dee* (short for lady, if they are seen as more feminine). In Baan Nua, no such terminology was current. What the girls did with their friends was simply *sanuk* (fun) and did not replace their view that their future involved a husband and children of their own. However, discussion of these lesbian interludes was the only time that I heard the children identify sexual experience with personal fulfilment. On the whole, sexuality and the possession of sexual responsiveness were not considered salient issues for the children and they did not necessarily expect sexual satisfaction in personal relationships. Unconsciously, however, the children did appear to create a way of having more satisfying sexual experiences by turning to their own peers, who had the same background and lifestyle, for sexual gratification. These relationships were unstable and inadequate in the long term, but they did temporarily produce a safe space for the children to explore a sexual part of themselves which was given no other outlet.

In twenty-first-century Western ideology, sexuality is fundamental to identity and personality and one cannot be understood without reference to the other (Foucault 1981, Weeks 1981, Jackson 1989). Until recently, however, this view of sex was not widely considered in Thailand and few people would conceive of a conflation of the two. This is shown most clearly in discussions of gay sexuality, which I touched on previously. There has been a traditional tolerance of homosexual acts in Thailand because they were no threat to the social order. The majority of 'gay' men married and had children and did not claim any special or separate gay identity. They performed their socially accepted roles of son, father and husband, and homosexual acts outside this structure were tolerated because they did not threaten it, (Jackson 1989, cf. Weeks 1981). As Jackson writes:

> Thais do not in general judge their actions by any abstract criterion of right and wrong, sin or virtue. Instead they are much more concerned with how they appear to others and how they measure up

to others' expectations. "Rightness" and "wrongness" thus tend to be socially specific rather the morally abstract notions in Thai culture, being more closely aligned with notions of propriety than of sin. (1989: 29).

Recently, however, there has been a growing acceptance within the media, and in middle class Thailand, of Westernised concepts of psychology, and sexuality is becoming increasingly thought of as fundamental to personality (ten Brummelhuis 1993). Such a discourse is crucial in understanding the clash between the children's view of prostitution and that of the campaigners. In Baan Nua, neither the children nor their mothers perceive their sexuality to be integral to their personality so it is not the focus of their identity. Identity is so bound up in status, prestige and hierarchy that sexuality is a means to those ends rather than an end in itself. The campaigners against child prostitution, however, have a very different ideology. In their understanding, children are 'ruined' through child prostitution because their sexuality is identified very closely with their personality and, therefore, if one is damaged, the other will be too.

Sexuality, however, does also have a moral aspect that the children are aware of. Whatever their actual behaviour, they acknowledge that chastity is the ideal for women. I asked Lek one day about her feelings towards her former sister-in-law, Tik, who had a series of affairs while married to Lek's brother, Tam. She said:

> What Tik did while Tam was away is a sin. It is a sin for a women to go with men other than her husband. I suppose it is also a sin to for a man to go with women other than his wife but I don't know. But with money it is different, I think it's not sinful because it is just for money. She's not really being sinful because it's just her body.

Her mother Saew echoed this, saying "a woman who goes with a man for money is not wrong because she is not being unfaithful, it is only her body, not her heart". There are many different views on sexuality and exchange in Baan Nua and it would be wrong to imply that there is one coherent or consistent view on sexuality within the community. Views are often contradictory, the same person at one time would claim "it is only a body" while, at another time, they would attach a definite morality to sexual relations. While they see themselves as part of the wider society and aspire to the dominant ideology of mainstream society, they also feel excluded by it. The women and children of Baan Nua emphasise a form of chastity by stressing the ideal of the exclusivity of marriage, but at the same time they know this ideal is unattainable for them and that the society they aspire to rejects them because they are prostitutes and, because of this, considered unchaste.

Middle class attitudes towards sexuality and prostitution did start to have an effect during my time in Baan Nua, and the children did begin to feel vulnerable and insecure. They were aware that being a prostitute was considered shameful by wider society and that inappropriate sexual acts, such as prostitution, would be policed and punished. The children became increasingly wary about talking about prostitution towards the end of my time with them. During my final month in Thailand, they stopped talking about it altogether, calling it an ugly (*nakliat*) thing that they did not want to discuss. It was a process that was only just beginning when I left but the children were rapidly becoming aware of the shame that they would suffer if their private lives were exposed publicly. The intention of the state was explicit, it would interfere in the family if the family was failing the state. The fear at the end was palpable. One day I went to the slum with a foreign friend, as I had done on other occasions, and was greeted with Malee asking me, "Have you betrayed us then?" She believed that any strange foreigner would be there to punish them. At this time, fear of exposure was certainly stronger than when I arrived. The fear came less from being prosecuted than from being held up to public censure. Whenever prostitutes are 'rescued' from brothels, pictures of them, usually desperately trying to hide their faces, are on the front pages of all the newspapers. Even within the poorest slums, and maybe especially there, the importance of not losing one's dignity and 'keeping face' was paramount and the thought of public exposure was hard to bear.

Gender, Prostitution and Identity

Too often there is a conflation between child prostitution and girl prostitution, and similarly, there is a tendency to look at gender only in relation to women. There is little information on boy prostitutes in Thailand, except in isolated, anecdotal cases reported in the media: see for example, 'Young Men Following in their Sisters' Footsteps,' (Narvilai 1994), 'Boy Prostitutes on the Rise, says study,' (*Bangkok Post* 1994c) or 'Boy Prostitutes Still Playing the Dangerous Game,' (Bai-ngern 1994). Yet in Baan Nua, boys do work as prostitutes along with their sisters, although their experiences of it and expectations are different from those of the girls. Nevertheless, the particular difficulties that boy prostitutes experienced is a much under-researched area, and it is important to acknowledge the special problems that they face, both within prostitution and within a wider context. The girls work within an ideology of reciprocity and duty which allows them to identify themselves as dutiful daughters, loyal family members and upholders of both their community and their religion. For boys, the construction of their identity is more problematic as different roles are expected of them which are harder to fulfil in the context of Baan Nua.

Within the broader Thai society, the most important social role for a boy is his entry into the monastery. For any Buddhist, the greatest amount of merit comes from nurturing the Buddhist religion; by giving food to the monks, contributing to the temple, or for men, becoming a monk. In Thailand, this need not be a lifetime vocation but can be for a limited period after which the monk leaves the monastery and resumes normal life. Becoming a monk is the most important way to make merit, and becoming a monk imparts merit not only to the novice himself but to his parents and especially to his mother (Tambiah 1970). Women cannot enter the monastery, and therefore this source of merit-making is closed to them, but by giving up their sons to the temple, their role as nurturers of the Buddhist religion is publicly acknowledged and the merit made by her son can accrue to her (Kirsch 1982, Keyes 1984a). Through his ordination, he can repay his mother the debt of gratitude that he owes her for giving him life, while his sister has a lifetime of commitment. Becoming a monk is also the traditional transition into adulthood for boys, before which he is considered 'unripe' (*mai suk*) and not fully adult (Keyes 1986 – see Chapter Two).

In Baan Nua, ordination rarely happened and only one child I knew had entered a monastery, Sompot, who had become a novice for just one week. It was, therefore, much harder for the boys to carve out an identity for themselves and to fulfil adult roles. The most important source of prestige and advancement was closed to them, and there was a much greater confusion about their roles than there was for the girls. In the rural communities of Thailand with which the families of Baan Nua still had links, the most important status marker for girls was motherhood. Motherhood brought prestige and status to a girl, and it also marked her as an adult. In Baan Nua, therefore, early motherhood was not viewed especially negatively. When I asked Saew if she was worried about Lek giving birth so young she said, "No, I married at twelve and gave birth at thirteen. I don't think it is an unusual or difficult thing". Thirteen in Saew's experience was old and mature enough to take on the ultimate trappings of adult-hood – a child of one's own.

Fatherhood does not bring the same status change as mother-hood and men with children are not necessarily considered adults because they have fathered a child. In Baan Nua, there are so few young men who have fathered children and then helped to raise them. Fatherhood seemed to imply fewer of the burdens of reci-procity and filial duty. Children in the slum do feel some sense of duty towards their fathers, but it is never as strong as their feel-ings towards their mothers. Many of the fathers are absent, and this may have affected relationships between fathers and chil-dren, but within Baan Nua, men are usually peripheral. They can-not work within the slum and rarely hold down jobs outside it, and they leave all the important decisions about finance to their female relatives. These men have no role as merit givers (by becoming monks), or as economic providers, and little as fathers. It is extremely difficult for them to be committed to a community which does not need them and, unsurprisingly, many young men drift off to other slums or occasionally to find work in other areas of the country.

The boys who are still needed are those who continue in pros-titution and who therefore continue to play a role in their families through the money they earn. However, there is a significant dif-ference in the expectations placed on child prostitutes according to their gender. Boys, for example, are supposed to be much more independent in finding clients and are given a freedom to solicit that the girls do not have. Finding clients in the town is much more dangerous, and girls are not expected to have to take this risk as often. Boys, however, are expected to be more resourceful and are afforded less protection than their sisters. It was notice-able, for example, that Lek, Kob and Nong, all pimped for other girls only and only Sompot was found clients by his mother.

The expectation of support is also very much less for boys. Boys and girls are seen as having very different relationships to their homes and families, and the self-sacrifice that is expected of girls is not anticipated for boys. Girls are not necessarily more exploited than their brothers, but their duties and rewards are seen differently. A girl cannot bring merit to her parents through entry into a monastery and therefore she is expected to give more practical help. Girls are seen as having much closer ties with their families than boys, who are expected to be independent at a much earlier age. Previously, therefore, the family has always been a Thai woman's power base because of the customs of matrilocal residence and because women tend to inherit from their mothers. In rural Thai society, especially in the North and the Northeast, significant household property is held by women and passed on to daughters. The youngest daughter almost always gets the house when she marries, on the understanding that she will care for her parents there until their deaths.[6] Due to this pattern of inheritance, it is expected that girls will contribute greater time, labour and money to their families while they are growing up (Hanks 1964, Potter 1979) because they have more invested in their families and will eventually inherit from them (Potter 1979, Blanc-Szanton 1985).

The women and girls in Baan Nua have maintained this tradition and have held onto their traditional position at the centre of the family after entering an urbanised environment. The permanence and stability of the women in comparison to the men in Baan Nua is noticeable, and it is the women who dominate the slum. There are limited earning opportunities for men and boys in Baan Nua, and while a few leave and work on construction sites around the country, most have a series of casual relationships with women from surrounding slums, move in with them for a few months and then leave. The women of Baan Nua have the potential to earn money in a way men do not, and because of this men are placed in an ambiguous position. Although younger boys can earn money from Western paedophiles, the gay bars in town tend only to employ young men between seventeen and twenty-one.

Men and boys are placed in a difficult and indeterminate position. None of the boys in Baan Nua identify themselves as gay, but they do perform in gay sex shows and they have gay customers. Many dislike doing this, and the older ones especially express their disgust at these "dirty foreigners". Like their sisters, they make a clear distinction between what they do and who they are. Most have girlfriends, or partners, in Baan Nua or in surrounding slums, and claim that clients are just work. This view is accepted by most people and those young men who do work as prostitutes are treated with some respect because of the money they have. They spend this money very conspicuously, buying stereos or motorbikes. Very rarely do these boys contribute to their families, and if there is any money left over they spend it gambling over cards in the slum at night, or on cock fighting or playing snooker.

---

6. In the 1970s, however, this traditional power base began to be eroded. The government passed a law requiring that all children inherit equally and that any land transfer needed a male signature for it to be legally binding (Blanc-Szanton 1985).

Notions of masculinity and femininity and the proper roles for each gender are clearly evident. Boys are supposed to be independent and self-centred with obvious outward material trappings of masculinity, in the form of consumer goods, while girls are expected to sacrifice for their families and to think of the implications of their behaviour on others. Even eight-year-old Sompot spends some of the money he earns on sweets and junk food for himself, whereas his sister gives all her money straight to her mother. What they do with their bodies and notions of sexuality are much less important in this regard than status, money and outward appearance. Men who do not work are thus further marginalised in the community and are treated with much more unease. Those who live off the earnings of their partners or daughters are said 'to eat a woman's money' (*kin ngun phuu ying*). They are seen as parasites who live off the work of the women and, while no-one ever challenges them directly, they are seen as less worthy than the men who work as prostitutes themselves in order to earn money.

Tam

None of the girls in Baan Nua transgress notions of femininity in the way a few of the men flout rules of masculinity; as a result the girls seemed more integrated and committed to their community than the boys do. Lek's brother, Tam, is one of the few men who seems to have settled permanently in Baan Nua and is viewed with a mixture of contempt and envy by others. He is twenty-one and has a twenty-eight-year-old Belgian girlfriend, called Christine, who works in a casino in Belgium. They met when she bought him out of a gay bar, and she comes back to Thailand for two months in every year. She speaks a little Thai but he speaks no English, so communication is limited. I once asked if he cared about her and he said, "I suppose so. She is very good to me". Like his sister, money buys affection or at least, gratitude, and he never makes pejorative comments about Christine's unmarried status in the way other people do in the slum. She once spent the night in Baan Nua and brought in food and alcohol for everybody as well as giving Tam 30,000 *baht* (about £800). Again, there was a very mixed response to this: on the one hand envy that Tam had found a Western woman who added to his prestige and supported him so well and, on the other, a contempt that he could lower himself to being a kept man in the power of a woman on whom he was dependent. The community was prepared to come to the party and eat and drink with her, but at the same time resentment was felt that she

could afford the things that she had brought. There were whis-
pered comments about her age and why she was not married,
and all sorts of rumours and stories were started and embell-
ished. Tam himself is very confused about it, and consequently
feels obliged to prove that he is not dependent on her by having
sexual relationships with other women when she is away. He
has married another Thai woman who moves into Baan Nua
with him whenever Christine is back in Belgium. He is also
ashamed of the money that Christine gives him, and hands it
over to his mother immediately, which is considered strange and
slightly ridiculous. As an adult man, it is felt that he should keep
his money and not be dependent on his mother. If Tam used the
money to enhance his prestige in the community by building a
big house for his family or buying an expensive television for
himself, or if he used that money to buy favours or services from
others and prove his power in that way, then the source of the
money would not have been referred to. The fact, however, that
he has 'eaten a woman's money' without making proper use of
it makes people look down upon him. By apparently rejecting
the opportunities for power and status that this money could
have brought him, he has earned himself a reputation as "aloof"
and "stupid".

Social Identity

The most common assumption made about child prostitutes is
that their whole identity and being is dependent on their prostitution and that they have no life away from prostitution. The
stereotype of the child caged in a brothel reinforces this; these
children do not have a life outside the brothel in any sense and
prostitution is their sole identifying marker. In stories about these
children, they are typically forced to receive twenty customers a
day, meaning that they have no time for anything else; their isolation in the brothel means that they have no family life and few
friendships; and, by finally contracting AIDS, they have no life
even after they have left prostitution. Status, filial obligations and
personal identity mean nothing in these stories because these
children are interesting only for their prostitution. This was
clearly illustrated in the story of the Phuket fire, one of the most
important events in the history of the campaign against child
prostitution. In 1984 a brothel in Phuket burned down. On entering the building after the blaze, fire-fighters discovered the
charred remains of five young prostitutes who had been unable to

escape the blaze because they had been chained to their beds. It is a gruesome story and one that has been endlessly repeated to show the 'typical' horrors of brothel life. The Foundation for Women even fictionalised the story in their book *Kamla* (1990), which was distributed amongst girls in the North and Northeast to warn of the danger and likely outcome of entering prostitution. This case generated a public outcry, and it was the first time that pimps and procurers had been prosecuted and made to pay compensation to the victims' parents. One mother claimed 90,000 *baht* for her daughter but no-one came forward as the relatives of the other four girls (Rattachumpoth 1994). These were young women without identity, known only as prostitutes. Who they were and why they were in that brothel was irrelevant. They were simply a variation on the perfect image of a child prostitute: unidentified, unclaimed, nameless, faceless and dead.

This particular case was horrible and tragic, and it generated large amounts of public anger. The abuses that went on in this brothel were indefensible, and the ten-year-sentences handed out to the pimps and brothel owners were clearly inadequate. It is equally clear that lessons from it have still not been learned and similar abuses continue throughout the country, although they are less well reported and create much less fury. In 1994 another fire claimed the lives of other young women trapped in a brothel and, again, there was evidence of serious human rights infringements (Sakhon 1994). However, the way in which the deaths of these prostitutes are reported decontextualises prostitution and robs the children and young people involved of any individual identity. Readers are given no information about who these children are, except when fictionalised in books like *Kamla,* and are told nothing of why or how they became prostitutes.

Child prostitution has been marked as the ultimate horror for children; worse than sweatshops, scavenging or begging. It has been set aside as something special and unique, an especially dreadful form of abuse. There is little need to place it in any wider context because it can be viewed as different from anything else, standing above and beyond all other forms of exploitation. This ideology rejects prostitution as a form of labour or as one of several forms of economic exploitation from which the poor suffer and places it instead as a form of slavery which must, inevitably, degrade, corrupt and destroy the humanity of those involved. The idea that factory work, or even domestic service, may do exactly the same is rarely countenanced; anything, in this ideology, is better than prostitution. Wider issues of who individual child prostitutes are, where they come from or why they enter prostitution, do not matter and are subsumed under assumptions that all child prostitution must be involuntary, that all children would rather do anything than enter prostitution, and that all child prostitutes think of themselves as prostitutes and as nothing else.

This view, however, contrasts dramatically with the children of Baan Nua, who did not locate their personal identity in prostitution and who did place their lives and their prostitution in a much wider social context, even though they did not have full knowledge of that context. These were children caught between opposing ideologies, whose lives contained many contradictions: between a rural past and urban present, between their current poverty and their future aspirations, and in the mutual exchange of fantasies between themselves and their clients. To study child prostitution in Baan Nua without looking at these other issues, makes understandings of the lives of these children meaningless. This is not to condone child prostitution but this approach does focus attention on the child as a social actor rather than as a passive prostitute, and it suggests ways of integrating the moral aspects of child prostitution with the social, political and economic. There is no separate world of child prostitutes or a special category of children, cut off from society and living in abused isolation. Child prostitutes are part of their communities, vital members of their families, and are subject to the same economic and social forces as others in society.

The children of Baan Nua are neither rural people nor yet fully urbanised. Despite living in an urban environment they are caught in a similar position to other migrants who find adaptation to city life difficult but who have left behind the security of village life. Many children in Baan Nua know little of village life, having been raised all their lives in slums, but they are inculcated with the values of their rural born parents, who stress reciprocity and help from relatives as the basis of family and community life. Their parents still identify with the rural communities that they refer to as home, while this 'home' is one that the children have rarely seen and never lived in. The values that these parents have taught their children become extremely problematic in a slum like Baan Nua. The social structures that support reciprocity and obligation in rural life, such as an extended family and work on the family farm, are not to be found in the slum, where the children find that they have little external support but many internal obligations. This is not to paint too romantic a picture of village life. There is often assumed to be a direct correlation between migration and prostitution as if the former inevitably leads to the latter (see for example Asia Partnership for Human Development

1992); the implication being that children who stay in their rural communities will be safe from exploitation. However, this safe and happy peasant community is idealised and imagined, and it no longer exists, if indeed, it ever did. Rural people are subject to increased pressure on their land, and families cannot offer to support unproductive relatives. People like Saew in Baan Nua did not have enough land to support her large family, so she migrated to seek better income-generating opportunities. Given the macro-economics of Thailand's development, this choice was entirely understandable. The World Bank reports that non-agricultural, real income is twelve times per capita higher than that in agriculture (Lewis and Kapur 1990: 1373). In the poorest Isan region of Thailand which is dependent on agriculture, Ekachai (1990: 21) estimates that 85% of people earn less than they need to survive and that two million a year migrate seeking work and a better way of life. Nor is migration just a choice between survival and starvation; it is also a choice between the more conservative rural world and the supposed sophistication of the big city where there is a chance to experiment and escape the limits of the village (Ford and Saiprasert 1993: 11). Muecke writes:

> There is strong evidence that non-elite women not only desire the status markers of the elite, but also have strategies for obtaining them. That is, the majority of disadvantaged are making rational choices to achieve status. The choices include the practices of abortion, urban prostitution, and urban migration for employment. (1984: 470).

In Baan Nua, returning to a home village is not an option for many children whose parents no longer have land there to farm or who have lost touch with relatives when they migrated. Even those, like Sompot and Fon, who have returned for short periods of time, find that they no longer fit in there. Village life was boring for them, lacking in the discos and karaoke bars which they enjoyed visiting from Baan Nua. They are not rural children any longer. They have no experience of farming, of raising chickens, of understanding the social hierarchy and expectations of village life. Yet they are not accepted in the urban environment either. They have not been successful, built new houses, moved out of the slum, or obtained prestigious or even socially acceptable jobs. They have few contacts with the state other than though the police. Some children do go to a state-run school, but they depend on welfare to buy uniforms and books and feel themselves pitied and despised. They are neither rural or urban and live instead on the margins of Thai society, overlooked and ignored except when child prostitution is uncovered there. Once again, these children are nothing to anybody, other than when working as prostitutes.

In a similar way, they are caught between the contradictions of being Thai but dealing exclusively with Western clients. They belong to neither world. They community sees itself as very Thai; all the houses in Baan Nua are decorated with pictures of the King and Queen, as almost all Thai homes are, and most people see themselves as being very much connected with the traditions and culture of the Thai countryside. Yet they are rejected by wider Thai society, dismissed as degenerates who sell sex and whose parents will be severely punished if they fail to prevent prostitution happening. They are given no help from their own society; there are few ways for them to earn their living, and there is no safety net provided for them by the state. In the absence of any state help, it is their Western clients who enable their families and community to function. Despite the children's claims that these men were friends who will help them in the long term, their clients, most probably, would not help them once they had ceased to find them useful, as the case of Paul showed. All they can do is strive for the trappings of Western consumerism but this world is not one they can ever fully enter. They can aspire to a Westernised lifestyle but in the long term, they do not have the money to support such an ambition. They can buy the trimmings, in the form of motorbikes, televisions and stereos, but on a daily basis, they will never be able to shop where they want and buy what they like. It is a contradiction of which they are very aware, but which they rationalise by claiming that one day, their clients will marry them and take them away to a better life or, that in their next incarnation, life will be materially much more comfortable. They may be deluding themselves but their aspirations remain high, despite their current circumstances.

CHAPTER 6

PROTECTING INNOCENCE

Innocence and Freedom

Child prostitutes are problematic because they challenge many notions about childhood itself, especially what is considered to be appropriate behaviour for children. They are children who are out of place, both physically, because they work when they should be in school and conceptually, in that while they are emotionally and physically children, they have the responsibilities of adults. The contradictions that the children of Baan Nua struggle with as they try to form an identity and self-image are mirrored on a wider conceptual level regarding the very nature of childhood. Child prostitutes who are tricked into brothels and helplessly await their fate are tragic because they are still recognisably children. They are innocent, passive victims controlled by adults, their innocence shattered and their lives coming to a premature end. The children in Baan Nua have no such tragedy about them because, in surviving, they have given up their claims to being children. They have none of the attributes and hence appeal of victims. They are placed in an ambiguous position; they are children who know what it is to act like adults, despite their age, but, in doing this, they have sacrificed the sympathy that childhood otherwise confers on them.

The children of Baan Nua, like child prostitutes or homeless youths in the West (Hall 1998), are anomalies in the discourses about children and childhood. They exist in an ambiguous category which challenges notions of childhood and which threatens Western constructions of children. They have none of the attributes that are expected of children and, as a consequence, they are

threatening and disturbing. These are children who blur the categories of adult and child, knowledge and innocence, force and
choice (Hall and Montgomery 2000). In some senses, they are not
still children, but neither are they yet adults. There is no external
stereotype into which these children fit, and their own sense of
identity is confused and contradictory. An analysis of their lives
demands a fundamental examination of the nature of childhood,
questioning its constructions and stereotypes and thereby com-
plicating a supposedly straightforward moral issue. A simplistic
emotional appeal against kidnapped children raped in brothels is
much less problematic than a systematic scrutiny of the expectations and projections that adults place on children.

Innocence, like dignity, is a phrase much used in discussions of
childhood, yet it is rarely defined or discussed (Ennew et al.
1996). It is seen as the pre-eminent quality of childhood, closely
linked to notions of purity, artlessness or ingenuousness. Children are separated from adults, not just because of their age or
size, but also by these less tangible qualities. Childhood should be
a time of happiness, of freedom from responsibility, of a lack of
knowledge of the adult world. Children are supposed to live in a
carefree world, sheltered from the harsh realities of labour, and,
ideally from abuse and exploitation. Children whose lives follow
different patterns are said to be 'robbed of their childhood',
'deprived of their right to be a child' or 'raped of their innocence'.
The children who live in 'especially difficult circumstances' such
as street children, child prostitutes or refugee children, are cast as
pitiable victims whose tragedy is their early entry into the adult
world. These are children who have been forced to face responsibility early; their innocence has been substituted for experience
and knowledge. When this occurs, they lose not only their innocence but also their childhood, and with it the sympathy of the
adult world. Unless they remain victimised and pitiful, they are
ignored. If they survive and lose the helplessness expected of children, then they are once more cast into an ambiguous and disturbing category. As Holland writes of abused children:

> The image [of the distressed child] operated in a dangerous area
> between sympathy, guilt and disgust. In abandoning the attrac-
> tiveness of childhood, these pictured children may well have sacri-
> ficed the indulgence childhood commands. (Holland 1992: 154).

When childhood is seen as a time of innocent freedom and a
release from the pressures of the adult world, issues of child
labour and child sex cause a great deal of anxiety. In the ideal

construction, both are seen as concerns which belong exclusively to the adult world and must be forbidden to children; but in many instances this is not possible. The twenty-first-century Western conceptualisation of the child is as a non-worker, yet for many children, work is not a choice but an economic and social necessity. This ideology assumes a separation between parents and children into dichotomous spheres of work and play and its implications, especially for children in developing countries, where such a division is not always possible in reality, are immense. The image of an innocent child, free from the responsibilities of labour, has little resonance in communities such as Baan Nua, where children cannot afford to stay in school and have to work to support their families.

As argued previously, childhood as a concept must be understood in terms of its cultural and historical specificity. There is no universal 'childhood' and no one way that children mature. Even within the same country, there are marked differences between the childhoods that children actually experience, depending on their class, gender and ethnicity. In Thailand, there is a great divergence of views on what is a child's proper role. The urban middle classes have very different concepts of children from those of the rural peasantry, or urbanised former peasants, such as the people in Baan Nua. Within cities, the middle class have accepted many Western notions of childhood and the correct role for children. Middle class children are sheltered; they attend school and go on to university. They rarely work, and if they do, it is not to ensure the survival of their families. They do not have to confront the dreadful choices that daily face the children in Baan Nua.

In Thailand, children are expected to complete at least six years of schooling. However not all children can afford even this primary education, and many start work much younger (UNICEF 1989). Economic necessity and cultural norms sanction this early entry into the work place, and work during childhood is a reality for the majority of children (cf. Elson 1982, Lai 1982, Ennew and Milne 1989, Fyfe 1989). Some work on family farms, where it is assumed, but never proved, that they are not exploited, while others go into more dangerous forms of work, such as factory work, scavenging on constructions sites, or prostitution (Banpasirichote and Pongsapich 1992). In all these jobs, children can only be employed illegally and therefore there is no regulation of their work. They cannot join trade unions, complain to the government inspectorate, or take measures to protect themselves, and it is very likely that they will be exploited. The World Health Organisation has emphasised that child workers do have different health risks from adults, even when they are doing the same work (1987). Child workers are very vulnerable, and there is a high risk that work involving children can lead to them being exploited. They often work for very low wages, have poor working conditions, and lack control over their conditions of labour.

There is a crucial difference between child labour and child exploitation, although it is obvious that the former may turn into the latter without regulation. It is equally clear, however, that whatever the ideal, work is a part of many children's lives in Thailand, and that forbidding children to work under the age of fourteen does not safeguard them from exploitation. Rather, it is likely to push them into the illegal workforce where they have less protection and are more likely to be exploited. Children's innocence is no barrier to their exploitation, and may indeed be a contributing factor to their abuse. Working children, whether they work in factories or on the streets, do not need innocence. They need knowledge of their rights, appreciation of all their options and ways of protecting themselves. UNICEF estimated that 95% of children who work do so because of family poverty, and of those children 93% claim to work willingly (UNICEF 1989). Child labour is a difficult issue because it involves conceptualising the child as an active social agent who can make choices and decisions and who needs to be empowered rather than protected. As long as the notion of 'the child' involves notions of weakness, dependency on adults, helplessness and innocence of the adult world, then child labour remains a problematic contradiction.

There are similar difficulties when looking at the connections between child sex and child prostitution. There is clearly a difference between them, yet there are also links and ways in which conceptualisations of child sex inform the debate about child prostitution. Sex, like work, is increasingly seen in middle class Thailand as something that should have no place in the world of children. Such reasoning however, assumes a level of affluence to protect children and a certain lifestyle which is alien to many children. The children in Baan Nua, for example, were introduced to both sex and work at an early age. They had to work when they were very young, selling in the streets or scavenging, and sex also formed an early part of their lives. In the one or two rooms of the houses in which they live, they saw their siblings and mothers having sex, and they heard older children discuss it. The mechanics of sex were no great mystery to them; they were certainly not innocent of knowledge about sex.

Many studies carried out throughout Thailand have shown that children are having sex more regularly and at younger ages than before (Chompootaweep et al. 1988, Havanon et al. 1992, Ford and Saiprasert 1993). The construction of childhood as a time of no knowledge of sex, and no participation in sexual activities, is under threat. However, recognition of this has been slow. Instead, new terminology has sprung up to explain the phenomenon of 'promiscuous' teenagers or children who have sex early. Phrases such as *dek jai taek* – a child with a shattered or broken heart – have come into common use as a way of explaining this aberrant behaviour. Rarely is it acknowledged that this behaviour is not aberrant, and that a child who is knowledgeable about sex is now commonplace. Similarly, the double standard is not noted so that this phrase, despite its neutrality ('dek' simply means child), is used exclusively to refer to girls. The phrase is used by adults in the media and in the NGO movement about a child who has lost her virginity. So much has been invested in this, that when a girl loses her virginity people may suggest that the child can *bloi tua*, literally free her body and do anything, no matter how inappropriate or shocking. Her heart is shattered and her behaviour symbolises this. Unlike Western concepts such as 'broken-hearted', the Thai phrase has more serious connotations. It suggests someone whose whole personality has been shattered and who cannot be put back together. It is a dangerous state to be in because the person may not be aware of the full implications (Fordham 1995: personal communication). A child can be called a *dek jai taek* by others even if they are in a happy and loving relationship. It is the fact that virginity has been lost that condemns the child in the eyes of the observer. It is assumed that a *dek jai taek* is out of control. Having lost her all-important virginity, she might become promiscuous and act in ways that are considered unacceptable in middle class society. By experiencing sexual activity, this new terminology implies that the child becomes a *dek jai taek*. Through sex, her heart is shattered, and thus promiscuity and prostitution become easy options. For the onlookers, it can explain away unacceptable behaviour as an aberration, while leaving the ideology of an asexual childhood intact. Sex is not something that can be entrusted to children as, like work, it is inherently corrupting to a child and so must be avoided. Experimentation and sexual experience can only lead to harm, to a girl becoming a *dek jai taek*, and so, like work, it is forbidden to the child, for her own good.

The distinction between labour, sex and exploitation becomes blurred by such reasoning. If all sex and all work are exploitative, then intervention in both is a necessity and a moral imperative. In fighting all child labour, the middle classes are fighting the traditional independence and autonomy of the working or peasant classes. In tackling the problem of child prostitution, they are also tackling the problem, as they see it, of promiscuous, lower class youth. Brody goes as far as to claim that the middle classes 'define prostitution into existence as a class problem. It is working class men who lack bodily control and are compelled to relieve their urges.' (1995: 3). Similarly, it is peasant and working class children who work as prostitutes, leaving the middle class as the guardians of morality. It is instructive to note that they do so using very Westernised terminology while claiming a purely Thai perspective. 'Amazing also is the growth of a middle class morality which develops in an osmotic relationship with selective adaptations from Western middle class patterns' (ten Brummelhuis 1993: 15).

Such attitudes to prostitution have little relevance to lower class and rural Thais for whom a visit to a brothel is an accepted part of life (Fox 1960, Havanon et al. 1992, Limanonda 1993, Podhisita et al. 1993, Boonchalaksi and Guest 1994, Fordham 1993, 1995). Attitudes towards child prostitution are very different for those who work as prostitutes, and those who attempt to stop them doing so. Again, there is a sense of the middle and working classes talking at cross purposes. There seems to be a willing blindness to the sexual experience of the children and youth of the elite classes, although, from time to time, I was told of rumours of young women from private schools working as prostitutes in order to get money for designer clothes and jewellery. I never came across these girls and I suspect that these rumours had more to do with another concern of the middle classes, fear of consumerism and Westernisation, than any observed reality.

There is obviously a clear distinction to be made between the sexual experimentation between peers, however young, and child prostitution, but to many observers it is the sexual act itself which is viewed as inherently corrupting. The loss of virginity, in whatever circumstances, is viewed as crucial to the child's life and, therefore, prostitution is only an extreme form of the deviant behaviour that takes place after virginity has been lost. It is the innocence of the child that is important, and once that has been lost, through sexual experience, then that child is innocent and childlike no more. Some NGOs have claimed a direct connection between loss of virginity and prostitution. One has suggested that if a girl has caused shame, prostitution may be seen by her parents as a way of getting rid of their socially undesirable daughter (DEP n.d). Others have made similar implications in case studies of young prostitutes. Sereewat gives the case of 'Suwana' who became a prostitute by choice at fourteen, because 'While going astray, at thirteen, she lost her virginity to a man she did not know before' (1993). The avoidance of young sex and indeed labour is a peculiarly middle class attitude, based on wealth and the possession of resources which shield children from such things (Brody 1995). Middle class children can be kept at home until they are adults, they live in a large enough house so that their parents' sexual activity goes unnoticed, and the family income is high enough to ensure that they do not need to work.

Buying Innocence

The ambiguities inherent in child prostitution and in the construction of childhood are further apparent in any discussion of the clientele of child prostitutes. Again, despite the repetition of certain stereotypes, there is next to no information on who buys sex with children and why. Childhood has been constructed as an asexual state where children have neither knowledge or experience of sex, and therefore child prostitution is a deviation that can only occur under force. In this scenario, children must be innocent of sex and their clients must be deviant abusers. Yet the boundary between childhood and adulthood, and between sexual innocence and sexual desirability, is not fixed, and in the West, as much as in Thailand, it causes difficulties.

> [As] a child, sexuality is forbidden to her, and it is that very ignorance that makes her the most perfect object of male desire, the inexperienced woman. Thus the fascinating exchange between knowledge and ignorance reaches beyond the boundary between girl and woman and towards the forbidden attraction of innocence itself. (Holland 1992: 127).

Innocence itself is therefore seen as sexually desirable. Children are not precluded from adult desire because they are children; instead, the very quality of innocence that is projected on to them can be both fetishised and normalised. As Wilson and Cox write, 'A certain degree of attraction to well developed thirteen and fourteen-year-old girls is very common, if not endemic, in the male population.' (1986: 18). However, children have no say in these images of themselves; both innocence and adult desire are forced upon them, leaving them with no protection against adults who wish to abuse their vulnerability.

The majority of adults do not abuse this power sexually, but it is interesting to examine what qualities in children are found sex-

ually attractive and how they relate to child prostitutes, especially
those in Baan Nua. Some commentators have suggested that
there are two main types of offenders against children: preferential and situational (Finkelhor and Araji 1986, Wilson and Cox
1986, Ennew 1986, Ireland 1993). Preferential abusers are men
who actively seek out sex with children of a particular age (also
known as paedophiles) while situational abusers may have sex
with a child if offered, but such intercourse would not be their
sexual preference. This distinction is an important one when discussing child prostitutes, and it once again raises the issue of the
unstable boundary between adults and children and the importance of innocence in the construction of childhood.

The clients who come to Thailand are as concerned with innocence and childishness as the campaigners against child prostitution.
The notion of innocence, with its connotations of artlessness and
trust, is deliberately played upon by the tourist industry and is
encouraged by Thai patterns of prostitution where prices are rarely
stated and time limits rarely imposed (Cohen 1982). Prostitution in
Thailand has none of the negative connotations that it has in the
tourists' home countries. It is common for women to stay with
clients for a week or two, refer to them as boyfriends, and, like the
children of Baan Nua, claim that their payment is not income, but a
gift. In the Thai sex industry, especially that catering for foreigners,
the line between romance and paid sex is thin and flexible: it is a situation fraught with tension and the possibility of misunderstanding
(Cohen 1982). Yet the tourist resorts of Thailand sell an image of
beautiful young women who are submissive and uncomplaining.
The distinction between child and woman is often deliberately
blurred in prostitution, but then it is a profession which places a premium on youth and where desirability and youth are closely linked.
A study among Thai men claimed that 'Many males felt that child
prostitutes between 15 and eighteen were more desirable than
adults, but that it was wrong to sleep with younger ones' (under
14). (Sittitrai and Brown 1994: 4). For foreigners, bars refer to their
dancers as girls, and they emphasise that they are 'very young' or
fresh. Some bars advertise that they have virgins for sale; one
researcher noted that a bar in Bangkok had a sign outside reading,
'5 fresh virgins, 4 down one to go.' (Gilkes 1993: 30). Whether or
not this is true is impossible to verify: there is always an element of
macho bravado and a desire to shock at such bars. What is clear,
however, is that both campaigners against child prostitution, and
bar owners and clients, are using the same doctrines which associate youth, virginity and innocence as something unique in children,
and whose destruction is therefore the ultimate taboo.

For the men who desire child-like prostitutes, Thailand is a place where they can fulfil these fantasies. That these women are prepared to act out the role of submissive and pliable girls, for such a small price, increases their desirability. In many of the interviews that I and other researchers conducted among sex tourists in Thailand, the men mentioned many similarities in the qualities that they are looking for in Thai women. 'Childish', 'powerless' and 'without body hair' appear over and over again in descriptions of what Western men find attractive in Thai women; qualities which are usually associated with children. Wilson and Cox's study (1986) of seventy-seven paedophiles found that the physical traits that were listed as attractive included good looks, smooth skin (hairlessness), and smallness, while the personality traits included innocence, openness and curiosity (1986: 19). The similarities between them and the clients of Thai prostitutes are noticeable:

> Dealing with Thai women is like dealing with thirteen-year-old school kids. You treat them just the same and they are quite happy. The mentality is just the same. Still, they're better than Australian women, who go on about being liberated the whole time and then just walk round the house in a track suit getting fat. I mean, who wants one of them? (Fifty-year-old Australian, interviewed by the author, November 1993)

> Tom [a bar owner] criticised *farang* [Western] women as snotty They wanted to attract you and then cut you down when they did. Tom sexually preferred Thai women because they didn't have body hair. (Odzer 1990: 180).

> Since I got back to New Zealand I have gone out with several English, German and local women but find they're extremely finance oriented, selfish, untrustworthy and basically not what I've been looking for. I was in Thailand with the army until recently and found the women most appealing, beautiful and faithful, just what I'm looking for. (Walker and Ehrlich 1994: 51).

Here are unthreatening and childish women with whom to have sexual relationships without the difficulty of relating to an adult woman. Many of these men are very hostile to men who do use young children, especially young boys (O'Connell Davidson 1994), but, nevertheless, their own interest in women seems to focus on their non-adult qualities. Another client of adult prostitutes once told me:

> All this child prostitution stuff is the invention of the media. They come here not knowing anything about Thai culture. They look at

the women and think that they are very young, whereas they are twenty or so. Take my mate, Jim. He owns a bar and has a Thai wife. The first time I met her, I said to myself, what's that ten-year-old school girl doing here? Only when I was introduced to her as Jim's wife, did I realise that she's had many birthdays since her tenth. But you really can't tell with these girls, you know. That's where the media makes its mistakes.'

There is a sense in which Thailand, in the Western mind, has long been associated with infantile simplicity. Since the seventeenth century, it has been portrayed as an infantile place inhabited by child-like people (Raynal 1776). Such portrayals find direct parallels in modern imaginings, where tourists claim that all Thai people are like children and therefore child prostitution is 'an invention of the media'. There is an obvious and crucial difference between men who actively seek out sex with children and those who might have sex with a young child if it is offered, but in the bars of Thailand's red-light districts this latter category is deliberately obscured. The very qualities that are so appealing about children, their dependency, powerlessness and their loyalty, are all to be found among Thai prostitutes, both adults and children. What is prized is their 'littleness'; they are often much younger than their clients, and they are inevitably much smaller. Women who look like pubescent girls are admired and paid for, so that even men who claim to despise the clients of child prostitutes buy women with the bodies of girls. If a woman appears so young, then it is an easy step to have sex with a girl who really *is* that young, either by pretending that she is older or by seeing no difference between a twenty-year-old and a twelve-year-old.

Such a deliberate obscuring of the boundaries between women and children causes a situation where men are willing to have sex with a child in a foreign context. Indeed, the clients themselves deny and obscure these boundaries. Men such as the Australian quoted previously, deny the child status to all children because they convince themselves that all Thais are older than they look. With this reasoning, it is not surprising that there is some evidence that men abroad give in to impulses that they would not act on at home. Ennew (1986) quotes two studies which suggest that, away from home, men are more likely to have sex with children because the boundaries are blurred. Ireland (1993) concurs with this, stating that:

… the dynamics of international tourism itself, particularly that to countries of another race, with significantly different cultures, pro-

duces conditions in which the sexual exploitation [of children] can
more easily occur.' (1993: 18).

As many Thais, both women and men, seem so small to foreigners, issues of racial difference become extremely important.
Men who have been charged with paedophile crimes, especially
those against boys, have tended to claim that they thought the boys
were over fifteen, the legal age of consent.[1] Youthful sexuality
commands a price in which age, except to a small group of preferential abusers, is not the main issue. Women who appear young
may well be as sought after as those who really are young, but to a
foreigner who is unable, or does not want, to guess ages, it is the
youthful, child-like qualities that appeal, not the actual age.

The paradox is that this innocence is very false, and it is a commodity for sale, much like any other. The vast majority of women
working in the red-light districts are over eighteen and many have
had a child already. The crackdown on underage sex in Thailand
during the last eight years has targeted these bars, and it is rare now
that any bar owner will take a risk in having underage girls on the
premises. However, the illusion of innocence and inexperience is
still desired. Many bar girls, when telling their stories, emphasise
that they are new recruits, forced into the professions by poverty
(see, for example, the stories in Walker and Ehrlich 1994) and not
'really' prostitutes. The Trink column, in the *Bangkok Post*, regularly
exposes the scams of bar girls along with a weary misogyny and a
disbelief in family hard luck stories. Trink may be right, to a limited
extent, but to put it less cynically, most women who work in the
bars are aware of what is expected of them and play up to this
image, partly because they are indeed supporting their families,
and partly also because they know that their customers wish to
believe that paying for sex in Thailand is not 'really' prostitution.

Innocence is the key to this mutual exchange of fantasies. Paul,
the client of both Nuk and Lek in Baan Nua, showed how crucial
the appearance of innocence is to some clients. While he was prepared to pay for sex with the two girls and then also with Tik, he
pulled out of the deal when he found out that Tik was twenty and
already had a child. She appeared so much younger that as long
as he could believe that her youth and inexperience were gen-
uine, he was willing to pay. When he found out how old she was
and he could not sustain his illusions, he refused to have sex with

1. The case of a Swede, Beng Bolin, was an example of this. Caught with a naked
boy in his bed, he claimed that he had been led to believe that the boy was over
fifteen and therefore of legal age. However the Swedish court did not accept
this defence, and on June 22 1995, he was sentenced to three months in jail.

her. Not only was she older than he thought, but the artlessness and innocence he expected from a child were not there. Tik's sexual appeal to Paul was based not on her appearance, which was that of a child, but on the qualities of childhood which he expected from her, especially her inexperience. Like the women in the bars, she was expected to play a role, and when that could not be sustained, she lost her client.

The line between innocence and experience is illusory and men who wish to buy sex in Thailand are given every opportunity for desiring women who look very young, and who have bodies, which in the West, are associated with children. Illusions that these are not child prostitutes, or even prostitutes, are easy to sustain. These illusions become much harder to uphold when discussing the children of Baan Nua, especially the very young ones. They are not glamorous, untouched or virginal in the way that child prostitutes are imagined to be. Rather they are dirty, ridden with lice and often have ugly, open sores on their arms and legs caused by their bad diet and the bad sanitation of their slum. It is hard to know what their attraction is except for their smallness and their pliability. Some of them are undoubtedly beautiful, but there are many other beautiful and young looking women and men who are not underage, or as desperate or physically damaged. For some men who want sex with a very young child this does not matter. These are men who do have boundaries: once a child is beyond a certain age, these paedophiles are no longer sexually interested. When children are the 'right' age, however, these men are prepared to have sex with children, whatever the physical state of that child, and whatever the consequences might be. The men who want a genuinely young girl or boy not only have to be prepared to pay a high price for it, but they must also be prepared to acknowledge the terrible difficulties and dilemmas that these children face. The child prostitutes of Baan Nua make no pretence at innocence, and their clients cannot help but to be aware of their desperation and poverty. They do not project an air of virginal innocence or even of adolescent sexuality; those too are artificial qualities that have to be purchased. It is not surprising that the children of Baan Nua are so difficult to help, or even to categorise. They have the bodies of children but not their expected qualities.

Maintaining Innocence

Innocence is a quality projected onto, and expected of, children by adults; it fulfils adults' needs much more successfully than children's. It is the quality which is expected of all children and whose existence ensures children are given sympathy and help, while its lack causes them to be overlooked and ignored. Children who are not perceived as innocent, such as children in Baan Nua, homeless youths in the West, and child prostitutes on the streets of London, become 'problem' children who threaten and disgust. Innocence and passive victimisation are demanded of children, and lives presented in this way do not threaten or problematise constructions of childhood. Child prostitution is presented as a problem so urgent and so serious that action must be taken immediately. It is so evidently an abuse of power and so dreadful a threat to so many children that the assumptions behind the campaign need not be made explicit. They are so widely shared and so obvious, that they do not need to be mentioned, and certainly not examined critically. Yet embedded in the discourses around prostitution are many suppositions about children, about families, and about the state which must be deconstructed and questioned in view of the data on the children of Baan Nua. As Ennew has written of stereotypes of child prostitutes:

> [They] assume the image of chattel slavery, in which a traffic in children steals them away from parents and keeps them in chains to cater for uncontrolled adult sexuality ... [It uses] powerful opposing images of family and strangers to reinforce not only the idea that the family is the correct locus for sexual activity, but also the need to strengthen the institution of the family as the basic unit of society. (1986: 66).

The children of Baan Nua, and their prostitution, dramatically threaten this discourse and these assumptions. These are children whose sexuality is controlled by their parents, but in a way of which the state disapproves. There is no simple dichotomy in Baan Nua between good parents and bad strangers; both parents and clients can inflict terrible damage on their children. It is possible to view these parents as an aberration and to target and punish them, but this brings no help to the children. If individual children are to be given access to help, then the debate about prostitution must move away from abstractions and symbols and into the tangible realities of child prostitution in communities such as Baan Nua. The clients can continue to be targeted also, but the long term help that these children need must not be denied to them because their stories complicate adult discourses.

One reason why child prostitution has aroused so much feeling is that representations of it rely on images of innocence betrayed. The depth of tragedy is great because the loss that these children suffer is so great. They have lost everything; their innocence, and with it their childhood and their lives. These children are nothing because they have lost the core of their being: their childhood innocence. The only end that will heighten their tragedy is death, and despite the outrage and sorrow expressed in so many stories about child prostitutes, this is usually undercut by a mawkish sentimentality. These stories are tragic but inevitable: the children are pitied but no help is offered to them. Their tragedy is inevitable from the moment they enter the brothel; anything that breaks this pattern, such as a child leaving to marry or to go home, lessens the impact of the story because it destroys the expectations of a pitiful and unhappy ending, complete with opportunities for sentimental moralising. The children in Baan Nua do not fit this image, and they exist in a complicated and ambiguous position because they have clearly lost their childhood innocence, yet they have refused to reclaim it by presenting a picture of passive victimisation. They both are, and are not, children, and this blurred distinction is disquieting to be confronted with. Adults, and especially adults who claim to speak for children, have a set of criteria which must be met before a child is given help. A child must be innocent or tragic; there is no room for a child who is neither. The children of Baan Nua were abused and exploited, but they refused to be pitied and it is therefore hard to know how to deal with them.

Children who have been tricked or forced into brothels present no problems in discussing rehabilitation. If they contract AIDS, they will die anyway, so issues of long term help and the long term effects of sexual abuse do not need to be raised. If, as campaigners claim, they cannot be rehabilitated after so much abuse, then there is no point in trying. Again, the children of Baan Nua contradict both these assumptions. They do need help, in both the short and the long term. Some of them will not conveniently die of AIDS; some will leave prostitution, and many will go on to have children of their own. It is vital that the cycle of abuse is stopped in communities like Baan Nua, but this involves complex long term intervention which punishes neither child nor parent, which accepts the children's justifications of their lives as valid and which does not rely on limiting stereotypes of what a child prostitute should be. This is an expensive process, and it will take many years to see the effects. It will involve understanding and questioning the assumptions that adults take for granted in their dealings with children. Given that, it is hardly surprising that the media and NGOs prefer neat stories in which there are no loose ends, or prefer campaigns which lock away abusers and leave the children to die off stage. Child prostitution is not simply an issue of good and evil, of wicked abusers versus wronged innocents. While it is presented as a moral issue, unrelated to other concerns, it is, in fact, based on unspoken and unquestioned assumptions and particular ideologies. When these are deconstructed, it is clear that campaigns against child prostitution are linked to certain views of children and families and to wider discourses about Thai society and the nature of that society as it has come into contact with the West and with globalisation. This is intended as no criticism of these campaigns. Their morality is widely shared, and few would condone the sexual abuse of children under any circumstances.

One of the most obvious symbolic uses of child prostitution is as a metaphor for social confusion and the fear of foreign influence. In 1994, a letter appeared in an English language newspaper, the *Bangkok Post,* which, for me, encapsulated many of the ideas about cultural crisis which I see as the key to an understanding of the campaign against child prostitution. The letter appeared in May 1994, half way through Thai Cultural Promotion Year. It read:

> 'Sir: What's Wrong with Thailand? Once Thailand was known as the 'Land of Smiles'. People were broad-minded, selfless and so lovely, smiling at one another everywhere.
>
> I wonder what is happening to Thai people today. What on earth is affecting the roots of Thai culture? Our way of life, behaviour, values, ethics, language, etc; all are changing.
>
> The more our technology improves, the more Thai culture is affected ... Thai kids start to imitate the lifestyles of kids in foreign countries ...
>
> Nowadays, I hardly see Thai people with beautiful smiles, acting selflessly and being broad-minded like before. What is going on? Thai culture is so charming: Why don't we Thais try to strengthen it to preserve our delightful culture?.' (Suwannachairop 1994).

The sense of loss and confusion felt by many Thais appears to have been growing greatly in previous years, and it was debated most vigorously in this government-sponsored year when Thai culture was to be definitively defined. In 1993 alone, there were a series of articles in the English language Thai newspapers, the *Nation* and the *Bangkok Post*, with titles like 'Culture in Crisis' (Cheang 1994), 'Observations on Thailand's Cultural Dilemma' (Asavaroengchai 1993), 'Lost in the Urban Jungle' (Ekachai 1994) and Northern Villagers put their Heritage up for Sale,' (*Bangkok Sunday Post* 1993b) all expressing the same fears that Thailand was losing its identity and becoming 'Westernised'. Likewise, when I asked middle class Thais what was wrong with Thailand, they would say 'it is becoming too materialistic', 'people aren't concerned about their culture anymore', or 'young people want TV sets and don't respect their elders any more'. The cause of this distortion was always the same: Western influence through the media and through consumer goods. As a friend once put it 'Thailand was always Thai until 7–11s[2] arrived'.

The pressure to be Thai does not manifest itself in the same way for the middle classes, who see themselves as the guardians of Thai culture, who must educate the poor and the marginalised and encourage them to accept their versions of culture (Nartsupha 1991). Again, the newspapers are full of alarmist quotes claiming that there is an 'inevitable lack of self confidence and pride among Thais of the younger generation' (*Bangkok Sunday Post* 1993b: 20). One University professor wrote:

> People of the former generation knew who they are and what they wanted. The younger generation don't know themselves. So they lose confidence and import foreign culture and adopt it as their own. (Asavaroengchai 1993: 24).

In a similar way, the peasants are urged to keep their traditional culture and are criticised for not doing so, even when they cannot or do not want to do so. In a newspaper article entitled 'Northern Villagers put up their Heritage for Sale,' a teacher in Chiang Rai in the North bemoans the fact that 'students and their parents never pay any attention to art, culture and tradition. They do not want to waste time studying art and culture but would rather concentrate on such things as computers' (*Bangkok Sunday Post* 1993b: 20). What it is to be Thai, or what it means to be a child, are questions which have become increasingly politicised. Thai culture, and therefore Thailand itself, is under threat, and this allows 'experts' to step in and define Thai identity definitively. Those who are not Thai, such as the hill tribes, or those who do not follow the prescribed patterns, become easier to identify and stigmatise.

The fundamental philosophy behind what it means to be Thai is never questioned or explicitly defined, however, and those who promote a national Thai identity usually do so with a political agenda. However, there is a fundamental contradiction in this promotion of what it is to be Thai. While the peasants are romanticised as the quintessential Thais (Hirsch 1993), Thai culture is

---

2. Twenty-four-hour convenience stores, imported from America.

defined as the traditional pursuits of the upper classes. In 1994, the Thai Cultural Promotion Year, the events that were staged and encouraged were all fine arts, such as displays of Thai dancing, historical plays, and events focusing on the historical Thai centres such as Ayudhaya and Sukothai.[3] The peasant populace had rarely taken part in traditional Thai dancing which was nurtured in the Royal Palace, yet the idea of Thai culture is still promoted as if the peasant were the cultural centre of Thailand: the definitions of what it means to be Thai come from the village and not the city.

However, activities such as dancing or handicrafts are recognisable and concrete activities which can be adhered to. It is these aspects of culture that can be saved from the creeping cultural imperialism of the West as something to protect which is recognisably Thai. Yet even this aspect of culture is threatened, and along with it, the integrity of Thai society. The threat, as ever, comes from outside and not from the peasants, who are too uneducated to see what they are doing: 'some traders have persuaded abbots to exchange ancient objects in their temples for televisions. Some monks aren't aware of the real value of the antiques and agree to the exchange' (*Bangkok Sunday Post* 1993b: 20); nor from the youth who 'lack confidence'. It is the West, either through tourism or economics, that is to blame for the decline. A professor of archaeology complained in the press that he is:

> ... deeply hurt when the younger generation feels indifferent whenever there is an insult to past sacred rituals, which have been circumvented into commercialised tools to attract tourists. (*Bangkok Sunday Post* 1993b: 20).

Another article in the same newspaper argued that:

> Art, tradition and culture are the root of society. Once the root is severed, people lose their knowledge of their own roots and rapidly accept a new culture, usually from the West, aggravating social problems such as prostitution. (*Bangkok Sunday Post* 1993b: 20).

There is an understandable fear of globalisation in Thailand, proved justified by the recent collapse of the Thai economy. As the country opens itself up to Western influence and Western investment, ways of life inevitably change. Bangkok is now a

---

3. Former Thai capitals and important historical centres: Sukothai was Thailand's first capital (between 1238 and 1378), Ayudhaya was the royal capital of Thailand between 1350 and 1767.

modern, industrialised city, filled with Western-style boutiques and shopping centres, yet this has brought huge social problems with it. There are large slum communities surrounding the city where levels of poverty are high, and there are huge problems with traffic congestion and pollution. It is not surprising that some Thais blame Western involvement for these social problems and are fearful of globalisation as a form of neo-colonialism or cultural imperialism. One of Thailand's most respected social critics, Sulak Sivaraksa, wrote:

> Although more and more Westerners come to Siam; and our economy benefits in the short run, the long range effect is undesirable. Economic advantages go to the few, while the many are faced with rising prices. Tourists may convert their travellers cheques – but their ready cash induces further erosion of our traditions. (1980: 201).

While he is correct in one sense – Thailand has become more Westernised and this has brought a huge social cost with it – there is little acknowledgement that the effects of defining and reinforcing this supposedly 'pure' version of culture do nothing to challenge the entrenched status quo. It is easy to look back to an idealised and static past where the peasant lived happily in his or her community, did not aspire to own consumer goods, and did not migrate to cities looking for work. This world, however, is largely imaginary. Peasants have always migrated and aspired to better ways of living, although their options were always limited. Social mobility has always been a dream, if not a possibility, for many people, and while industrialisation and Westernisation have brought many social problems, they have also increased the options available to peasants. Indeed, these are the very conditions which have also produced a new and wealthy middle class, some of whom are now exhorting the peasantry not to aspire to similar lifestyles. The view of culture and tradition which is now being presented is limited and reactionary, and in promoting such an ideal any form of social change is ruled out. For example, rural children can be discouraged from learning new technologies because they are untraditional and 'un-Thai', and therefore these children will not try to compete in the job market with the urban educated Thais who are trying to claim their sole right to use new technologies. The peasants will be kept in their place and consigned to a life of producing 'traditional culture', even if it is economically impractical and unrewarding.

The arguments about Thai identity are presented as a battle for 'the marginals' – the young, the tribal people or the Northeast-erners (which are also the groups most at risk from prostitution). Other research, by Ford and Saiprasert (1993) or Mills (1993), suggests that young people are very aware of the difference between the traditional and the modern, but that they somehow manage to integrate this into their daily lives and do not see themselves as less Thai because of their adoption of certain foreign fashions or even behaviours. Despite this, there is a widespread belief that young people are 'losing their culture'. There is a sense that by taking on Western role models and dressing in Western clothes, Thai young people are behaving in ways that are contrary to Thai values. One of the key sites of this struggle is sexual behaviour. Prasoet Bunsom, the former Deputy Minister of Education, has been quoted as saying that homosexuality and pre-marital sex are Western phenomena which have no relevance to Thailand. Speaking of these, he said, 'free sex, as in America ... [as a] type of behaviour might be such an ordinary thing that no-one takes much interest in it. But in Thailand, it may be seen as something detestable and a social abnormality' (Jackson 1989: 33).

It is not coincidental that the rise in concern about child prostitution has happened at almost the same time as concerns about Thai identity and Thai society are raised. The two are intimately linked. One of the reasons that the ECPAT campaign has succeeded in ways in which its predecessor, ECTWT, did not, is that it has avoided wider issues of foreign involvement in Thailand, concentrating instead on one where unrestrained resentment of foreigners is acceptable and encouraged. As ECPAT said in its founding statement, 'The issue of child prostitution is a symptom of the broader oppression which face people in developing countries, but it may be a starting point for this wider debate.' (1991: 1). However, there has not been a widening debate in Thailand: rather it has narrowed down to a focus on the individuals who have come there to abuse children. The very pertinent issues raised by the form and rapid rate of development in Thailand have not been adequately debated (Jacobs 1971, Turner and Ash 1975, Luther 1978, Pongsapich 1990). Instead, the whole force of the middle class resentment of, and contradictory attitudes towards, Western influence can be directed onto this one, supposedly noncontroversial issue. The perfect symbol for this resentment has been the child-sex tourist, 'a potent symbol of touristic excess' (Black 1995: 20). Child prostitution, like so many 'moral' problems, is not the straightforward issue of good and evil, standing above politics and economics, that some campaigners claim. Focusing on it is a conscious political decision, with a particular agenda and subtext which must be acknowledged. Muecke writes:

[The Thai middle classes] interpret prostitution as a function of both the low education and poverty in Thailand as a Third World country and as a function of the greed of the individuals who sell, procure or buy girls for labour in the prostitution industry. These views implicitly discount class responsibility for prostitution by globalising it to the scale of the Third World, and by individualising it to detestable characters. This stance also safeguards the women's groups members' relationships to their male partners and peers. By championing the cause of *child* victims of prostitution, the elite activists protect the disadvantaged children of the nation and protect the ideology of women – and themselves as nurturing mothers. And by restricting their activism to child prostitution, they avoid impugning male friends and relatives, that is those of their own class, and elitist systems (such as police, government officials surreptitiously involved in the sex entertainment trade) for supporting adult prostitution. (1992: 896).

In a society where public expression of anger and confrontation are considered unacceptable, the success of ECPAT has been in finding the one issue where such anger is justifiable. ECPAT and others have successfully harnessed the fear and resentment of foreigners by focusing on the individual men involved in exploitation of Thai children. This is not to accuse ECPAT and other campaigners of cynicism or opportunism. There is a real problem of child prostitution in Thailand, of which the children in Baan Nua are but a small part. Equally, Thailand's rapid industrialisation has caused divisive and long term social problems. However, it is extremely difficult for NGOs to generate interest about an issue on an international level, especially if it is seen as a national or local concern. Raising protests about cultural identity being distorted tend to fall on deaf ears, as do pleas to help certain other exploited groups, no matter how severe the exploitation. However, in targeting individual Western men, they are encouraging a justifiable anger at one man and encouraging it to expand into a more general resentment. Thais do have a right to get angry about foreign paedophiles who come to their country and indulge in behaviour that would not be tolerated in their home countries. However, the campaigns against these men are not as clear cut and single issue as they claim; the agenda of resentment is skilfully employed. There is no more emotive image than the innocent Thai child abused by the rich Westerner on holiday (Black 1995), but the advertising that accompanies the ECPAT campaigns is ambiguous. Their posters depict a sign that says 'For Sale' over some Thai children. This applies to the abuse of children, but it also applies to the society in general. They imply that what is promised in terms of economic gains will turn out to be a very false illusion.

It is also unsurprising that the battleground of culture involves images of the body, and especially images of the unpolluted body of a child. One of the reasons for the emphasis on the perfect virginal victim is that a child with previous sexual experience exists in a grey area and loses much of his or her symbolic power. The child's body has taken on a symbolic value above and beyond that of the exploitation of the individual child. The use of the human body as a metaphor for society in general is not unique but it remains very powerful (Douglas 1973). The activists against child prostitution are fighting a social battle, using the image of a violated child. In this battle, there is no room for nuances and no place for symbols which do not fit. The child's body has taken on the symbolic role of Thailand itself, and the images of violation are used, by association, to refer to the defilement of Thailand in general. The analogies that are drawn between tourism and rape, such as 'tourism is the rape of culture, the environment, women and children' (Srisang and Srisang n.d: 11), come into even sharper focus when used in relation to child prostitution. Westernisation and tourism are not just social nuisances but become forms of moral pollution which taint and defile. Child prostitutes are defiled by their experiences and yet any responsibility for them is dismissed and they are viewed as being beyond rehabilitation. By casting child prostitution as a moral issue above and beyond all other forms of exploitation and using these metaphors of pollution, the poverty and vulnerability to exploitation of communities such as Baan Nua are glossed over.

In this scenario, little emphasis needs to be placed on individual children or their circumstances. The emphasis has shifted away from child prostitutes themselves, and is now focused on child prostitution as a metaphor for other concerns. Child prostitution has become a way to discuss other issues, and it is being used a vehicle for raising other, less tangible, anxieties about societal change. There remains a horror of child abuse and a determination to stop it, yet the focus on foreigners abusing innocent children has been overwhelming. There has been no concurrent concern with children used by Thai or Asian clients, despite suggestions that these men form the majority of customers (Black 1994). Instead the image of 'the child and the tourist' has gained its own momentum, focusing hostility and resentment onto individual men rather than onto the faceless and nameless forces of globalisation. Industrialisation or Western economic involvement have brought frightening changes, yet it is easier to voice fears of a shadowy, international, paedophile conspiracy. In the latter case, the issue is much more straightforward. There is no excuse or justification for their actions; no-one benefits from what they do but the men themselves. The modernisation and Westernisation of Thailand are more problematic. The people who have benefited most from this are also the people aware of its drawbacks, and who are now trying to prevent the peasantry aspiring to the 'modern' way of life. Child prostitution is a focus for these fears. It can be presented as the ultimate horror, an inevitable consequence of further Westernisation, which must be prevented at all costs. The hidden message is that the poor must give up their aspirations and accept their place in society. That the lives of young prostitutes are very different from the image presented of them, is not surprising. The realities of different circumstances and daily life detract from the impact of the symbol. The image of a violated child as a symbol of social distress is extremely powerful, but this image must be unambiguous, and the child must be fully innocent, in every sense of the word, for this symbol to retain its power.

CHAPTER 7

CONCLUSION

The children with whom I worked in Baan Nua were undoubt-edly exploited and forced into lifestyles that exposed them to many forms of abuse and oppression. There has been no intention or attempt to justify this in writing this book. However, this abuse does not exist in a vacuum and it needs to be contextualised in order to understand what motivates these children and their families. This is not 'academic voyeurism' but an attempt to look at the very few options available to the poor and powerless. Unless other realities and discourses in discussions of child prostitution are acknowledged, any help or assistance is rendered meaningless. The process of understanding these children needs to start with a critical examination of the notion of what is a 'correct' childhood for children, especially in relation to sexuality and to work. Over the past twenty years, there has been an explosion of interest in various forms of child sexual abuse, largely influenced by the feminist movement of the late 1960s and early 1970s, which high-lighted the sexual abuses of power inherent within patriarchy. The exposure of such abuses has been vital and has transformed dis-cussions of child abuse. What was previously ignored or denied is now acknowledged as having damaging long-term emotional and physical effects. It is now viewed, in the West, as being the worst possible form of abuse, more emotionally damaging than physical or mental abuse. Given this, it is quite understandable that child prostitution evokes such horror. However, discussions of child prostitution which use this paradigm have a tendency to view it in isolation from other factors, thereby implying that anything is bet-ter than prostitution, even if this means a life in sweatshops or on the streets. While child prostitution is usually presented as a clear cut choice between good and evil, it is, in fact, a far more complex and ideologically motivated issue.

The exposure of child abuse is so closely linked conceptually with feminism, that important questions of how closely women and children can be linked ideologically have rarely been asked, but they must be problematised. While the practical and social links between women and children should be acknowledged, I have purposely avoided a gender-based analysis throughout this work. Like Ennew (1986) and La Fontaine (1990), I find that there are serious analytical difficulties with an uncritical acceptance of much of the feminist agenda.

> There are two problems in this refusal to disaggregate women and children as groups. The first is that it continues the association between women and children as minors in need of protection, which is a necessary correlate of male power. The second is that it does not acknowledge the importance of power relations based on age. (Ennew 1986: 57).

Despite similarities in their lack of structural power, children's issues and interests are very different from gender ones, and a feminist explanation of child prostitution places it very firmly in a discourse about child sexual abuse which is in turn linked with wider issues of 'male damage' (Jenkins 1992: 47). However this takes no account of the fact that it is not only girls who are prostituted and it is not only men that exploit. It could be argued that, because the women in Baan Nua do most of the recruiting, and are the ones that encourage their children to bring home family income, it is they who are most culpable. Gender is only one of the many forms of power relations in Baan Nua and it would be misleading to prioritise gender over age where children are concerned.

Currently the moral climate in the West is such that anything other than outright, unqualified, condemnation of child sexual abuse in all circumstances is impossible. This can hardly be faulted except that in placing a premium on child sex, it ignores many other forms of exploitation that children suffer. By placing prostitution firmly in the realms of morality, any discussion of economics, or structural inequalities, can be ignored. One of the reasons that children end up as prostitutes is that there are no other forms of well-paid labour available to them. Children are denied access to regulated employment and therefore their work options are limited to family farms, sweatshops, scavenging or prostitution. Without a functioning welfare state to protect children who have to work, the informal economy, in whatever form, fills the gap. In Baan Nua, the children's decision to prostitute themselves is a dangerous one for many reasons; health, risk from the police, or risk of further abuse from clients. Therefore in no sense would I suggest that it is a good choice or one that will be beneficial to children in the long term. Although prostitution earns them more money than other jobs, ultimately, it does not alleviate their poverty or lead to long term financial benefits. However, children who become prostitutes do so because they are already exploited and already alienated from other forms of work. In presenting child prostitution as a unique evil, all other social patterns and inequalities are ignored, and thus the fundamental status quo of the prevailing social relations remains unquestioned. When child prostitution is seen as an issue of economics, then serious discussions of child labour and regulated work for children will occur and state funds will need to be pledged to ensure that children will be protected from abuse. However, by placing it within a moral agenda and viewing it in terms of good and bad parenting, the economic factors inherent in prostitution are glossed over. The unease with which child prostitution in Britain is discussed is indicative of this. There are very clear indications that child prostitution is intimately linked with an inadequate and abusive system of care where low-paid and unqualified staff are placed *in loco parentis* over vulnerable children. The abuse that has come to light in the welfare system is not simply about the immorality of individual 'carers', but is an inevitable result of underfunding and of a conscious, political, decision to deny adequate resources to children in need.

In Baan Nua, the children make no absolute distinction between economics and morality and they do not choose between them so much as trade off one against the other. The economic benefits from prostitution can be used for very moral ends if they are used to provide for dependants. Prostitution, for the children themselves, is not an issue of morality versus immorality but of turning a socially unacceptable form of earning money into a way of fulfilling their familial obligations. Economics is tightly bound up with morality, and there is no clear division between the two. There is an awareness among some of the prostitutes that what they do is immoral in the eyes of wider society and that their private behaviour is in conflict with public opinion. Yet, private and public morality and behaviour are not opposites: people live with both. Behaviour that is publicly abhorred by the state is privately welcomed and supported in the family, even though people are aware of the social sanction against it.

The importance of children as social actors is central to this book, and although child prostitutes are portrayed as helpless and passive victims forced along by circumstances beyond their control, this is not the case in Baan Nua. It would be going too far to claim that prostitution is a 'free' and fully informed choice for these children, but, nevertheless, many of them do see it as the least of many evils. Their analyses of their motivations are based on a very partial knowledge of what they do, but even so, they use skill and power to capitalise on what little control over their actions they do have. Issues of choice and force are difficult to deal with in regard to child prostitution. It is possible to argue that, given the circumstances, any decision the children make is a forced one. Their earning options are so limited that they may be 'forced' into prostitution, just as they may be forced into collecting rubbish or working in a sweatshop. This is compounded by the fact that, as children, they are also subject to the influence of their parents. It would be easy to view these children as acquiescent victims of their circumstances and of their parents, unable to resist and therefore passively complying. Yet the children themselves specifically reject this categorisation, and although their choices are extremely restricted, they do struggle to take control of these decisions.

The two most important of these are the negotiation of relations between themselves and their clients and the emphasis on status and hierarchy. In these circumstances, the children exercise their choices: in the case of child pimps by deciding which clients are desirable and can be dealt with personally, and which are of lower status and to be given to younger children. For other children, it is the decision whether or not to go and actively find clients or wait for them to come to Baan Nua. For other children, there is the choice of whom to do favours for, and which patron to be adopted by. This could be an older child in the village, such as Lek, who will pass on the clients she no longer deals with, or it could mean becoming part of Julio's or James's entourage and providing sexual favours for them in return for financial protection. Again, it could be argued that the children are victims of a form of false consciousness, unable to see their own oppression, or knowing it, refusing to acknowledge it. Their justifications and rationalisations of prostitution did not sit comfortably with their extensive drug and alcohol use. However, even taking that into account, it is important to believe the children when they talked about their decisions, and to see their attempts to control certain aspects of their lives as active and informed choices among very limited options.

The importance of relative status is also central and is vital for an understanding of how the children viewed themselves. It has often been assumed that child prostitutes are an undifferentiated category and yet the children themselves place much emphasis on hierarchy. Prestige is based on what children are able to avoid and what they can get others to do in their place, so that Nong, the pimp, is considered much better off than five-year-old Ning (Dam's grand-daughter) who is without any power to coerce. Stages of prostitution are clearly marked and the children struggle to raise themselves in this hierarchy by associating with certain patrons or forming their own entourages. For those outsiders who see what they do as uniformly bad, such distinctions are irrelevant, but for the children, they contribute to a strategy for survival. For many in Baan Nua, and throughout Thailand, morality is not an absolute concept. It involves a compromise between the public and the private and is based more on the public reaction to their actions than to private conscience. Within Baan Nua, child prostitutes are judged not so much on what they do but how successful they are at doing it. Therefore the positive consequences of their actions can outweigh the negative labels that their behaviour attracts. Kob is admired because she has found herself a rich foreigner who paid for a new house for her parents. That is more important within her community than what she has done to obtain that money.

Without an understanding of these forces, any discussion of child prostitution in Thailand is incomplete. So many people who campaign against child prostitution treat 'children', 'sexuality' and 'prostitution' as unproblematic categories which they clearly are not. The archetype of a happy, innocent, childhood is a product of Western ideology which is an impossible ideal to impose cross-culturally. There is little cross-cultural agreement about what constitutes a proper childhood, or even what establishes a bad one (Korbin 1981, Ennew and Milne 1989, La Fontaine 1990). Likewise, as many other researchers have written, sexuality and prostitution are constructed very differently in Thailand from the West (Odzer 1990, Havanon et al. 1992, Muecke 1992, ten Brummelhuis 1993, Fordham 1993, 1995, 1996) and it is only in Western discourses that money and sexuality are so distinctly separated (compare La Fontaine 1974 with Bell 1987). Thailand has a long history of prostitution, polygamy, concubinage and what Cohen calls the 'fuzzy margins' of prostitution (Cohen 1982: 409), where sex is bartered for money and gifts in an established relationship (Phongpaichit 1980, Hantrakul 1983). However, new cultural ideals in Thailand are of monogamous, non-commercial sexual relationships, which once again have few historical or cultural precedents.

A clash is inevitable therefore between the middle classes, represented by the state and the NGOs, which have adopted many Western definitions of these subjects, and others, like the people in Baan Nua, who continue to use older models of the role and status of the child. There is a contradiction within the activist ideology between their rejection of all things foreign and their enthusiastic, if unacknowledged, adoption of almost all Western discourses on childhood, sexuality, labour and prostitution. The idealisation of 'the golden childhood' is very much a Western notion which has been imported into Thailand and one which finds little historical basis within Thai society. Work has always been a part of a poor Thai child's life, and although the forms of it have changed dramatically over the last thirty years, the idea of a work-free period of innocence and leisure in everyone's life is a myth. Despite claims to the contrary by campaigners against child prostitution, commercial sexual abuse is not a new phenomenon imported by foreigners, but it is, rather, a contemporary distortion of many cultural norms in Thailand. Children have always been sold by their parents, and daughters have always been sent to provide sexual services to pay off their parents' debts or to cement alliances (Fox 1960, Miles 1972, Turton 1980, Phongpaichit 1982, Hantrakul 1983, Truong 1990, Muecke 1992). The child traditionally had no privileged or independent status in Thailand and remained under his or her parents' care and control. While this traditional scenario may have lost its relevance in recent years, vestiges of it remain, and the people of Baan Nua certainly did not view children as autonomous.

There is a fundamental contradiction in the middle classes between the espousal of traditional Thai values and the speed with which Western discourses on morality have been adopted. Ten Brummelhuis claims there is

> ... a tendency among professionals and leaders of opinion to see the "problem of prostitution" as one of loose morals. The reasoning behind and defence of this position gives the impression of a Western discourse characterised by notions of sexuality, monogamy and marriage which have only been recently introduced in Thailand. (1993: 5).

Images and norms of sexuality have become Westernised at the same time that Western sexual mores are seen as a problem. The West is blamed for almost all of the 'deviant' sexuality in

Thailand, from homosexuality to the institutionalised rape of young Thai children by paedophiles, and yet Western discourses on child-sex, pre-marital sex and prostitution appear to be becoming accepted unquestioningly. This contradiction is largely unacknowledged, but social apprehensions about Western influences are explicit, and displayed in the NGOs' and their supporters' fear and distrust of influences from the West. However, there is also a realisation that the battle against these influences will be lost. Bangkok is an international city with over one hundred thousand resident foreigners, and more than five million tourists visit Thailand every year. For better or worse, therefore, Thailand cannot remain untouched by Western influence. Indeed many people do not wish it to, and are dependent on the money that foreigners bring in. To launch a battle against foreigners, therefore, would at best be ignored, like the Ecumenical Council on Third World Tourism's 'National No Golf Day' against the Japanese, and at worst it would be divisive and unpopular. Even the issue of sex tourism cannot be guaranteed to unite public opinion. Tourism is Thailand's largest foreign currency earner, and there are vested interests in allowing it to continue unchanged and in continuing to allow the prospect of Thai women to persuade overseas men to travel to Thailand. There is also the issue of indigenous prostitution, which would have to be tackled if sex tourism were prohibited and which would be hard to achieve without serious social disruption. The government's attempts to change sexual practices in the wake of the AIDS crisis have been largely rejected by many rural Thai men because, in Fordham's words, the state's 'penetration of the private sphere in order to manipulate sexual behaviour [removes] one of the few free spaces left to the poor for the construction of self' (1996: 4).

Thailand has changed dramatically over the last thirty years; it has opened itself up to Western influence both in the economic and the social spheres. The pride that Thailand, the land of the free, has never been colonised is proving harder to sustain when everything that was traditionally held to be Thai, such as the centrality of village life or the family farm, are coming under increasing pressure (Hirsch 1993). They have been replaced by the urban rat race and jobs among strangers in Bangkok or other major cities, alongside widespread internal and external migration and economic catastrophe caused by external market forces. The influences that shape these new social conditions are identifiably foreign whether in the form of capitalism, tourism or other cultural factors. For some members of the middle classes, this has brought economic benefits, but it has also precipitated an identity crisis. One Thai intellectual claimed that NIC did not stand for Newly Industrialised Country but for 'Newly Insecure Culture' or 'New Identity Crisis' (Santasombat 1990). It has led to a re-defining of what it is to be Thai which is highly elitist and reactionary, and has little to do with the people who have suffered most in the social upheavals of the last thirty years, such as the farmers who have been forced off their land, or the foresters who are no longer given access to the forests which had previously provided a livelihood. People like the inhabitants of Baan Nua are caught up in the process of industrialisation and are subject to the increasing emphasis on consumer goods that this has brought. Their responses to these new situations have been migration, prostitution and dependence on their children's labour. None of these are new phenomena, and yet those who do migrate or become prostitutes are attacked as undermining the very foundation of Thai society. In attempting to improve their position and opportunities, they are seen as both a symptom and a cause of the growing consumerism in Thai society.

It is unsurprising that the middle classes and those they claim to speak for have very different agendas. For those who work as prostitutes, prostitution is one difficult choice among many. For the middle classes, however, it is something very different. The increasing furore about child prostitution has very little to do with concern about the exploitation that the poor suffer under the new industrial conditions, and everything to do with the insecurities of the middle classes. By abdicating all class responsibility and blaming outsiders, the middle classes have avoided all questions of their own culpability.[1] They are the ones who benefited financially from the changes in Thailand, embracing the new consumer society, and yet they are also leading calls for a return to traditional Thai values. In the eyes of the middle classes, people such as the inhabitants of Baan Nua form a dangerous underclass, complete with the 'economic marginality, alternative values and deviant behaviour that appear in some combination in almost all discussions of the underclass' (Morris 1994: 80). Although, in reality, the villagers that I know share many similar values with the dominant society, such as the importance of the family, and a profound respect for Buddhism and for the Thai monarchy, the gulf between the two groups is seen as unbridgeable.

---

1. Equally in contemporary Britain, analyses which are sympathetic to the situation of child prostitutes abroad take up a very different position when discussing child prostitutes at home, who are often poor and disadvantaged. Whereas these children in Thailand are considered helpless victims, those in Britain are often condemned as delinquents and social drop outs who reject the social order.

Child prostitution has become an international problem in the 1990s. It is no longer confined simply to Thailand, and the emphasis on the role of Western tourists has forced the West to acknowledge some culpability for the problem. However, while the West does have a responsibility to act, it also has a responsibility to understand: not only the situation of child prostitutes in Thailand but also its own response to them. Undoubtedly there is a horror of child abuse but the continual emphasis on the suffering and degradation of child prostitutes is worrying. Unless there is a real understanding of the complexities of the issue of child prostitution in Thailand, and elsewhere, there is a great danger of voyeurism and titillation in stories of prostitution. Distorted child sexuality is of great concern to Western nations, as the recent scares about ritualised or Satanic child abuse have shown (Jenkins 1992). However, this concern is not just about child abuse, but is also about adults' expectations of children. Children are viewed as both asexual and sexually exciting, and the emphasis on child sex, which is always present when talking about prostitution, does not only disgust: it can also excite. As Foucault (1981) suggested, sometimes the forbidden is deliberately masked to increase the excitement of its exposure. More emphatically, Scheper-Hughes and Stein have drawn a link between the emphasis modern Western culture places on uncovering child sexual abuse and the unconscious desire for such abuse to happen. They write:

> Child abuse, of course, began as a fact, and not as the product of group fantasy. However, as it has become fuelled by unconscious wishes, projections of endangerment and rescue, it has become inseparable from the collective unconscious which has used child abuse towards its collective ends. If there is a prevalent fantasy that "a child is being abused", " a girl is being molested", then whatever the actual incidence or prevalence of such occurrence we must also address and understand the combined fear and wish that such occurrences take place. (1987: 351).

The stories that are presented of child prostitutes stress the sexuality of the children and their death. Like many AIDS discourses, these twin fears are continually returned to and emphasised. The clients are strangely absent, although supposedly, it is they who are of primary concern under the new extra-territorial laws to prosecute clients in their home countries for offences abroad. What happens to them? Do they too contract AIDS and die abandoned? It is one of the many areas about which nothing is known. Child prostitutes are defined only in terms of their sexu-

ality and their death. Other issues such as their families, their
clients, their economic situation, or their community, are sidelined
and overlooked. This tells us next to nothing about the children
themselves, and very much about the readers and writers of these
stories. Although the stereotype is well known, there are still calls
for 'awareness' to be raised and, consequently, it is still claimed
that there is a necessity for more stories about child prostitutes.
There is not, unless these stories are more profound, better contextualised, and set out to inform rather than titillate. There is a
public appetite for stories of child sex and child abuse, often intermingled with concern and calls for action, but these must be handled carefully. Foreign children must be given the same protection
as their Western counterparts. Newspaper or television articles, or
indeed NGO case studies, which use images of children, must protect their identity and should not further exploit these children by
emphasising their degradation and suffering.[2]

The image of threatened children and childhood innocence,
under attack from evil foreigners, has a long tradition from the
anti-Semitic blood libel onwards (Schultz 1986). It is a symbol
which allows the blame to be passed onto the 'unclean other'
without attaching any guilt or responsibility to insiders. It is
supremely divisive in that it separates everyone into the good and
the bad; those who do belong and those who do not. It allows for
no middle ground. Child victims are also potent symbols because
their image neatly side-steps many issues of the right of the state
to interfere in private behaviour. To those who are concerned
with a publicly supported and monitored system of morality, children provide ready-made potential victims in whose name protective laws can be passed. In the Thai context, child prostitution
provides the perfect symbol and focus for fears about foreign
influences and insecurities about the Thai identity. Here is an
issue that is anti-foreigner and which does not involve condemnation of Thais. It allows popular anger to focus on the stereotype
of a rich foreigner exploiting innocent children's bodies for his
own perverted pleasure, and it even draws in the support of many
Westerners. Black writes:

> ... no society wants to admit that it practices "child prostitution".
> And where the evidence is undeniable, it is more bearable to blame
> the "unclean other" – decadent foreigners with their incompre-
> hensible tastes and misbehaviours. Where there is an overlay of

2. For an intelligent and sensitive overview of media responses to these issues, see
White and Holman (1996).

> North-South exploitation – the Western tourist ruining innocent
> paradise with his credit card and unleashed libido – this version
> plays easily in certain well-meaning ears. (1994: 13).

With the success of so many campaigns in Western countries
against their own men, here is an issue that makes even Westerners acknowledge the corruption inherent in their own societies. There is nothing in the West for 'real' Thais to want to
emulate: Western society can be shown to be synonymous with
decadence and moral pollution.

Whether the campaign against child prostitution will be as successful within Thailand as it has been overseas remains to be seen.
With many Thais still expressing scepticism about reports of
forced prostitution and seeing the problem as far removed from
themselves (see Sittitrai and Brown 1994), there does not appear
to be the consensus on morality that many in Bangkok hope for.
However, the fact that it is seen as a problem by the participants
in the same survey does suggest that people are taking heed of
middle class discourses on the subject. The people of Baan Nua
are certainly affected by the changes and understand that their
resistance to the version of morality that is presented to them will
not be tolerated. It is always hard to see social change during the
course of fieldwork, and yet changes in the behaviour and attitudes of the villagers were evident as they began to feel the pressure of disapproval. Towards the end of my fieldwork, they would
not discuss prostitution as freely as they once would, and they
became very distrustful of strangers. Their fear of outsiders
increased as did their fear that they would be caught and punished for what they did. They were aware that prostitution was
viewed negatively by outsiders, and they knew that the penalties
for it were becoming harsher. Despite this, however, both the
children and their families were motivated by a complex and
occasionally contradictory view of private and public morality.
What was seen by some children as a highly moral way of earning money for their parents was viewed by others outside their
community as a public vice of the severest magnitude which
stained the child, his or her family, and, most of all, Thailand
itself. The relationship between the worlds of public morality and
private behaviour began to change, and, although the interface
continued to be a compromise between public and private morality for the children, for the activists it did not.

The voices of the children themselves have become largely lost
in this battle that is being fought in their name, but then the battle has never been fully about them. As one of the most tireless

campaigners against child prostitution has written, 'Irresponsible treatment of our children today will become tomorrow's nightmare. Prostituting a child is prostituting our own future' (O'Grady 1992a: 5). In this vision, the future of Thailand is being spoiled by selfish and irresponsible Westerners, ostensibly through child prostitution but also, by implication, through Westernisation and its concurrent consumerism. Child prostitution is presented in this scenario as an issue about which there can be no disagreement or dissent. The subject of child labour produces a passionate debate, as does adult prostitution, but neither of these issues are clear cut. The image of a child prostitute is perfect, however, because the parallels are explicit, and it is emotionally and morally impregnable, There are few people, except paedophiles with their own ulterior motives, who want to condone or justify child prostitution. Child prostitution has became a problem because there needs to be a potent symbol of Western excess. The exploitation of children is a moral outrage, but so is a prurient, sensationalist and politicised description of it that ignores the mundane face of poverty and focuses only on the 'exotic', sexual side.

The first step towards helping child prostitutes is to understand them, in their own terms. Only after this is done can there be any form of useful intervention. It is not enough to condemn child prostitution if it is not properly understood, and if children, with all their contradictions and inconsistencies, are excluded from discussions about their future. It is not necessary to agree with the children of Baan Nua in order to take their explanations seriously and to offer them help based on their own understandings. Concentrating only on children rescued from brothels, or those with foreign clients, helps only a small minority of the children in Thailand, and indeed, throughout the world, who are currently working as prostitutes. The different paths into, and out of, prostitution taken by many children, must be recognised and intervention tailored accordingly. Emphasis should be transferred from prostitution and back onto children. This means that children in general, and child prostitutes especially, should not be treated as a homogenous group with similar needs and priorities. Notions of the universal nature of women's oppression and subordination have been abandoned in response to a recognition of the diversity of women's experience. Similarly, studies of children, even child prostitutes, must acknowledge the differences between them, not least those depending on age or gender. Although based on a worthy ideal of protection and assistance, the categorisation of all people under eighteen as children is of limited use when dealing with children who use very different categorisations.

Currently, most attempts to end child prostitution focus on finding someone to blame and punish. Sometimes this is the children themselves, who are breaking the law by working as prostitutes. Given the sensitivity of this issue, however, and the lack of public support, nationally and internationally, for such measures, the recent emphasis has been on the police rescuing children rather than arresting them.[3] Not only does this fit in with popular stereotypes of passivity in children, it also draws attention away from the many charges of police collusion in child prostitution (Centre for the Protection of Children's Rights n.d., Hantrakul 1983, Heyzer 1986, Ennew and Milne 1989). Other attempts have been made to punish the parents of child prostitutes, removing parental rights, or even giving jail sentences to parents who allow their children to become prostitutes ('Parents Warned Not to Sell their Children,' (*Nation* 1989). Yet this is difficult, and there is little popular support for such measures. Focus group discussions on child prostitution, conducted in 1993 and 1994, revealed a high level of integration between the families of child prostitutes, their clients, and 'ordinary' members of the public. The authors of a study based on this research reported that, out of their seventy-nine participants, made-up of students, office workers, and residents of a slum area, 'A number reported being clients or neighbours of child prostitutes, former child prostitutes themselves, or procurers of child prostitutes' (Sittitrai and Brown 1994: 3). With so many people implicated in child prostitution, there is a marked reluctance to target individual parents.

Punishing parents, or indeed, Thai clients, means admitting that there is a degree of Thai culpability, which there is a reluctance to do. For foreign NGOs, this is quite understandable. They would be easy targets for accusations of interfering in internal politics and would have to answer charges of hypocrisy. Many countries in the West have a far from impressive record on dealing with child sexual abuse and children's rights. However, viewing the problem entirely as an issue of foreigners abusing Thai children places unhelpful limitations on the issue and focuses a great deal of resources on a few individual men. The extra-territorial laws have made some impact and there have been some successful prosecutions.[4] It is impossible

3. See, for example, '60 girls Rescued in Police Crackdown,' (*Bangkok Post* 1992), '2 Girls Sold to Sex-Seeking Foreigners Rescued by Police,' (*Bangkok Post* 1993), 'Secret Raid Rescues 19 Girls from Brothel in Chiang Mai,' (Holt and Khaikow 1995).

4. See, for example, the prosecutions in 1990 in Norway, June 1995 in Sweden, April 1996 in Australia and October 1997 in France. The first (and, to date, only) successful prosecution in Britain resulted in the conviction of Durham Wragg in January 2001. He was sentenced to thirty months imprisonment for making child pornography while in the Philippines (Chrisafis 2001).

to know the preventative value of such campaigns, but the realisation that they can and will be prosecuted if they buy sex from children abroad, may well have warned off some paedophiles. The number of prosecutions has been relatively small and, even if figures of one million children a year becoming prostitutes are questionable, clearly the prosecution of a few men has had a negligible impact on the numbers of children involved in prostitution.

Individual paedophiles make a more acceptable target than Thai clients or poverty-stricken parents. Yet it is questionable whose needs are fulfilled by these prosecutions. For the child prostitutes themselves, compensation may be offered or they may feel a certain satisfaction in seeing their abusers go to prison. Set against this, however, is their risk of exposure, of the traumas of being made to give evidence in a foreign and often intimidating court, and the issue of what happens to them on their return to their home countries. Are they placed in care, given counselling and alternatives to prostitution? Are they stigmatised in the eyes of the government and their communities? Or are they simply forgotten? It is one of the many areas which needs reflection. For NGOs and governments, however, there are more tangible benefits to prosecution. Although there are legal and constitutional difficulties involved in passing extra territorial laws, the differing legal systems of Scandinavia, Australia and New Zealand have coped with these. Indeed the difficulties in making such changes to their laws are used as evidence of their commitment to ending child prostitution. Prosecutions are proof that something palpable is being done. In the court, child prostitution can be removed once again from its economic and social context and argued over simply as a matter of law. The complexities of individual cases become irrelevant as legality becomes the only salient issue. There is also a satisfaction in accusing these men; they will have few defenders and there is a sense of justice in seeing them imprisoned for crimes against children. Again, there is a satisfaction in prosecuting these men and from publicly repudiating them as appropriate members of society.

> The field is cleared for the abusers (who, God knows, are real enough) to come to bear the entire burden of the public's displaced guilty conscience about the institutionalized abuse of the weak, the young, and the vulnerable to which, they too, are party. There is also suggestion of the projection of a fantasy – the wish to abuse, to hurt, to torture the weak and vulnerable that is concealed in the aggressive tracking down of the "evil" perpetrators of the "crime". In seeing abusers and molesters hunted down and severely punished, members of the social mainstream are able to experience a

symbolic sacrifice and thus feel themselves cleansed, stabilized and whole. (Scheper-Hughes and Stein 1987: 345).

Trying and condemning individual men has a neatness to it which is appealing: it unites Western NGOs with their Thai counterparts, and it makes a symbolic gesture that this is also the West's responsibility. It also makes the accused paedophiles confront the seriousness of their abuse, and, one would hope, make other men reflect before they travel. It is one of several steps that are necessary to combating child prostitution. However, it is only one of many, and a disproportionate amount of interest and activism has been directed at this one issue, while other, more fundamental areas have been overlooked. The prosecution of these men encounters none of the problems of helping children at grass roots level. It is not good enough to target paedophiles while the children they have abused are forgotten. The emphasis on their contracting HIV is a convenient veil for the fact that there is no knowledge of how to treat children when they leave prostitution, and little inclination to try. By claiming that they are going to die anyway, the need for financial and social help for them is obviated. Similarly, claims that they are so abused that they can never be rehabilitated, remove the will to look at ways in which they might be helped. Helping child prostitutes is a long term process which must go beyond an easy satisfaction at prosecuting a handful of paedophiles. Even if a child prostitute has contracted HIV, this does not mean that nothing can be done for them. On the contrary, these are precisely the children for whom medical and social help is most needed. However, this does not have the high profile that prosecuting a paedophile does, although it is probably much cheaper and more beneficial to the child.

The emphasis on prosecuting paedophiles also obscures the issue of child prostitutes who do not have foreign clients. This is a difficult area to examine, especially for foreign researchers and NGOs, who lay themselves open to charges of interference in other cultures.[5]

5. The dangers inherent in such an approach are illustrated by the parallel issue of female circumcision in Africa which has been widely commented on and condemned by Western feminists. Their campaigns against it provoked a backlash from African's women's groups who criticised them for their focus on the sensational aspects of oppression. African Women's groups such as AAWORD (Association of African Women for Research and Development) argue that circumcision must be placed in the context of 'ignorance, obscurantism, exploitation, poverty' (Davies 1983: 219) and claim that Western groups only take the sensational (and salacious) aspects of oppression and not the mundane ones. They further claim that it is an African issue which Westerners should be wary of commenting on.

Nevertheless, there is, at the moment, only a partial picture of child prostitution: this needs to be expanded and properly understood. There is little point in targeting the children of foreign clients if they are simply pushed back into the brothels for local clients as a result. Schemes to tackle child prostitution must encompass all children, whatever their clients. It is not acceptable to choose easy political targets while deliberately ignoring wider abuses. This must mean looking honestly at the structural social inequalities as well as indigenous patterns of prostitution and notions of sexuality. There is no need to 'blame' Thailand or to see this only as a Thai problem. Child prostitution has existed in other cultures and histories also. However, claiming a direct causal relationship between tourism and child prostitution is equally partial and obfuscatory. The causes of child prostitution are multiple and attempts to alleviate the problem must reflect this.

Ending all child prostitution is a worthy ideal, but there is no-one, simple, solution. The problem must be tackled from many angles: prevention, rehabilitation, and support for children when they still work as prostitutes. Focusing only on the morality of the issue is understandable, but it over-simplifies the issue, and encourages notions of uncomplicated causes and straightforward solutions. It is probably impossible to stamp out all child prostitution, just as it has proved impossible to end all forms of exploitative child labour. However, it is possible to take a multi-faceted approach to the problem which would increase the options available to poor children and ensure that some children were given real alternatives. In 1996, The World Congress Against the Commercial Sexual Exploitation of Children produced an ambitious and challenging declaration which called for different strategies to tackle child prostitution, and which recognised 'that the different types of perpetrators and ages and circumstances of victims require differing legal and pragmatic responses' (1996: 5). It is a brave and useful document which provides a framework which encompasses all children working as prostitutes, and which acknowledges that child-sex tourists are only part of a much bigger problem. It admits the complexities of child prostitution and recognises the various ways in which children become prostitutes; it draws no distinction between those who are trafficked and debt-bonded and those who are technically free and who work part-time. Most importantly, Article Six of the agenda for action calls for 'the participation of children, including child victims, young people and their families, peers and others, who are potential helpers so that they can express their views' (1996: 7).

It is hoped that this declaration for action will eventually lead to an end of the repetitive stereotypes and endlessly told stories of helpless and hopeless children, waiting to be rescued and spoken for by adults. However, this means challenging many notions of the nature of childhood and the rights of adults over children. Few societies take children seriously or give their views weight, and this problem is confounded when the children involved are vulnerable, inarticulate and fearful of repercussions when they do speak. 'Listening to smaller voices' becomes even harder when children's and adults' views diverge considerably. This was a constant problem when dealing with the children in Baan Nua. Their support for their families was evident, yet clearly abuses occurred. They wanted to stay with their families, yet ultimately they might have been better off had they been taken away. The concept of the 'best interest of the child' is a difficult one, which must be considered carefully if it is not to be used as an excuse to replicate patterns of adult power over children in the name of children's rights (Montgomery, forthcoming).

So far, the most successful schemes in Thailand have been those which work with both parents and children, aiming to provide financial alternatives to prostitution. A system of scholarships has been set up which provides money to families who keep their daughters in school, and hence out of the brothels. This is expensive, and has, so far, largely relied on private charity to supply the funds.[6] It is also too early to know how successful it will be in the long term. It is impossible to know at this stage if this will keep girls out of the sex trade permanently, or simply keep them out of prostitution for a few more years. If the girls go on to become prostitutes at sixteen, rather than thirteen or fourteen, has this project been a success? There have also been criticisms that not enough money is given to parents so that it is still more profitable for their daughters to enter prostitution. However, by emphasising prevention and recognising that economic hardship and parental encouragement are two of many factors which contribute to child prostitution, schemes such as these make welcome steps away from punitive intervention. It is worth noting further that recent studies (Baker 2000) have claimed that increased educational opportunities and a decline in the population of girls aged between ten and sixteen have also led to a decline in the overall numbers of children entering prostitution from the Chiang Rai region. Fear of AIDS and of prosecution under the 1996 Prostitution Prevention and Suppression Act have also influenced parents and made them more reluctant to allow

6. See for example, 'Princess Offers Scholarships for North Girls,' (*Nation* 1994b) or 'Ministry Seeks B3,100 m to Hand Out Scholarships,' (*Bangkok Post* 1994b).

children to become prostitutes. Nevertheless, Baker notes that his findings are controversial and the perception in North Thailand among NGO workers is that child prostitution is still increasing.

It is too late for prevention schemes in Baan Nua, and these children would not be eligible for such projects. Yet there is a clear need for help targeted at these children, for their own sakes and also for the next generation of children, such as Oy, born in the slum to a young mother who knows no way of life other than prostitution. To take these children seriously means accepting their views of their families and, at least in the short term, doing everything possible to keep their families together. Whatever others' opinions of the role of the parents in the prostitution of their children, punitive sanctions against parents will put even greater pressure on these children. If obtaining help means the arrest of their parents, they are highly unlikely to seek it out. Likewise, they are clearly unwilling, at this stage, to testify against their abusers, whom they still claim as friends.

The children of Baan Nua are extremely difficult. It is probable that they would not be able to cope with schooling, even if they were offered scholarships. Their lifestyles and their addiction to drugs have left them with short attention spans and erratic behaviour. They are frequently violent and have little respect for authority. Any help that is offered to them must be both intensive and long term, and should enable them to deal with their anger and frustration, without adding to their suffering. Their physical health is poor and their emotional state is vulnerable: intervention must be handled extremely carefully, if they are to acknowledge the abuse without blaming or hating themselves. They have built up a certain self-image and ways of coping and surviving, and while these are not ideal, it is important not to destroy them, if nothing can be put in their place. Indeed, whatever they have suffered, their resilience and their roles as dutiful children and pivotal members of their communities should be celebrated. Only when this process is completed will these children be ready to decide whether continuing to live with their parents is best for them. This is, however, a decision they must make for themselves. If it is forced upon them when they are not ready, it will only lead to further resentment and greater unwillingness to accept intervention.

In some cases, prostitution has been the source of income for families in Baan Nua for three generations. The children are given few other options by their parents, or indeed, by the state or the free market. By understanding what is important to these children – familial duty and status – it becomes possible to suggest options which might be acceptable to these children. Clearly menial jobs in service industries which reinforce their sense of alienation and low social status are no way out. Menial jobs are inevitably badly paid and bring in too little money to support a family, which is a primary concern. This is a concern also if the children are ever persuaded to testify against their abusers. They risk being permanently stigmatised as former child prostitutes, and as a consequence find themselves unemployable. They need access to jobs that they think will bring them prestige, such as working in department stores, and which bring in enough money to look after their parents. However, few companies are prepared to take on such children without the necessary academic requirements, and it is indeed risky taking on such children when their behaviour can be so unpredictable. These children are adult in so many ways, yet their compacted childhoods mean that they have not had time to learn and accept the responsibilities of adulthood gradually. They have had to deal with both work and sex at an early age, and although they have coped with both, there is no indication what long term effects this will have. For this reason, they need intensive psychological help and counselling before any form of income-generating scheme can be countenanced.

Declarations and agendas for action have noble intentions, but if they are to have any practical effect at grass roots level they must face up to the multitude of problems that child prostitutes face, and work to overcome the very real difficulties that these children present. The children of Baan Nua are a few children among many. Like children everywhere, their lives are complex and influenced by many social, political and economic forces. They are much more than simply prostitutes, and excessive focus on that alone robs them of any individuality or of other identities. They are difficult children to help; they fit into no neat conceptual categories and their problems are multiple, making intervention complex and challenging. It may be the case that there is no effective intervention that outsiders can offer to these children. Yet it is always possible to attempt to understand them, and to accept the validity of their stories. Rather than trying to destroy those stories and replace them with versions that adults want to hear, it is important to acknowledge the variations that exist between different forms of prostitution and between different children's experiences of it.

The Declaration at the World Congress was a useful step in this direction. It showed that some advocates at least were prepared to move away from limiting and unnecessary stereotypes and were prepared to embrace all aspects of this problem. However, the disjunction between theory and practice is still apparent, and there is still an unwillingness for adults to give up, or even acknowledge, their power over children. The image of a passive, victimised child, totally dependent on either the cruelties of abusive adults or the kindness of their advocates and rescuers, remains central to campaigns and newspaper articles about these children. It still remains possible for campaigners to say that 'prostituting a child is prostituting our own future' thereby writing children out of their own story. The effects of prostituting children should be understood in terms of their future, not ours. It is their future, just as it is their present, and their past, which should be the primary focus of concern. Instead, too often, child prostitutes are understood only in so far as they relate to and reflect adult concerns; they are adored as victims but scorned as survivors.

BIBLIOGRAPHY

Allsebrook, A. and Swift, A. 1989. *Broken Promise*. London: Hodder and Stoughton.

Archavanitkul, K. and Havanon, N. 1990. *Situation, Opportunities and Problems Encountered by Young Girls in Thai Society*. Bangkok: Terre des Hommes.

Ariès, P. 1979. *Centuries of Childhood*. London: Penguin.

Asavaroengchai, S. 1993. 'Observations on Thailand's Cultural Dilemma.' *Nation*, 18 March 1993.

Asia Watch. 1993. *A Modern Form of Slavery: Trafficking of Burmese Women and Girls into Brothels in Thailand*. New York: Human Rights Watch.

Asia Partnership for Human Development. 1985. *Awake*. Sydney: APHD.

—— 1992. *Awake 2*. Philippines: APHD.

Bai-ngern, C. 1994. 'Boy Prostitutes Still Playing the Dangerous Game.' *Nation*, 3 April 1994.

Banpasirichote, C. and Pongsapich, A. 1992. *Child Workers in Hazardous Work in Thailand*. Bangkok: Chulalongkorn University Social Research Institute.

Baker, S. 2000. *The Changing Situation of Child Prostitution in Northern Thailand: A Study of Chiang Rai*. Unpublished draft manuscript.

Bangkok Post. 1992. '60 girls Rescued in Police Crackdown.' *Bangkok Post*, 16 November 1992.

—— 1993. '2 Girls Sold to Sex-Seeking Foreigners Rescued by Police.' *Bangkok Post* 3 November 1993.

—— 1994a. 'Russian Women Face Prostitution Charges.' *Bangkok Post*, 4 March 1994.

—— 1994b. 'Ministry Seeks B3,100 m to Hand Out Scholarships.' *Bangkok Post*, 11 March 1994.

—— 1994c. 'Boy Prostitutes on the Rise, Says Study.' *Bangkok Post*, 29 April 1994.

Bangkok Sunday Post. 1993a. 'PM Hails Children as Most Important Resource.' *Bangkok Sunday Post*, 10 January 1993.

—— 1993b. 'Northern Villagers put their Heritage Up for Sale.' *Bangkok Sunday Post*, 3 October 1993.

Barry, K. 1984. *Female Sexual Slavery*. New York and London: New York University Press.

Beesey, Alan. n.d. *Women and Buddhism in Thailand*. Unpublished manuscript.

Bell, L. 1987. *Good Girls/Bad Girls: Feminists and Sex Trade Workers Talk Face to Face*. Toronto: The Women's Press.

Black, M. 1994. 'Home Truths.' *New Internationalist* February, 11–13.

——— 1995. *In the Twilight Zone, Child Workers in the Hotel, Tourism and Catering Industry*. Geneva: ILO.

Black Shadow. 1949. *Dream Love: The Book for Men Only*. Bangkok: Vitayakorn.

Blanc-Szanton, C. 1985. 'Gender and Inter-generational Resource Allocations: Thai and Sino-Thai Households in Central Thailand,' in *Structures and Strategies: Women, Work and Family in Asia*. L. Dube and R. Parliwala (eds.) New Delhi: Sage, 79 – 102.

Boonchalaksi, W. and Guest, P. 1994. *Prostitution in Thailand*. Mahidol University, Bangkok: Institute for Population and Social Research.

Boyden, J. and Bequele, A. 1988. *Combating Child Labour*. Geneva: ILO.

Brody, A. 1995. *Problematising Thai Masculinity, with Specific Reference to Prostitution in Thailand*. Paper presented at the International Conference on Gender and Sexuality in Modern Thailand. Australian National University, Canberra.

Campagna, D. and Poffenberger, D. 1988. *The Sexual Trafficking in Children*. Dover, Massachusetts: Auburn House.

Cannell, F. 1990. 'Concepts of Parenthood: the Warnock Report, the Gillick Debate, and Modern Myths.' *American Ethnologist*. 17:4, 667–86.

Caplan, P. 1987. *The Cultural Construction of Sexuality*. London: Tavistock.

Carsten, J. 1991. 'Children In-Between: Fostering and the Process in Kinship on Pulau Langkawi, Malaysia.' *Man*. 26:3, 425–443.

Catholic Commission for Health. 1993. *Factors and Sexual Behaviour that Contribute to the AIDS Contraction by Students in Catholic Schools*. Bangkok: Catholic Commission for Health.

Centre for the Protection of Children's Rights. 1991. *The Trafficking of Children for Prostitution in Thailand*. Bangkok: Unpublished manuscript.

——— n.d. *Prevention of Trafficking and Sale of Children in Thailand*. Bangkok: Unpublished manuscript.

Cheang, W. S. 1994. 'Culture in Crisis.' *Nation*, 24 January 1994.

Christian Aid 1995. *An Abuse of Innocence: Tourism and Child Prostitution in Thailand*. London: Christian Aid.

Chompootaweep, S., Yamarat, K., Poomsuwan, P. and Dusitsin, N. 1988. *A Study of Reproductive Health in Adolescence of Secondary Students and Teachers in Bangkok*. Institute of Health Research, Bangkok: Chulalongkorn University Press.

Chrisafis, A. 2001. 'Global Child Porn Ring Broken.' *Guardian*, 11 January 2001.

Chuenprasaeng, P. 1993. 'Ignored in the Fracas, Prostitutes Define their Feelings.' *Nation*, 18 July 1993.

Chutikul, S. 1992. *Child Prostitution in Thailand.* Paper presented at The International Conference on Children in Prostitution. Sukothai University: Bangkok

Cohen, E. 1982. 'Thai girls and Farang Men – the Edge of Ambiguity.' *Annals of Tourism Research.* 9:3, 403–42.

———— 1987. 'Sensuality and Veniality in Bangkok. The Dynamics of Cross-Cultural Mapping of Prostitution.' *Deviant Behaviour* 8:3, 223–234.

Cumming-Bruce, N. 1995. 'Thais' Uphill Battle Against Sex Slavery,' *Guardian,* 4 February 1995.

Connerton, P. 1989. *How Societies Remember.* Cambridge: Cambridge University Press.

DaGrossa, P. 1989. 'Kamphaeng Din: A Study of Prostitution in the All-Thai brothels of Chiang Mai City.' *Cross-roads* 4:2, 1–7.

Daniel, N. 1996. 'Vietnamese Children Sold into Sex Slavery.' *Daily Telegraph,* 1 December 1996.

Davies, M. 1983. *Third World, Second Sex.* London: Zed.

Day, S. 1994. 'What Counts as Rape? Physical Assault and Broken Contracts: Contrasting Views of Rape Among London Sex Workers,' in *Sex and Violence: Issues in representation and experience.* P. Harvey and P. Gow (eds.) London: Routledge, 172–189.

Delacoste, F. and Alexander, P. 1988. *Sex Work: Writings by Women in the Sex Industry.* London: Virago.

de Mause, L. 1976. *The History of Childhood.* London: Souvenir Press.

de Zalduondo, B.O. 1991. 'Prostitution Viewed Cross-Culturally: Towards Recontextualising Sex Work in AIDS Intervention.' *Journal of Sex Research* 28:2, 223–248.

DEP (Daughters Education Project) n.d. *Programme Report.* Chiang Rai: Unpublished manuscript.

Dollimore, J. 1991. *Sexual Dissidence: Augustine to Wilde, Freud to Foucault.* Oxford: Clarendon.

Drummond, A and Chant, A. 1994. 'Child Sex Britons Freed with Bribes.' *Evening Standard,* 7 March 1994.

Douglas, M. 1973. *Natural Symbols: Explorations in Cosmology.* London: Barrie and Jenkins.

Dutter, B. 1996. 'Girls as Young as 12 'Sold for Sex'.' *Daily Telegraph,* 21 August 1996.

ECPAT (End Child Prostitution in Asian Tourism). n.d. *Report on International Conference to End Child Prostitution in Asian Tourism* Bangkok: Unpublished manuscript.

———— 1991–5. *Newsletters* Bangkok: ECPAT.

ECTWT (Ecumenical Coalition on Third World Tourism). 1983. *Tourism, Prostitution, Development.* Bangkok: ECTWT.

———— *Contours: Newsletters of the Ecumenical Coalition on Third World Tourism.* Bangkok: ECTWT.

Edwards, J. 1993. *Technologies of Procreation: Kinship in the Age of Assisted Conception.* Manchester: Manchester University Press.

Ehrenreich, B. and English, D. 1979. *For Her Own Good.* London: Pluto Press.

Ekachai, S. 1990. *Behind the Smile: Voices of Thailand.* Bangkok: Thai Development Support Committee.

——— 1994. 'Lost in the Urban Jungle.' *Bangkok Post,* 19 May 1994.

Eliot, D. 1978. *Thailand: Origins of Military Rule.* London: Zed Books.

Elson, D. 1982. 'The Differentiation of Children's Labour in the Capitalist Labour Market.' *Development and Change* 13:4, 479–497.

Engels, F. 1977. *The Origin of the Family, Private Property and the State.* London: Lawrence and Wishart.

Ennew, J. 1986. *Sexual Exploitation of Children.* Cambridge: Polity Press.

——— 1998. *The African Context of Children's Rights.* Seminar January 12–14 1998. Harare, Zimbabwe

Ennew, J, Gopal, K, Heeran J and Montgomery, H. 1996. *The Commercial Sexual Exploitation of Children: Background papers and annotated bibliography for the World Congress on the Commercial Sexual Exploitation of Children.* Oslo: Childwatch International and UNICEF.

Ennew, J. and Milne, B. 1989. *The Next Generation: Lives of Third World Children.* London: Zed Books.

Fawcett, J., Khoo, T. and Smith, P. C. (eds.) 1984. *Women in the Cities of Asia: Migration and Urban Adaptation.* Boulder: Westview Press.

Fentress, J. and Wickham, C. 1992. *Social Memory.* Oxford: Basil Blackwell.

Fernand-Laurent, J. 1983. *Report on the Suppression of the Traffic in Persons and the Exploitation of the Prostitution of Others.* Geneva: United Nations E/1983/7.

Finkelhor, D. 1979a. *Sexually Victimised Children.* New York: Free Press.

Finkelhor, D. 1979b. 'What's wrong with sex between adults and children? Ethics and the problem of sexual abuse.' *American Journal of Orthopsychiatry.* 49:4, 692–697.

Finkelhor, D. and Araji, S. 1986. *A Source Book on Child Sexual Abuse.* London and Delhi: Sage.

Firestone, S. 1971. *The Dialectic of Sex.* London: Jonathan Cape Ltd.

Ford, N. and Saiprasert, S. 1993. *Destinations Unknown: The Gender Construction and Changing Nature of the Sexual Lifestyle of Thai Youth.* Paper presented at the Fifth International Conference on Thai Studies. SOAS, London.

Fordham, G. 1993. *Northern Thai Male Culture and the Assessment of HIV Risk.* Paper presented at the IUSSP Working Group on AIDS: Seminar on AIDS Impact and Prevention in the Developing World.

——— 1995. 'Whisky, Women and Song: Alcohol and AIDS in Northern Thailand.' Unpublished draft manuscript. (Later published in a modified version in *Australian Journal of Anthropology.* 6:3, 154–177.)

——— 1996. Northern Thai Male Culture and the Assessment of HIV Risk: Towards a New Approach. *Cross-roads.* Unpublished draft manuscript. (Later published in a modified version in *Crossroads.* 12:1, 77–164).

Foucault, M. 1981. *The History of Sexuality: An Introduction.* London: Penguin.

Foundation for Children. 1989. *Asian Symposia on Children in Distress: Past Experiences and New Directions.* Bangkok: Foundation for Children.

Foundation for Women. 1990. *Kamla.* Bangkok: Foundation for Women.

Fox, M. 1960. *Problems of Prostitution in Thailand.* Bangkok: Department of Public Welfare.

Franklin, S. 1997. *Embodied Progress: A Cultural Account of Assisted Conception.* London: Routledge.

Fyfe, A. 1989. *Child Labour.* Cambridge: Polity Press.

Gibsonainyette, I., Templer, D.I., Brown, R., Veaco, L. 1988. 'Adolescent Female Prostitutes.' *Archives Of Sexual Behavior* 17: 5, 431–438

Gilkes, M. 1993. *Prostitution in Thailand.* Southampton: BA Thesis Long Island University.

Gonzales, P. 1993. *Social, Political, and Ecological Impacts of Tourism.* Bangkok: Contours.

Goody, J. and Tambiah, S.J. 1973. *Bridewealth and Dowry.* Cambridge: Cambridge Papers in Social Anthropology No. 7.

Goonatilake, H. 1993. 'Women and Family in Buddhism,' in *Buddhist Perceptions for Desirable Societies in the Future.* S. Sivaraksa (ed.) Bangkok: Thai Inter-Religious Commission for Development, 224–243.

Graburn, N.H. 1983. 'Tourism and Prostitution.' *Annals of Tourism Research* 10:3, 437–42.

Grant, L. 1995. 'Girls, Girls, Girls.' *Guardian,* 10 July 1995.

Green, P. n.d. *Prostitution: Children the Victims: The Effects of Prostitution and Sexual Exploitation on Children and Adolescents.* Bangkok: Rahab Ministries.

Grimshaw, A. 1992. *Servants of the Buddha: Winter in a Himalayan Convent.* London: Open Letters.

Guest, P. 1993. *Guesstimating the Unestimateable: The Number of Child Prostitutes in Thailand.* Mahidol University, Bangkok: Institute for Population and Social Research.

Hall, T.A. 1998. *Accommodating Inequality: An Ethnography of Youth Homelessness and Hostel Provision in South-East England.* Cambridge: PhD Dissertation, Department of Social Anthropology, University of Cambridge.

Hall, T and Montgomery, H. 2000. 'Home and Away.' *Anthropology Today* 16:3, 13–15.

Hanks, J. 1964. *Maternity and its Rituals in Bang Chan.* Data Paper 51, South East Asia Programme. Ithaca: Cornell University.

Hanks, L. M. 1962. 'Merit and Power in the Thai Social Order.' *American Anthropologist* 64:6, 1247–1261.

Hantrakul, S. 1983. *Prostitution in Thailand.* Melbourne: Paper presented to the Women in Asia Workshop, Monash University.

———— 1993. 'Feudalism and the Politics of Sex in Thailand.' *Nation,* 1 August 1993.

Havanon, N. and Chairut, W. 1985. *Nuptiality and the Family in Thailand.* Bangkok: Chulalongkorn University Press.

Havanon, N., Knodel, J. and Bennett, T. 1992. *Sexual Networking in a Provincial Thai Setting.* Bangkok: AIDS Prevention Monographs.

Hart, A. 1998. *Buying and Selling Power: Anthropological Reflections on Prostitution in Spain.* Boulder: Westview Press.

Hart, K. 1973. 'Informal Income Opportunities and Urban Employment in Ghana.' *The Journal of Modern African Studies*. 11:1, 61–89.

Hecht, T. 1994. *At Home on the Street: Street Children of Recife, Brazil.* Cambridge: PhD Dissertation, Department of Social Anthropology, University of Cambridge.

Herdt, G. 1984. *Ritualised Homosexuality in Melanesia.* Berkeley: University of California Press.

Herdt, G. and Leap, W. 1991. 'Anthropology, Sexuality and AIDS.' *Journal of Sex Research* 28:2, 167–169

Heyzer, N. 1986. *Working Women of Southeast Asia: Development, Subordination and Emancipation.* Milton Keynes: Open University Press.

Hirsch, P. 1993. 'What is the Thai village?' in *National Identity and its Defenders: Thailand 1938–89.* C. Reynolds (ed.) Chiang Mai: Silkworm Books, 323–340.

Holland, P. 1992. *What Is A Child?* London: Virago.

Holt, S. and Khaikow, T. 1995. 'Secret Raid Rescues 19 Girls from Brothel in Chiang Mai.' 3 March 1995.

Hornblower, M. 1993. 'The Sex Trade.' *Time.* 21 June 1993.

Hyam, R. 1990. *Empire and Sexuality: the British Experience.* Manchester: Manchester University Press.

International Save the Children Fund. 1991. *Position Paper on the Commercial Sexual Exploitation of Children.* London: Save the Children Fund.

Ireland, K. 1993. *Wish you Weren't Here.* London: Save the Children Fund.

ISIS. 1990. 'Poverty and Prostitution.' *Women's World* 24. Geneva: ISIS.

Jacobs, N. 1971. *Modernisation Without Development.* New York: Praeger.

Jackson, P. 1989. *Male Homosexuality in Thailand: An Interpretation of Contemporary Thai Sources.* New York: Global Academic Publishers.

James, A. and Prout, A. 1995. 'Hierarchy, Boundary and Agency: Toward a Theoretical Perspective on Childhood.' *Sociological Studies of Children.* 7, 77–99.

Jenkins, P. 1992. *Intimate Enemies: Moral Panics in Contemporary Great Britain.* New York: Aldine de Gruyter.

Jinakul, S. 1994. 'Foreign Flesh in Thai Sex Trade.' *The Bangkok Post*, 15 March 1994.

Joshi, V. 1993. 'Childhoods Sacrificed to Labour.' *Bangkok Post,* 27 July 1993.

Jubilee Action Trust. n.d. *Child Prostitution in Thailand.* London: Jubilee Trust.

Kandre, P. 1976. 'Yao (Iu Mien) Supernaturalism, Language and Ethnicity,' in *Changing Identities in Modern Southeast Asia.* D. Banks (ed.) Mouton: The Hague, 171–197

Kennedy. D. 1996a. 'European Widows Exploit Sri Lankan Teenagers for Sex.' *The Times,* 29 August 1996.

——— 1996b. 'Child Abuse Tourists Boast to Undercover Researchers.' *The Times,* 30 August 1996.

Keyes, C. F. 1984a. 'Mother or Mistress but Never a Monk.' *American Ethnologist* 11:2, 223–41.

———— 1984b. *Thailand: Buddhist Kingdom as Modern Nation State.* Bangkok: Duang Kamol.

———— 1986. 'Ambiguous Gender: Male Initiation in a Northern Thai Buddhist Ceremony.' In *Gender and Religion: On the Complexity of Symbols.* C. Bynam, S. Harrell and P. Richman (eds.) Boston: Beacon Press, 66–96.

Kirsch, A.T. 1975. 'Economy, Polity and Religion in Thailand,' in *Change and Persistence in Thai Society.* G.W. Skinner and A.T. Kirsch (eds.) Ithaca: Cornell University Press, 172–196.

———— 1982. 'Buddhism, Sex Roles and the Thai Economy,' in *Women of South East Asia.* P. van Esterik (ed.) Occasional Paper No. 9. Illinois: Centre for South Asian Studies, Northern Illinois University, 16–41.

———— 1985. 'Text and Context: Buddhist Sex Roles/the Culture of Gender Revisited.' *American Ethnologist.* 12:2, 302–20. Paper No. 9. Illinois: Centre for South Asian Studies, Northern Illinois University Press.

Komin, S. 1991. *Psychology of the Thai People.* Bangkok: National Institute of Development Administration.

Koompraphant, S. n.d. *A Just World for Our Future.* Bangkok: CPCR.

Korbin, J. E. 1981. *Child Abuse and Neglect: Cross-Cultural Perspectives.* Berkeley: University of California Press.

La Fontaine, J.S. 1974. 'The Free Women of Kinshasa,' in *Choice and Change.* J. Davis (ed.) Monographs in Social Anthropology, London: Athlone Press, 89–113.

———— 1986. 'An Anthropological Perspective On Children,' *Children Of Social Worlds.* M Richards and P. Light (eds.) Cambridge: Polity Press, 10–30.

———— 1987. 'Preliminary Remarks on a Study of Incest in England,' in *Child Survival: Anthropological Perspectives on the Treatment and Maltreatment of Children.* N. Scheper-Hughes (ed.) Dordrecht: D. Reidel, 267–290.

———— 1990. *Child Sexual Abuse.* Cambridge: Polity Press.

———— 1994. *The Extent and Nature of Organised and Ritual Abuse: Research Findings.* London H.M.S.O,

———— 1998. *Speak of the Devil: Tales of Satanic Abuse in Contemporary England.* Cambridge; Cambridge University Press,

Lai, A. E. 1982. 'The Little Workers: A Study of Child Labour in the Small Scale Industries of Penang.' *Development and Change* 13:4, 565–587.

Landon, K. 1939. *Siam in Transition: A Brief Survey of Cultural Trends in the Five Years since the Revolution of 1932.* Oxford: Oxford University Press.

League of Nations. 1933. *Report of the Council by the Commission into the Traffic in Women and Children in the East.* Geneva: League of Nations.

Lee, M. and O'Brien, R. 1995. *The Game's Up: Redefining Child Prostitution.* London: Children's Society.

Lee-Wright, P. 1990. *Child Slaves.* London: Earthscan Publications.

Lewis, G. 1980. *Day of Shining Red: An Essay on Understanding Ritual.* Cambridge: Cambridge University Press.

Lewis, J. and Kapur, D. 1990. 'An Updating Country Study – Thailand Needs and Prospects in the 1990s.' *World Development.* 18:10, 1363–1378.

Limanonda, B.1993. *'Female Commercial Sex Workers and AIDS: Perspectives from Thai Rural Communities.'* Paper presented at the Fifth International Conference on Thai Studies, SOAS, London 1993.

Lowman, J. 1987. 'Taking Young Prostitutes Seriously.' *Canadian Review Of Sociology And Anthropology.* 24:1, 99–116.

Luther, H. 1978. *Peasants and State in Contemporary Thailand: From Regional Revolt to National Revolution?* Hamburg: Institut fur Asienkunde.

Lutkehaus, N. and Roscoe, P.B. 1995. *Gender Rituals: Female Initiation in Melanesia.* London: Routledge

Macfarlane, A. 1987. *Marriage and Love in England: modes of reproduction 1300 -1840.* Oxford: Basil Blackwell.

Malee. 1986. *Tiger Claw and Velvet Paw: The Erotic Odyssey of a Thai Prostitute.* London: Headline.

Mayall, B. 1994. *Children's Childhoods: Observed and Experienced.* London: The Falmer Press.

Mead, M. 1962. *Male and Female.* London: Pelican.

────── 1977. *Coming of Age in Samoa: A Study of Adolescence and Sex in Primitive Societies.* London: Penguin.

Mead, M. and Wolfenstein, M. (eds.) 1955. *Childhood in Contemporary Cultures.* Chicago: University of Chicago Press.

Miles, D. 1972. 'Yao Bride-Exchange, Matrifiliation and Adoption.' *Bijdragen tot der Taal: Land und Volenkunde* 128, 99–117.

Mills, M. B. 1990. 'Moving Between Modernity and Tradition: The Case of Rural-Urban Migration from North-eastern Thailand to Bangkok.' *AUA American Studies* 2, 52–71.

────── 1993. *We Are Not Like Our Mothers.* PhD Dissertation, Department of Social Anthropology. Berkeley: University of California.

Millward, D. 1996. 'Hundreds Abused in Care Homes.' *Daily Telegraph,* 10 June 1996.

Michael Sieff Foundation. 1996. *Child Prostitution.* London. Michael Sieff Foundation.

Montgomery, H. (Forthcoming). 'Imposing Rights? – A Case Study Of Child Prostitution In Thailand' in *Culture and Rights.* J. Cowan, M.B. Dembour and R. Wilson (eds.) Cambridge: Cambridge University Press.

Morgan, R. 1985. *Sisterhood is Global: The International Women's Movement Anthology.* London: Penguin.

Morris, L. 1994. *Dangerous Classes: The Underclass and Social Citizenship.* London: Routledge.

Morrow, V. 1995. 'Invisible Children? Toward a Re-conceptualisation of Childhood. Dependency and Responsibility.' *Sociological Studies of Children* 7, 207–230.

Morrow, V and Richards, M. 1996. 'The Ethics of Social Research with Children: An Overview.' *Children and Society* 10, 90–105.

Mougne, C. 1978. 'An Ethnography of Reproduction: Changing Patterns of Fertility in a Northern Thai Village,' in *Nature and Man in South East Asia*. P. Stott (ed.) London: SOAS.

Muecke, M.A. 1976. 'Health Care Systems as Socialising Agents: Childbearing the North Thai and Western Ways. *Social Science and Medicine* 10:8, 377–383.

—— 1981. 'Changes in Women's Status Associated with Modernisation in Northern Thailand,' in *South East Asia: Women, Changing Social Structures and Cultural Continuity*. G.B. Hainsworth (ed.) Ottawa: University of Ottawa Press, 53–65.

—— 1984. 'Make Money Not Babies: Changing Status Markers of Northern Thai Women.' *Asian Survey* 24:4. 459–470.

—— 1992. 'Mother Sold Food, Daughter Sells Her Body: The Cultural Continuity of Prostitution.' *Social Science and Medicine* 35: 7, 891–901.

Mukherji, S. K. 1986. *Prostitution in India*. New York: Advent Books.

Mulder, N. 1979. *Inside Thai Society: An Interpretation of Everyday Life*. Bangkok: Duang Kamol.

Muntabhorn, V. 1992. *Sale of Children*. Report submitted by the Special Rapporteur. New York: United Nations E/CN.4/1992/55.

Murray, A. 1998. 'Debt-Bondage and Trafficking: Don't Believe the Hype,' in *Global Sex Workers: Rights, Resistance and Redefinitions*. K. Kempadoo and J. Doezema (eds.) London: Routledge, 51–64.

Nartsupha, C. 1991. 'The Community School of Thought,' in *Thai Constructions of Knowledge*. M. Chitakasem and A. Turton (ed.) London: SOAS, 118–141.

Narvilai, A. 1994. 'Young Men Following in their Sisters' Footsteps.' *Bangkok Post*, 2 July 1994.

Narvesen, O. 1989. *The Sexual Exploitation of Children in Developing Countries*. Oslo: Redd Barna.

Nation. 1989. 'Parents Warned Not to Sell Their Children.' *Nation*. 23 February 1989.

—— 1993a. 'Government Will Try to Educate Longman.' *Nation*, 7 July 1993.

—— 1993b. 'Ranong Brothel Raids Net 148 Burmese Girls.' *Nation*, 16 July 1993.

—— 1994a. 'Government Can't Keep Russian Women out of the Sex Trade.' *Nation, 21 February 1994*.

—— 1994b. 'Princess Offers Scholarships for North Girls.' *Nation*, 17 March 1994.

National Commission of Inquiry into the Prevention of Child Abuse. 1996. *Childhood Matters: Report of the National Commission of Inquiry into the Prevention of Child Abuse*. London: NSPCC

Oakley, A. 1994. 'Women and Children First and Last: Parallels and Differences between Children's and Women's Studies.' In *Children's Childhoods: Observed and Experienced*. B. Mayall (ed.) London: The Falmer Press, 13–32.

O'Connell Davidson, J. 1994. *British Sex Tourists in Thailand*. Unpublished manuscript.

Odzer, C. 1990. *Patpong Prostitution: Its Relationship to, and Effect on, the Position of Women in Thai Society.* New York: PhD Dissertation, New School for Social Research.

O'Grady, R. 1992a. *Address to the Summit Conference on Child Prostitution of the Vatican Pontifical Council for the Family.* Bangkok: ECPAT.

——— 1992b. *The Child and the Tourist.* Bangkok: ECPAT.

——— 1994. *The Rape of the Innocent.* Bangkok: ECPAT.

Parakh, D. n.d. *Does the Law Discriminate Against Thai Women?* Unpublished manuscript.

Patkar, P. 1991. 'Girl-Child in the Red-light Areas.' *The Indian Journal of Social Work* 52:1, 71–80.

Parker, R. 1991. *Bodies, Pleasures and Passions: Sexual Culture in Contemporary Brazil.* Boston: Beacon Press.

Pattaya Mail. 1993. 'Pattaya up in Arms About New Hours Regulations.' *Pattaya Mail,* 12 November 1993.

Paul, D. 1979. *Women in Buddhism.* Berkeley: Humanities Press.

Phongpaichit, P. 1982. *From Peasant Girls to Bangkok Masseuses.* Geneva: ILO.

Piker, S. 1975. 'The Post-peasant Village in Central Plains Thai Society,' in *Change and Persistence in Thai Society.* G. W. Skinner and A.T. Kirsch (eds.) Ithaca: Cornell University Press, 298–323.

——— 1979. 'The Relationship of Belief Systems to Behaviour in Rural Thai Society,' in *Modern Thai Politics: From Village to Nation.* C.D. Neher (ed.) Cambridge, Mass: Shenkman, 114–132.

Podhisita, C., Pramualratana, A. Kanungsukkasem, U, Wawer, M., McNamara, R. 1993. *Socio-Cultural Context of Commercial Sex Workers in Thailand.* Paper presented at the IUSSP Working Group on AIDS: Seminar on AIDS Impact and Prevention in the Developing World.

Pollock, L. A. 1983. *Forgotten Children: Parent-Child Relations from 1500 – 1900.* Cambridge: Cambridge University Press.

Pongsapich, A. 1990. 'Politico-Economic Development Impacting on Society and Traditional Values.' *AUA American Studies* 2, 79–98.

Potter, J. 1976. *Thai Peasant Social Structure.* Chicago and London: University of Chicago Press.

Potter, S. H. 1979. *Family Life in a Northern Thai Village: A Study of the Structural Significance Of Women.* Berkeley: University of California Press.

Qvortrup, J. 1994. *Childhood Matters: Social Theory Practice and Politics.* Aldershot: Avebury Press.

Rajadhon, P. A. 1965. 'Customs Connected with the Birth and Rearing of Children,' in *Life and Ritual in Old Siam.* William Gedning (ed.) Westport: Greenwood Press.

——— 1987. *Some Traditions of the Thai and Other Translations of Phya Anuman Rajadhon's Articles on Thai Customs.* Bangkok: Thai Inter-Religious Commission for Development.

Rattachumpoth, R. 1994. 'The Economics of Sex.' *Nation,* 3 February 1994.

Raynal. A. 1776. *A Philosophical and Political History of the Settlements and Trade of the Europeans in the East and West Indies.* Translated by J. Justamond. London.

Reeves, G. 1993. 'Impoverished Thai Parents Sell Girls into Prostitution.' *Dallas Morning Star*, March 21, 1993.

Reynolds, C. 1977. *A Nineteenth Century Thai Buddhist Defence of Polygamy and Some Remarks on the Social History of Women in Thailand.* Unpublished paper prepared for the Seventh Conference of the International Association of Historians of Asia.

Richter, L. 1989. *The Politics of Tourism in Asia.* Honolulu: University of Hawaii Press.

Rodgers, G. and Standing, G. 1981. *Child Work, Poverty and Underdevelopment.* Geneva: ILO.

Rogers, T. 1996. 'Lost Children of the Night.' *Daily Telegraph*, 24 August 1996.

Rozario, R. M. 1988. *Trafficking in Women and Children in India.* New Delhi: Uppal Publishing House.

Sachs, A. 1994. 'The Last Commodity – Child Prostitution in the Developing World.' *World Watch.* 7:4, 24–30

Saengtienchai, C. 1995. *Wives' Views on the Extramarital Sexual Behaviour of Thai Men.* Paper presented at the International Conference on Gender and Sexuality in Modern Thailand. Australian National University, Canberra.

Sakborn, M. 'A Silver Lining on Longman's Stormy Cloud.' *Nation*, 18 July 1993.

Sakhon, S. 1994. 'Two Burn to Death in Brothel Fire.' *Bangkok Post,* 13 June 1994.

Santasombat, Y. 1990. Traditional Values and Changing Thai Society. *AUA American Studies* 2, 71–79.

Save the Children Fund (UK). 1995. *Towards a Children's Agenda.* London: Save the Children Fund.

———— 1996. *Kids for Hire.* London: Save the Children Fund.

Scheper-Hughes, N. and Stein, H. 1987. 'Child Abuse and the Unconscious,' in *Child Survival: Anthropological Perspectives on the Treatment and Maltreatment of Children.* N. Scheper-Hughes (ed.) Dordrecht: D. Reidel, 339–358.

Schildkrout, E. 1979. 'Women's Work and Children's Work: Variations among Moslems in Kano,' in *Social Anthropology of Work.* S. Wallman (ed.) ASA Monograph 19. London: Academic Press, 69–86.

Schultz, M. 1986. 'The Blood Libel: A Motif in the History of Childhood.' *Journal of Psychohistory* 14, 1–24.

Sereny, G. 1984. *The Invisible Children: Child Prostitution in America, West Germany and Great Britain.* London: Andre Deutsch.

Sereewat, S. 1983. *Prostitution: Thai-European Connection: An Action-Oriented Study.* Geneva: World Council of Churches.

Sharp, L. and Hanks, L. 1952. *Siamese Rice Village: A Preliminary Study of Bang Chan 1948–49.* Ithaca: Cornell University Press.

Sittitrai, W., Wolff, B., Knodel, J., Havanon, N. and Podhisita, C. 1991. *Family Size and Family Well-being: The Views of Thai Villagers.* Bangkok: Institute of Population Studies, Chulalongkorn University.

Sittitrai, W., Phanuphak, P., Barry, J. and Brown, T. 1992. *Thai Sexual Behaviour and Risk of HIV Infection.* Bangkok: Thai Red Cross Society.

Sittitrai, W. and Brown, T. 1994. *The Impact of HIV on Children in Thailand.* Bangkok: Thai Red Cross Society.

Sivaraksa, S. 1980. *Siam in Crisis.* Bangkok: Komol Keemthong Foundation.

Sleightholme, C. and Sinha, I. 1997. *Guilty Without Trial: Women in the Sex Trade in Calcutta.* New York: Rutgers University Press:

Snell, C.L. 1995. *Young Men in the Street: Help Seeking Behaviour of Young Male Prostitutes.* Connecticut and London: Praeger.

Sommerville, C.J. 1982. *The Rise and Fall of Childhood.* London and New Delhi: Sage.

Soonthorndhada, A. 1994. *Factors Affecting Adolescent Sexual Behaviour in Thailand.* Project Proposal.

———— 1995. *The Discourse of Sexual Values: A Comparison Between Female Students and Factory Workers.* Paper presented at the International Conference on Gender and Sexuality in Modern Thailand. Australian National University, Canberra.

Srisang, S. and Srisang, K. n.d. *Prostitution in Thailand: Products of Power Manipulation and Spiritual Bankruptcy.* Unpublished manuscript.

Strathern, M. 1992. *Reproducing the Future: Essays In Anthropology, Kinship and the New Reproductive Techniques.* Manchester: Manchester University Press.

Sunday Age. 1993. 'Bo, 12, Taken to a Hotel and Forced to Have Sex.' *Sunday Age,* 18 April 1993.

Suwannachairop, S. 1994. 'What's Wrong with Thailand?' *Bangkok Post,* 30 May 1994.

Tambiah, S.J. 1970. *Buddhism and the Spirit Cults of North East Thailand.* Cambridge: Cambridge University Press.

Tanabe, S. 1991. 'Spirits, Power and the Discourse of Female Gender: The *Phi Meng* Cult of Northern Thailand,' in *Thai Constructions of Knowledge.* M. Chitakasem and A. Turton (eds.) London: SOAS, 183–212.

Tantiwiramanond, D. and Pandey, S. 1987. 'The Status and Role of Women in the Pre-Modern Period: A Historical and Cultural Perspective.' *Sojourn* 2:1, 125–147.

———— 1989. 'Dutiful but Overburdened: Women In Thai Society.' *Asian Review* 3, 41–53.

ten Brummelhuis, H. 1993. *Do We Need a Thai Theory of Prostitution?* Paper presented at the Fifth International Conference on Thai Studies. SOAS, London.

Tendler, S. and Ford, R. 1994. 'Police Link with Thailand to End Trips for Child Sex.' *The Times,* 5 March 1994.

Thitsa, K. 1980. *Providence and Prostitution: Women in Buddhist Thailand.* Women in Society. Series No. 2. London: Change International.

———— 1982. *Nuns, Mediums and Prostitutes in Chiang Mai: A Study of Some Marginal Categories of Women.* Occasional Paper No. 1. Canterbury: Centre of Southeast Asian Studies, University of Canterbury.

Thorbek, S. 1987. *Voices from the City.* London: Zed Publishers.

Tourn-ngern, S. 1989. 'Children's Day Means Work as Usual for Go-Go Kids.' *Bangkok Post,* 15 January 1989.

Truong, T.D. 1982. 'The Dynamics of Sex Tourism.' *Development and Change.* 14:4, 533–553

———— 1986. *Virtue, Order, Health and Money: Towards a Comprehensive Perspective on Female Prostitution in Asia.* Bangkok: United Nations.

———— 1990. *Sex, Money and Morality.* London: Zed Books.

Turner, L. and Ash, J. 1975. *The Golden Hordes: International Tourism and the Pleasure Periphery.* London: Constable.

Turton, A. 1980. 'Thai Institutions of Slavery,' in *Asian and African Systems of Slavery.* J. Watson (ed.) Los Angeles: University of California Press, 251–339.

UNICEF. 1989. *A Situation Analysis of Children in Thailand.* Bangkok: UNICEF.

United Nations. 1990. *Convention on the Rights of the Child.* New York: United Nations.

———— 1991. *Promotion of Community Awareness of the Prevention of Prostitution.* Bangkok: United Nations.

van Esterik, P. 1982. 'Laywomen in Theravada Buddhism,' in *Women of South East Asia.* P. van Esterik (ed.) Occasional Paper No. 9. Illinois: Centre for South Asian Studies, Northern Illinois University.

———— 1996. 'Nurturance and Reciprocity in Thai Studies,' in *State, Power and Culture.* E. P. Durrenberger (ed.) New Haven: Yale University Southeast Asia Studies, 22–46.

Vance, C. 1989. 'Pleasure and Danger: Towards a Politics of Sexuality,' in *Pleasure and Danger: Exploring Female Sexuality.* London: Pandora, 1–28.

———— 1991. 'Anthropology Rediscovers Sexuality: A Theoretical Comment.' *Social Science and Medicine* 33:8, 875–884.

Vichit-Vadakan, J. 1990. 'Traditional and Changing Values in Thai and American Societies.' *AUA American Studies* 2, 27–52.

Wahnschafft, R. 1982. 'Formal and Informal Tourism Sectors: A Case Study of Pattaya, Thailand.' *Annals of Tourism Research.* 9:3, 429–451.

Waksler, F.C. 1991. 'Studying Children: Phenomenological Insights,' in *Studying the Social Worlds of Children: Sociological Readings.* F.C. Waksler (ed.) London: The Falmer Press, 60–69.

Walker, D. and Ehrlich, R. 1994. *Hello My Big Big Honey: Love Letters to Bangkok Bar Girls and Their Revealing Interviews.* Bangkok: White Lotus.

Walkowitz, J. 1983. 'Male Vice and Female Virtue: Feminism and The Politics of Prostitution in Nineteenth Century Britain,' in *Powers of Desire: The Politics of Sexuality.* A. Snitow, C. Stansell and S. Thompson (eds.) London: Virago, 419–438.

Watson, H. 1994. 'Separation and Reconciliation: Marital Conflict among the Muslim Poor in Cairo,' in *Muslim Women's Choices: Religious Belief and Social Reality.* C. El-Solh and J. Mabro (eds.) Oxford: Berg, 33–54.

Weeks, J. 1981. *Sex, Politics and Society: The Regulation of Sexuality Since 1800*. New York: Longman.

Weisberg, D. K. 1985. *Children of the Night: A Study of Adolescent Prostitution*. Massachusetts: Lexington Books.

West, J. 1997. 'Sri Lankan Children for Sale on the Internet.' *Daily Telegraph*, 26 October 1997.

White, A and Holman, K. 1996. *Prime Time for Children: Media, Ethics and Reporting of Commercial Sexual Exploitation of Children*. Paper presented at the World Congress Against the Commercial Sexual Exploitation of Children, Stockholm. Prepared by the International Federation of Journalists for UNICEF.

Widom, C.S. and Ames, M.A. 1994. 'Criminal Consequences Of Childhood Sexual Victimization.' *Child Abuse and Neglect* 18:4, 303–318.

Wikan, U. 1980. *Life Among the Poor in Cairo*. London: Tavistock.

Wilson, G.D. and Cox, D.N. 1986. *The Child Lovers: A Study of Paedophiles in Society*. London and Boston: Peter Owen.

World Congress Against the Commercial Sexual Exploitation of Children. 1996. *Declaration and Agenda for Action*. Stockholm 28/8/96.

World Health Organisation. 1987. *Children at Work*. Geneva: WHO.

Wyatt, D. 1984. *Thailand: A Short History*. New Haven and London: Yale University Press.

INDEX